An Armful of Babies
and a Cup of Tea

An Armful of Babies and a Cup of Tea

Memoirs of a 1950s Health Visitor

MOLLY CORBALLY

First p
Just Vi
as
'0s

A CIP catalogue record for this title is available from the British Library

Paperback ISBN 9781473671492
eBook ISBN 9781473671508
Audio Digital Download ISBN 9781473671515

Typeset in Stone Serif by Hewer Text UK Ltd, Edinburgh
Printed and bound by CPI Group (UK) Ltd, Croydon, CR0 4YY

Hodder & Stoughton policy is to use papers that are natural, renewable
and recyclable products and made from wood grown in sustainable
forests. The logging and manufacturing processes are expected to
conform to the environmental regulations of the country of origin.

Hodder & Stoughton Ltd
Carmelite House
50 Victoria Embankment
London EC4Y 0DZ

www.tworoadsbooks.com
www.hodder.co.uk

Contents

Glossary of terms (in order of appearance)

QAs	*Full name: The Queen Alexandra's Royal Army Nursing Corps*
POWs	*Prisoners of war*
WI	*Women's Institute*
SSAFA	*Soldiers, Sailors, Airmen and Families Association – the Armed Forces Charity*
ATS	*Auxiliary Territorial Service*
W(R)VS	*Founded in 1938 as the Women's Voluntary Service, later the Women's Royal Voluntary Service (2004) and since 2013 the Royal Voluntary Service*
MOH	*Medical Officer of Health*
BRCS	*British Red Cross Society*

Author's Introduction

There was a time when the only welfare officer was the school attendance officer, when the needs of children at risk were catered for by the NSPCC and the health visitors, when disabled children were provided for by the appropriate voluntary societies, and the British Red Cross spread its benevolent wings over all. At that time the health visitor had an undisputed responsibility for the health and welfare of everyone within her area.

It is of those days that this book is written, days when lice and fleas and scabies were so common that cleansing stations were operating all over the country, when TB was rampant, sanatoria were filled, and children died from diphtheria and whooping-cough. On new council estates, baths were frequently used to store coal. In those days health visitors were important in the community. We were consulted by doctors and magistrates, police and charities; we co-operated closely with all voluntary societies, with paediatricians and probation officers; the council employed and paid us, but we worked for the families under our care, and their needs took priority over statistics and economics in the council offices.

I have seen sanatoria close for lack of patients, diphtheria and whooping-cough eradicated by wholesale immunisation, cleansing stations disappear, and generations of clean, healthy children result from our years of intensive health education in homes and clinics. Today a proliferation of social workers and welfare officers have taken over much of the work which was once the province of the health visitors. Other fields are opening to them; they have new challenges to meet. As long as there are people, there will be challenges; there will be hope and despair, success and failure, laughter and tears. It is of such things that this book is about, because it is a book about *people*.

1

A Small Henhouse

It all began on Southport Pier. Eileen Newton and I had returned from overseas service with the QAs and had been posted to a makeshift hospital in Southport's Floral Hall, to look after POWs repatriated from Japan who were under psychiatric care. We had enormous fun together, playing with slot machines on the pier, drooling over Rex Harrison (who was almost continually on the screen in three different films) and laughing together over the vicissitudes of our temporary accommodation. After years of camp hospitals, even a narrow wooden bed in the dormitory of a children's home was comparative luxury.

Playing on the pier, walking by the sea, sitting by the bandstand in the Floral Gardens, we discovered each other, liked what we found, and decided to set up home together somewhere in Warwickshire, near my ageing mother and Eileen's married sister. After years of hospital living-in and of army messes, we longed for a little place of our own, for the home comforts we had so missed during the war, for our own front door which we could shut against the world, and lead our own lives in privacy and independence.

We were both demobilised in 1945. Eileen got a job in Birmingham as a Nursing Officer with the Ministry of Labour, while I went to London to do my health visitor's training. With the arrival of penicillin we felt the end was coming to the challenge of nursing as we had known it, and we had grown far away, in the easy comradeship of army life, from the narrow disciplines and etiquette of a civilian hospital. In our Territorial Army unit there were all sorts and degrees of nurses, and I had found the health visitors more outgoing, more companionable, more fun to be with than the average ward sister, whose outlook was apt to be limited by the four walls of her ward – and I liked what they told me about their work.

The training at the Royal Sanitary Institute lasted six months, followed by a period of close supervision in Solihull, with experienced staff always at hand to help and advise. In the busy clinics I observed and listened, and soon realised how little I had learnt on the training course. You can't learn about people from books and lectures, certainly not about baby people, who, not having read the books, invariably break all the rules.

It was frightening knocking on those first doors. Up till then my patients had come to me, not I to them, and these weren't even patients. They weren't ill and in need of my professional skill. What had I to offer, in my brand-new navy-blue suit and hat, with the Warwickshire badge on the hatband? They didn't need me, not like a district nurse is needed, or a midwife. Would they even want me? Strangely enough, they did, and the kindness of their reception, and the courtesy with which they

4

listened to what few suggestions I dared to offer them were a tribute to the service which the health visitors had been giving to the people of Warwickshire before I was even aware that such people existed.

I've always felt sympathy for salesmen knocking on doors trying to sell their wares to busy women with no time to listen to their patter, and no desire for their products. What had I to sell to these young mothers? Health for their precious babies. You can't carry health in a suitcase, nor display it on the kitchen table. In those early days I wasn't even convinced of the value of what I was doing, and after a morning of visiting polite but experienced and confident mothers, I would long to be back in a hospital ward, to be healing and comforting, to be needed and wanted and appreciated.

An early awakening to the value of my work came as a direct result of my diffidence. A first visit to a big house was not well received. The mother was a private patient and told me she would call in her doctor if she needed help. She did not actually ask me not to call again, and I left her my telephone number, but it was her first baby, and I should have made a follow-up visit. It was three months later, on hearing from a neighbour that the baby was in hospital, that I plucked up courage and rang the bell again. I was warmly welcomed and told, shamefacedly, that the baby had had severe digestive problems caused by incorrect feeding. The doctor had visited frequently but was unable to find the cause of the trouble and had called in a paediatrician from Birmingham. The feeding formula was wrong; the milk was too concentrated. It had all cost her a great deal of money, and the poor baby a great deal of pain.

'Why didn't you ring me?' I asked. 'I could have told you that over the telephone.'

She smiled ruefully.

'I know. "For twopence" – as the paediatrician pointed out. I'll know better another time.'

Too many people make the mistake of thinking that the more they pay for advice and treatment, the better it must be.

After a year's apprenticeship I was considered safe to be let loose on the public and was allocated my own field of work in Kenilworth and its surrounding villages and hamlets, responsible for my own clinics and schools. While I moved into digs in Leamington, Eileen and I got down to house hunting. As it happened, her sister and brother-in-law lived in Kenilworth and were keeping their eyes and ears open on our behalf. Leonard Smalley was a dedicated and much-loved doctor and my rather vague connection with him – sharing a home with his wife's sister – was to be of immense help in my professional life and opened all sorts of doors to me. Claire, Eileen's sister, was one of Kenilworth's leading citizens, a councillor, chairwoman of innumerable committees, governor of most local schools, a JP and twice a mayoress when Leonard wore the mayoral chain. They thought we were most unwise and held out no hope of our partnership being successful or lasting. Who can blame them? They knew Eileen, and they quickly assessed me, and we were both women of pretty average independence and obstinacy. On the face of it, it seemed a rash decision, but nursing, especially in wartime, is a great smoother of rough edges and teaches the give and take required in any partnership.

In spite of her misgivings, Claire was helpful, and it was she who found us the little house in Birmingham Road. I wonder what there is about a house that makes it somehow different from other identical houses in the same street? Before we had seen the number, we were both hoping that the honeysuckle-covered porch belonged to 149. Often, when we were living there, strangers would call to ask the way, to use the telephone or the loo, to borrow a safety pin. When we asked, 'Why pick this house?' The reply was always, 'There's something so friendly about it.' Yet, apart from the honeysuckle, 149 was exactly like 147 and 151, with its sloping roof and dormer windows, like surprised eyebrows, the formal little front garden and short drive to the garage. It was a little way out of the town, the road running through a ford, past the castle ruins and the green opposite – the scene of the annual Boxing Day meet, when it was bright with the gay new Christmas scarves and woollen caps proudly displayed by children of all ages. When the ford was full it was a great gathering place for children, who would watch with glee as rash motorists splashed through it – often, to the spectators' delight, getting trapped in the deceptively deep water. A sharp corner and steep hill beyond the ford, a hazard for cars with wet brakes, brought us to the clock and the main shopping street.

Alternatively, a hill opposite the house led to the High Street shops, old and picturesque. At the top of the hill, this road passed St Austin's Roman Catholic church, a little Pugin gem, with its attached school and presbytery in which reigned a gentle and holy old man. Canon Swift was well into his eighties and unable to do much active work in the parish, but he was ably supported by his curate, Father Pat O'Leary, a big, black-haired, curly-headed, boisterous and endearing young man with the physique of a prize-fighter and the heart of an angel. It was a treat to see him on Good Friday afternoon after the service, armed with great sticks, waylaying reluctant men who were trying to slink past him and pretending not to see the church carpets spread out on the grass.

'Come on now, you can help beat the carpets. Isn't that the great penance you can be doing for Good Friday?'

He was bigger than most men of the parish, and the carpets got beaten. But those strong hands could be so gentle in cradling a child or tending the sick and house-bound whom he visited and cared for with such love.

In those days, Kenilworth had not become the dormitory town for Coventry that it is today; it was an intimate little place where everyone knew each other and many people were related, in varying degrees of kinship. There were family businesses, like the firm of brothers who had built (and lived in) our own house, and another family of brothers running three businesses: plumbing, ironmongery and greengrocery. I discovered the intricacies of Kenilworth's relationships after a party Eileen and I gave for the builders, plumber, decorator, plasterer and carpenter who had helped to enlarge

149, much to the amusement of the Aitken brothers who had fitted in, five of them with their parents, without feeling cramped. We fed our guests on beer and sandwiches and entertained them with one of the early television sets, and everyone in Kenilworth knew about it. Every family I called on was full of it, being related in some obscure way to one or other of our guests. From my point of view that party was extremely good for business. But that came a lot later. In 1947 we were busy getting settled in. The idea of the extension resulted from the many friends we made and the need of a room large enough for party-giving and a guest room large enough for two.

There are problems and compensations in a 'henhouse', and one of the problems we met at the very beginning. People don't get wedding presents unless they are getting married! In 1946 furniture, china and household linen was all 'utility' – basic, drab, but adequate. Eileen's careful search for export rejects produced a complete service of rose-patterned china, of which we were very proud. A canteen of silver and some good pieces of furniture came from her old home. Clothing coupons were hoarded and exchanged for sheets and curtain material. For the rest we hunted round markets, bazaars and second-hand shops – and what fun it was! One of the joys of two women sharing a home is the shared shopping. In a henhouse there is no dividing line between the man's province and the woman's province. We were both women and every domain was shared – decorating, gardening, furnishing, sewing, catering. It is really much more fun playing with your partner among rolls of wallpaper and shelves of furnishing fabrics, even on limited means, than being alone among such excitements with only a husband's cheque for company, however generous.

In those days L-plates were not displayed on cars. Not only should outsize Ls, in bright red, have been in evidence on my Austin, and on my new navy-blue uniform, but also in the kitchen!

Even if brides have not taken a pre-marriage cookery course, their early mistakes are probably cushioned by the rapture of young love, and starry-eyed bridegrooms may fail to notice the culinary howlers which, should they occur a few years later, might be sent hurtling through the window. There were no stars in our eyes, but, as we were both learning and experimenting, no stars were needed. For our own self-protection we withheld criticism, remembering, nose curling over the burnt potatoes, how last night's over-salted soup had been swallowed without even a raised eyebrow. There were not too many casualties. We had a good cookery book and followed each recipe meticulously. We were used to following instructions to the last minim. Carelessness in the dosage of drugs and medicines can be disastrous. Not for us the unhelpful advice from experienced and blasé cooks: 'Chuck in a bit of this, and a handful of that, and bung it in the oven.' Eileen's hands and mine were different sizes anyway.

The garden provided us with fresh vegetables, apples and small fruit, and we planted a herb bed, which contained nearly every herb known to man – at least to English-dwelling man – even a root of incense given by a friend. I've never been good at remembering names, so, when I decided to flavour the stockpot for a good nourishing soup, I gathered leaves from all the herbs. It never occurred to me to plant the culinary herbs separate from the others, so in they all went: thyme, sage, mint, parsley, lavender, peppermint, rosemary, verbena, even a sprig of incense. It smelt wonderful and it tasted delicious, and we suffered no ill effects. The mints were a recurring problem. I could never remember which was which, and, in early summer when new potatoes and young peas were cooking, the kitchen would sometimes be filled with a strange and not unpleasant smell of peppermint.

Fortunately, we had a kind butcher who, like so many tradesmen and neighbours, was a grateful and admiring patient of Leonard's and took the doctor's wife's sister and her friend under his wing. Hitherto, meat, for me, had been something which just appeared on a plate in hospital dining rooms and hotels. It came as a joint in other people's houses. I knew, of course, that 'roasts' came as beef, lamb or pork, but sirloin, buttock, silverside, brisket, ribs, legs, shoulders and hands were not in my vocabulary, catering-wise. To me, a shoulder was a clavicle and a hand was something with five fingers that grew on the end of an arm. Listening to experienced shoppers in the queue giving their order, and seeing them receive goods that seemed totally unrelated to what they had asked for, I eventually found myself standing at the counter, wanting something simple like a 'Sunday joint'. Jake the butcher was a large man, his ample form covered with a striped

11

apron, eyes twinkling behind his glasses. I had met him before, in my childhood, in our pack of 'Happy Families'. But his eyes didn't always twinkle. I had seen them blazing with anger. No awkward customer lasted long in his shop, but he recognised a tyro when he saw one. There are tradesmen who make a nice profit from the ignorance of customers, but not Jake. Week by week he helped me through the intricacies of his trade, identifying joints and cuts, discussing quality and value, suggesting recipes, ensuring that his 'Favourite Girls' ate the very best that our money and our ration books allowed.

It was always fun when Eileen and I were able to visit the shops together, and tradesmen must have smiled in pleasurable anticipation when they saw us arrive. Together we always seemed to see things which, on my own, I would not have noticed. If we found a recipe we liked the sound of, we would go out and buy the ingredients, regardless. Such expeditions might have been disastrous for the housekeeping purse, but they did result in exciting meals. Eileen, on her own, was not safe in a shop. Asked to pop into the electricians one morning to buy an adaptor, she came home having bought a refrigerator. Admittedly, we needed a fridge, and it was going at a bargain price; nevertheless when I needed a spare bulb for my car I went to the garage myself. There just might have been a bargain in the showroom!

We were fortunate in our neighbours. At 151 lived a master-carpenter with his wife and small son; at 147 three bachelor brothers – the eldest, Charlie, being a decorator. Charlie adopted us from the very first, watching over us like a broody hen over her chicks. When we camped in the house one weekend before moving in, it was Charlie who hurried round before it got dark, concerned and embarrassed, to tell us that the uncurtained windows rendered us visible from the road. Charlie was the 'man about the house', ready to do any odd job that might be beyond the capabilities of two helpless little women. I hope he was not disappointed that there were so few. Helplessness is not a characteristic of a nurse, and wartime nursing in jungles and deserts requires a certain ingenuity in coping with minor practical difficulties. We graduated, quite undeservedly, from being Charlie's 'ladies' to being his 'angels'. After the episode of the uncurtained windows he never called at the house uninvited, but would materialise at the fence when we were in the garden to check on our well-being, and on that of our dog, our budgie, our guests of all ages. If there were any angels in the relationship, I think it was Charlie who wore the wings in his capacity as guardian angel of 149.

2

Early Days

Finding my way round Kenilworth was easy. Streets had names and most houses had numbers, but it was different in the villages, scattered over the wooded Warwickshire countryside. I had babies in council houses and flats, cottages and prefabs, Nissen huts, caravans and houseboats, manor houses and farmhouses. I had a particular love for the farmhouses, where I was always welcomed by mothers whose knowledge of babies and all young life was vastly greater than mine. After coping with the inanity that I sometimes encountered on my rounds, it would be refreshing to call at one of my farms and drink deep, not only of the tea or coffee that was always produced for me while I dried out or warmed up by a huge log fire, but also of the common sense and sanity and sheer naturalness of these homes. No feeding problems here.

'I check that the calves are suckling, and the piglets, put the bitch in with her pups, then come in and feed my baby . . .' was the way one farmer's wife described her morning routine. In those early post-war days of rationing, how valuable were the gifts without which I could never leave a farm – eggs, freshly made butter, a chicken. I received so much from these women and felt I had so little to offer them, but they always seemed glad of my visits, being too busy to get to the clinics.

However, the farmhouses weren't in streets, but down nameless lanes, and so were cottages; caravans were in fields, and houseboats tied up somewhere along the stretch of canal which bypassed Lapfold on its way between Warwick and Stratford. My best chance of finding the babies was to go straight to the Post Office as soon as I reached the village. A village post office is a world on its own, and, like the village pub, contains the whole atmosphere of the village life. Is the gossip exchanged with the postmistress concerned or malicious? Do the villagers drifting in and out greet each other? Lapfold was a happy community. I felt it that first day as I waited my turn at the counter. There were notices in the window announcing a jumble sale, a parish meeting, a Red Cross outing for the elderly, job vacancies for a part-time gardener and a babysitter, articles for sale. A table by the door displayed a selection of village crafts, pottery and exquisite bookmarkers made with pressed flowers from the surrounding countryside. Everyone greeted everyone else, their children and their dogs. A new coat was admired, invitations issued to a party, help enlisted for the jumble sale, the outing, the car pool which transported people, parcels and prescriptions to and from Leamington. I waited only because I chose to wait, happy to talk to people in the queue, to listen and observe and feel the pulse of this village, which was to be a part of my life for so many years. I was pressed to jump the queue, and when I reached the counter everyone crowded round giving different directions as to the quickest way to reach the houses I had come to visit.

'Past the pond, second on the left, a green gate . . .'

'Not now . . . I saw him painting it white while she was in hospital.'

'But they're nearly all white in that lane. How will Miss Corbally recognise the cottage?'

'The pink cherry tree by the gate.'

'That won't help in winter.' (That was the green gate lady.)

'It would be quicker to leave your car this side of the pond and take the path on your left across the field. It comes out opposite the cottage.'

There was a chuckle behind me. The postmistress smiled across my shoulder.

'Good afternoon, Vicar.'

'Afternoon, Mrs Down.' He turned to me, his hand outstretched. 'Our new health visitor, I presume? Miss Smart told us to expect you.'

'That's our nurse. You know where she lives?'

The voices started up again with conflicting directions to the nurse's cottage. The vicar laughed aloud.

'Lucky you're not in Ireland. When we lost our way in Donegal last summer and asked for directions, the young fellow, after offering the same sort of advice you've been getting, ended up saying: "Well, I wouldn't start from here . . ."'

While everyone laughed, Mrs Down handed me a small map she had been sketching while the conversation was going on, the houses and cottages I wanted

16

marked with the initials of the owner. I was immensely grateful for this help which was available, accompanied by the equally willing advice from whoever was in the post office, until I came to know my district so well that people could change the colour of their gates and front doors, and plant or cut down trees without confusing me.

My first call was to the midwife. Miss Helen Smart welcomed me into her cosy sitting room. She had had a busy morning, and a late lunch, so there was a freshly brewed cup of tea for us to share. Approaching middle age, her black hair already streaked with grey, Miss Smart was a tubby, bespectacled little person, solid, dependable, wise and tough, with a voice gentle to soothe away fear, sharp to check hysteria, melodious to lull a baby to sleep.

'I'm glad you called,' she said. 'Your predecessor rather kept herself to herself, she was sort of eaten up with professional jealousy. I think she resented the babies being mine before they were hers.'

Her eyes met mine, straight, challenging.

'They're always mine, you know – when you've delivered a baby.'

I smiled.

'I know. I've been a midwife, but it was in London, before the war. I've lost touch.'

'I never lose touch. They're all round me, nearly a generation of my babies.'

I felt a twinge of envy. I was so new, so untried. Every house I called on was strange, every family I met were strangers. She seemed to read my thoughts.

'You'll soon get to know them. They're nice people, warm and friendly.'

I felt she had been trying to tell me something. I had to know where we stood. My job was clearly defined. After the tenth day I had sole responsibility for the babies.

'Do you continue to visit your babies after the tenth day, Miss Smart?'

'Officially, no. That's when you take over. But . . .'

I smiled.

'Of course, they're your friends, your neighbours. You live here.'

She nodded. 'That's about it. I live here, as you say, and you come over . . . what, once a week or less?'

She refilled my cup.

'Do you mind?'

Did I mind? I'd been asking myself that since the conversation started, and I thought I knew the answer.

'No. No, Miss Smart, I don't mind. I think I'm going to like it, knowing you're around and still caring about the babies, our babies.'

She smiled suddenly, held out her hand.

'Our babies. Shake on it, Miss Corbally.'

We shook on it, but I too had my professional pride. After all, I was to be responsible from the tenth day onwards. We discussed feeding and general care, and I made quite sure that my ideas and principles and prejudices were clearly understood. We agreed on most points. The midwife assured me that nearly all her babies would be on the breast when I took over, or, failing that, she would start them off on my preferred brands of dried milk.

Professional possessiveness towards 'our' babies was no longer divisive, but a mutual bond, an exclusive bond which waived the statutory ten days ruling if one or other was on holiday, and I would take over at a week, or she would visit for two weeks, to exclude the need of a 'relief' trespassing on our domain. A brief rundown on the family and any snags that had arisen during or after the birth would precede my first visit, and she could always check on her babies' progress at the Lapfold clinic at which she was always a welcome visitor.

But there was a third person who might be involved professionally with our babies.

'What's Dr Stevens like?' I asked.

Miss Smart paused, and those few seconds of silence told me much that professional loyalty forbade her to utter.

'He's not all that strong. He had a bad time during the war, lost his home and his family in the Coventry blitz. It took the stuffing out of him, poor man. Now he's . . .' she hesitated. 'He's just not interested. He does what he has to do, and does it well. You could say he's a good doctor, but not a caring one, if you understand.'

I nodded. I'd got the picture.

'Is he pro- or anti-health visitors?'

She laughed.

'Health visitors? He doesn't know they exist. He'll not bother you . . . and he won't thank you for bothering him.'

I was glad to be forewarned. Miss Smart helped me into my coat.

'Let me know if there's any way I can help.'

I was glad of those words. One day, in the distant future, I would be saying the same words to the new tenant of the nurse's cottage. We walked down the flower-bordered path to my car. Miss Smart saw the little brown face watching for me at the window.

'A dachshund! My favourite breed.'

She knew the breed well enough not to open the car door, but waited to make Solow's acquaintance until I had released the very pregnant bitch and she stood inside the gate, receiving with dignity the homage of the knowing midwife, whose professional hands were busy while her voice caressed. Her verdict was unerring.

'She's got a bellyful! I'd guess there's six or seven in there.'

I'd not brought Solow to the midwife's cottage because she was pregnant, but because I brought her everywhere, as Eileen was now working all day in the surgery of a big factory in Coventry. A dog had not figured in the early plans we had made.

How could we have been so stupid? Having seized our independence in both hands, we sat down and rationally and logically discussed the advisability of buying a dog and irrevocably exchanging our treasured independence for total slavery!

The local paper was advertising a four-month-old dachshund puppy at a giveaway price, so, having acquired a basket and other dog belongings, we drove up to the farm to investigate. We were greeted by a pack of excited, wriggling, licking, rotund puppies, but they were another litter. The giveaway puppy stood apart, shy and shivering and painfully thin. The farmer's wife explained that the little bitch was very nervous. She had been ill-treated by one of the kennel lads and, although very well bred, was now valueless for showing or breeding. There was no hesitation. We signed a cheque and gathered the pathetic trembling little creature into our arms, and into our lives.

In spite of recurrent eczema and cankerous ears, we managed to keep our pet healthy until her odd behaviour forced us to get advice. She was listless and unhappy, refusing food, and making beds all over the house. The vet diagnosed a false pregnancy and advised an early mating. Remembering that we had not got her pedigree, I took our beautiful bitch to the farm from which we had bought her. The farmer's wife met us at the door.

'What a superb bitch. Where did you get her?'

'From you,' I replied.

She shook her head. 'I don't remember her. I wouldn't have forgotten if we'd bred that one.'

'You did breed her, and sold her to us for eight guineas.'

She remembered, and shook her head in disbelief. However, when I told her the purpose of our visit she still insisted that we would never have puppies from Solow. She said she had been breeding long enough to recognise a barren bitch.

So we mated Solow.

'Keep her quiet after the mating to make sure she takes,' we were told. Keep Solow quiet? She was far too elated and full of herself. She careered round and round the garden, into the house, up the stairs for a scramble under the beds, but in spite of her activity she 'took' in no uncertain way. She had indeed, to use the midwife's words, 'a bellyful'.

'Talking of a bellyful,' said Miss Smart, 'have you seen the twins?'

'Mrs Roche-Anderson? I'm on my way now.' I consulted my map. 'First right past the pond, the big house opposite the church. Right?'

'Yes. It's the old Glebe House. The gate will be open, you can drive straight in.'

'Girls, aren't they? Is everything OK?'

'Yes . . .' She didn't sound too sure. I waited, the car door open. 'They're identical, an enchanting pair, and she's an intelligent woman. You'll have a lot to do with her, since she is in on everything – president of the WI, secretary of the Welfare Centre committee, Red Cross, you name it, Mrs R-A is in it, up to the eyebrows.'

I quailed.

'Oh dear! She sounds rather formidable.'

Miss Smart chuckled.

'Formidable? Not her. She's not even terribly efficient, just adores people and finds fulfilment in doing things for them and with them.'

'Perhaps she'll find fulfilment in her babies now. Is she happy to have twins?'

The midwife hesitated.

'I think so . . . we had some trouble with the second. She was a breech. And the birth was difficult. She was

22

the bigger, the five-pounder, but has dropped behind in weight.'

'Why's that? Are they breastfed?'

'Yes. Mrs R-A's managing them both very well, but I've a feeling . . . I don't know . . . I suppose she concentrates more on the smaller one, and she's certainly a better feeder.'

She closed the car door and I settled behind the wheel.

'I'll be interested to watch those two develop. First twins we've had in the village for years. Good luck. They're all yours now.'

I smiled. '*Ours*, Miss Smart.'

'Ours.'

She was right about Mrs Roche-Anderson, who was anything but formidable. A warm, outgoing woman in her mid-twenties, she welcomed me into her lovely Georgian house, sat me down, and plied me with questions about myself and my work. Did I like the village? Where was I living? I was beginning to wonder who was visiting whom when the door was pushed open and we were joined by a beautiful black cocker spaniel who greeted me ecstatically, and, after two abortive efforts, jumped onto the sofa and settled happily with her nose on my knee.

'Smudge is losing a bit of her spring,' explained her mistress. 'We're expecting puppies in about three weeks. She must have caught the infection from me.'

I raised an eyebrow.

'She could have. I'm told it is catching. A doctor friend told me how a patient, being told his wife was

pregnant, could only think of one possible explana-
tion. His wife had been seeing a lot of the woman next
door, and she was six-months gone.'

In that gracious drawing room, with its chintzes and
old china and bowls of roses, I didn't feel like a health
visitor visiting a new mother, but like a guest in whose
affairs my hostess was so interested that I had to remind
her of the purpose of my visit. Patricia and Phillida
were, as Miss Smart had said, an enchanting pair. They
were asleep, so I accepted the assurance, and the
midwife's report, that all was well, but I noticed, before
we left the nursery, how the mother bent over the cot
and gently caressed one baby's cheek . . . Patricia's.

3

Dogs and Roses

It was strange driving out to the country without Solow, our dachshund, beside me. I would be glad when the puppies were weaned and my long companion restored to me. As I left Kenilworth behind me on that beautiful June morning and headed towards Lapfold, I mentally reviewed the babies I planned to visit. I really should look in on Mrs Roche-Anderson before running right into the centre of the village. Once my little blue car was spotted, I could be delayed by the usual requests for a visit, the knock on the door, the note left in the car, the child waiting beside it with a message from Mum. Last time I was in the village, I'd got so bogged down with unscheduled calls that I'd had to hurry back for the afternoon clinic in Kenilworth without seeing the twins. Not that I had been unduly concerned, as Mrs R-A was a very intelligent young mother and would have certainly rung me up if she had run into any difficulty. But the babies were getting on for two months. They should be starting their vitamins, and there was vaccination to discuss. Not urgent matters that would have required a telephone call, but important nevertheless.

I had barely rung the bell when Mrs Roche-Anderson herself opened the door.

'I saw your car drive in,' she explained breathlessly. 'I *am* glad to see you.'

My heart sank. Such a greeting meant one of two things. With friends of several years it could mean they were glad to see *me*. With new mothers, being glad to see their health visitor usually meant trouble. I was right; it did mean trouble. Seizing my arm, the frantic young woman propelled me round the back of the house towards the stables.

'It's Smudge. You remember Smudge?'

Indeed I remembered Smudge, the beautiful spaniel bitch who had greeted me at my first visit, herself heavy with pups. How familiar were the sounds emanating from the stable, the squealing, the nuzzling, the maternal growling reprimands. Familiar, too, was the anxious look on the bitch's face, the staring coat, the dull eyes. Solow had looked just that way when the vet had told us that she had more puppies than she could manage. I counted six squirming, blind, black bundles in the straw.

'She seems to have the same problem as our dachshund. Too many puppies.'

Kneeling to stroke and reassure the exhausted mother, I examined the puppies, looking for the smallest and weakest, which I kept in my hand.

'This looks like the one you'll have to sacrifice, unless you feel you could hand-rear the little fellow. We're bottle-feeding one of ours and he's getting along fine.'

She took the puppy from me, planting a kiss on the top of the tiny domed head.

'Of course I can hand-rear him! I was sure you'd know what to do for Smudge, having so recently had pups of your own, and being a midwife.'

I laughed, admitting that, in spite of my qualifications, I had consulted a vet about Solow and her babies, and it was his advice that I was now passing on to her. The standard textbooks of midwifery or health visiting do not include information on how many puppies bitches of various sizes can comfortably suckle!

'Hand-feeding's not difficult,' I assured her. 'It's rather fun really. We use a doll's feeding bottle, and you can get a special dried milk in the pet shop, or at Boots.'

The three of us made our way back to the house along the path which skirted the rose beds. Many lovely blooms hung limply from stems too feeble to support them. Their owner shook her head sadly at their plight.

'Do you know anything about roses, Miss Corbally?'

I admitted that I knew quite a lot about roses, my very favourite flowers. I recognised the trouble. I'd seen it often enough in my own rose beds.

'Epsom salts,' I said firmly.

My companion looked at me, obviously wondering if my mind was still on Smudge, or even, perhaps, on herself. I smiled at her astonishment.

'I mean it. They're suffering from limp stems. It's easily remedied by watering them with a solution of magnesium sulphate – Epsom salts to you – a quarter of an ounce to a gallon of water, about three pints to each rose bush. You can buy it at Boots when you get this young man's milk.'

As we talked, we reached the front of the house. I caressed the puppy's head as Mrs Roche-Anderson kindly opened the door of my car.

'Thanks for your help and advice.' Her eyes twinkled as I switched on the ignition. 'And, by the way, the twins are all right. They sleep all night now, and love their orange juice.'

I gasped as the enormity of my omission dawned on me.

'But it was the babies I came to see . . .'

She nodded understandingly. 'I guessed it was. Come again soon.'

She was still laughing as I turned to wave from the gate.

I wasn't altogether happy as I drove home for a quick lunch. It would have to be quick as there was shopping to do and Solow had to have a run before I left for the afternoon clinic at Chesford. I really should have seen those twins, but, under the circumstances, it would have seemed officious if I'd returned to the house. Smudge, or the roses for that matter, would be a good excuse for a follow-up visit in the near future, and in the meantime I'd sound out Miss Smart, who I knew was a frequent and always welcome visitor at Glebe House.

Fortunately, Chesford was nearer than Lapfold, but even so I had to hurry. It was my first session at that clinic, having been out of circulation with a heavy cold the previous month. No map was needed in Chesford, as nearly all the cottages lay on either side of the tree-lined street which wound up a steep hill to the old church and the rectory. It continued past the post office on the right, facing the wrought-iron gates of the Hall and the drive, climbing parallel to the village street. The imposing Tudor house with tall chimneys and the church spire rising above the trees was visible from a long distance. At the bottom of the hill, a group of ten council houses had recently been built round the village green, and beyond that, discreetly hidden behind tall lime trees, the council had erected a temporary camp of Nissen huts to shelter some of the families made homeless by the wartime bombing of Coventry.

The Hall had been owned by many generations of the Merlins, a Catholic family who had endowed and built the RC church and presbytery halfway up the hill. A corpulent bespectacled gentleman in the black Benedictine habit was standing at the gate as I drove past, deep in conversation with a young woman, her baby, and her Labrador puppy. 'Father Abbot' – as he was known in the village – had retired from his exalted position in a Benedictine monastery owing to ill health and been sent to recuperate in this peaceful village. He was father, mother and brother to all, irrespective of their religion, or lack of it, and even honorary son to the old ladies who lived alone in the L-shaped house next to the presbytery. He was invariably to be seen standing at the gate, pipe in mouth, watching the world go by, receiving offerings of fruit and flowers and eggs and news. Nothing was missed by those shrewd eyes behind his steel-rimmed glasses: the radiance of a young girl in love, a woman's eyes red from tears or dull with pain, a sickly child, a bandaged hand, a new dress, a missing dog. The joys and sorrows of the village were all taken to his big heart. I was sorry I could not stop as he waved to me, but I had to reach the church hall in time to meet my helpers and ensure everything was ready before we opened for the mothers at 2 p.m.

As I grabbed my white overall and hurried in through the side entrance I was greeted by the rattle of cups and saucers, a shy smile from the mousy little woman who was creating the clatter, and an impatient voice from the next room.

'Where's that new nurse? She's late.'

The Mouse looked sympathetic as I walked through into the main hall and came face to face with Lady Merlin. She was an imposing presence, a big woman in a well-cut, well-worn Harris tweed suit, dark brown hair set in formal waves, drawn back from her high forehead, a big nose, a big chin, a wide mouth, and eyes – no doubt big by nature – that had been narrowed by many years of frowning, scrutinising, and expressing disapproval or contempt. They narrowed as they rested on me, assessing.

I smiled and held out my hand.

'Lady Merlin? I'm Miss Corbally, the new health visitor.'

The handshake was cold, flabby, unwelcoming.

'You're late, nurse. Miss Hawkins was always here – punctually – at one forty.'

I did not say I was sorry. I wasn't. A stout middle-aged woman was arranging tins of milk on a trestle table, and the Mouse was hovering in the doorway. I waited for introductions. None being forthcoming, I shook hands with them both.

'It is so kind of you to help out, and get the hall ready.'

I quickly checked the arrangements, the weighing

30

scales and piles of fresh paper, bowls beside the chairs for the babies' clothes, all in order.

'Which room does the doctor use?'

The lady of the food table opened a door on her right and I took my case through with the syringes and needles to be sterilised. I came back into the weighing room just as Dr Lang came in from the kitchen to be greeted civilly, almost warmly, by Lady Merlin.

The doctor smiled at me; I knew her from the Kenilworth clinic.

'Welcome to Chesford clinic, Miss Corbally. You've met everyone?'

Her glance included the three helpers. Now helpers, in my book, are very necessary and highly valued, but the running of an Infant Welfare Centre must be the province of trained people.

Only ten mothers turned up with their babies, and two toddlers for injections. As the first baby was brought to the scales Lady Merlin took the record card from the file on her table. I held out my hand for it.

'I record all the weights,' she snapped.

I still held out my hand.

'I'd like to see the card if I may.'

'Whatever for? Miss Hawkins never bothered.'

I settled the baby on the scales, smiling at the mother. I felt her tenseness, the tenseness of the food-table lady, of the Mouse who was listening by the kitchen door. I turned to face Lady Merlin, who sat beside me, her gold fountain pen poised over the record card.

'Miss Hawkins knew these babies. They're all new to me. The names and histories on the record cards will help me to get to know all about them.' An embracing gesture included the little boy on the scales and the other babies in various stages of undress. 'They're my babies now.'

Silently, the card was handed to me, as was the card of each baby that was brought to be weighed. New babies, on their first visit, were sent through for a check-up with Dr Lang. I was not happy with the appearance of a four-month-old little girl. There were angry red marks on her legs which I was not experienced enough to recognise. I suggested Lady Merlin should show the baby to Dr Lang. A beringed hand reached out to take the card from me.

'It is our custom for the doctor to see the new babies only.'

I retained the card. The mother, looking scared, was about to lift the baby off the scales, when Dr Lang wandered in and crossed the room towards us.

'We're not busy. I'm just popping out to the car for a book.'

She greeted the mothers and glanced casually at the baby being lifted off the scales.

'Those legs look a bit sore. I'll have a look at them when I come back. Take her into my room, would you? I won't be a minute.'

She took the card from my hand, and, with a charming smile to Lady Merlin, went out to her car for one of the medical books that always accompanied her to the clinics, where every free moment was used to absorb more knowledge about the problems of the small people with whose health and well-being she was so passionately concerned. Next time I would recognise the superficial burning from being dressed and nursed too close to a fire, but how I blessed the sharp hearing, quick reaction and consummate tact that had prevented, or at least deferred, an unpleasant confrontation with 'her Ladyship'.

We were halfway through the session and tea had just been brewed, when a large black form appeared in the kitchen doorway, his pipe temporarily replaced by a cup of tea. The room lit up, the toddlers ran to him, grabbing at his cassock, forcing him to put down his cup to pick them up in turn, tossing them in his arms to their squeals of joy. Lady Merlin looked horrified.

'Really, Father! I don't think this is quite the place for a priest. One of the mothers might be feeding her baby.'

The priest was tickling the bare tummy of a baby boy. He didn't look up.

'Everywhere is the right place for a priest.'

He left the gurgling infant and came over to the weighing table.

'I've come to meet this young lady who, wisely and correctly, hurried past me to get to her job on time.'

I had a handful of baby so couldn't shake hands, but we exchanged smiles.

'If I can be of any help to you, in any way, you'll know where to find me.' A slight wink and movement of the grey, tonsured head indicated a possible cause for needing his help. As I drank my tea, I watched the monk, who seemed so much at home in this setting that was totally alien to the life he had chosen, and wondered if our Father Abbot had any lingering regrets for the joys of natural fatherhood which he had renounced in his youth.

4

An Englishman's Castle

The summer of 1947 was 'the summer of the puppies'. Solow was a conscientious mother, but not an affectionate one, all her love being concentrated on her human family, but she did her duty by her offspring, fed them as required, and, under protest, slept in their run with them at night. As soon as we put her into the run at bedtime she gave the babies their supper in the shelter of the overturned orange box, then threw them out, one by one, to spend their final pennies. Those tiny creatures, handled by us like precious china, came hurtling into the run, rolling over and over, squealing in protest, but they got the message, and if one of them sneaked back without performing, it was immediately thrown out again.

Weaning was a major operation, fitting six hungry puppies to six dishes, one to each, while the greedy ones tried to gobble their share and steal from the gentler siblings. The lunchtime feed was a problem when I was out in the country all day, and I don't know how we would have managed without our guardian angel, Charlie. He adored the puppies and was only too delighted to take over as nursemaid when the need arose. He would spend hours leaning on the fence watching them playing, enchanted when we placed one in his outstretched hands to be fondled, his face bent to receive the licks and nuzzles and bites of his diminutive new neighbours. The little bitch, Beauty, was the prime leader in all mischief, and I am sure it was she who led her brothers out of the run one evening. When we brought Solow out to join them at dusk there were no puppies to join. They had found a gap in the wire cage and were all set for a game of hide and seek in the shrubbery, a game in which both our neighbours joined with a will. It was nearly dark before we found the last culprit by torchlight, and we were getting very anxious as a busy main road passed the front of our house. For this reason they rarely played in the front garden, but when they did, passers-by would stop to watch and laugh. One afternoon a party of children cycled past.

'Look!' cried the first.

'Puppies!' cried the second

'Sausage puppies!' squeaked the third.

The sausage puppies were playing in the back garden when Father Pat called, at our request, to bless the house. He decided to bless the puppies, and his liberal sprinkling of holy water (most of which missed the restless little creatures, hopefully sanctifying the lawns and the flowerbeds) left only a few drops of the precious liquid for the operation he had come to perform. Going from room to room, watching nothing being sprinkled from an empty container, I was satisfied that the presence and prayers of a good man would be blessing enough for any house. His offer to christen our babies by total immersion in our lily pond was, however, firmly rejected, so he cheerfully settled for a cup of tea with us on the lawn, where we were entertained by the spectacle of a mound of sleeping, exhausted puppies, heaving rhythmically up and down as the one at the bottom hiccupped through his dreams. It was on that occasion that we discovered the young priest's addiction to sugar lumps, but the laughter we shared and his enjoyment of the antics of our graceless little sausages were worth a few days of unsweetened tea.

One morning I had just finished coping with the early feed, and was putting the last puppy back into the run, when the telephone rang.

'This is Mr Storey. The wife's been taken to hospital.'

I knew Mrs Storey well – and her three small children, ranging from four and a half to six months – a quiet little woman, browbeaten by her bullying husband. It was always: 'I must ask Mr Storey', or 'I'll see what Mr Storey thinks', whether we were discussing an anti-diphtheria injection or a change of soap powder. She was a frail wisp of a woman and never looked well, although she never complained. She was kept busy with her children and a demanding husband, who, far from giving her a hand in the house, would more likely give her the sharp end of his tongue, if not the back of his hand, if his tea was five minutes late or not cooked to his liking. Poor little Mrs Storey.

'I'm so sorry,' I said. 'I hope it's nothing serious.'

'That's no concern of yours. It's the kids that's your

business,' he replied. 'That's why I'm ringing, to tell you to get them sorted out. I've got to go to work.'

I drew in my breath, mentally reviewing, as I counted to ten, the morning's commitments. Two first visits, and they'd have to wait until after the school medical inspection in Chesford village.

'You still there? You heard what I said?'

'Yes, Mr Storey, I heard you, but—'

'Don't you go butting me, woman! It's your job to look after the kids, so just you get over here, and fast.'

'I'm sorry, Mr Storey, but I'm afraid you must sort out this problem yourself. They are your children, and you are the one to decide what is to happen to them.'

I held the receiver away from my ear as the insults and obscenities roared through it.

'Kids is *your* job. What do you think we lot are paying you for?'

'Certainly not to assume the responsibilities of the children's parents but to help and advise, and that I will do if you stop shouting for a minute and listen to me.'

I gave him the telephone number of the office of the Ministry of Health in Kenilworth, where the superintendent health visitor would have a full list of local foster mothers, and know where there were vacancies.

'There are also residential nurseries in the county, but they might be a bit far for you to visit.'

'I'm not bothered about visiting. I just want the kids out of the house.'

'You may not be bothered, but surely their mother will want to have news of them when you see her. With luck, you'll be able to get them into a foster home in Dodsworth, although three is a tall order, and we do like to keep families together.'

'You bloody well stop telling me what to do, and get on and do your job.'

'No, Mr Storey. You're their father, and it's your responsibility to see the home where your children are going to live, and the people who are going to look after them.'

I was trembling a little as I put down the receiver. Rudeness always upset me, and I was thankful that the spate of insults I had received had reached me over the telephone and not in personal confrontation. Poor Mrs Storey. I wondered, if I had been approached differently, would I, perhaps, have dealt personally with the crisis, seen the foster mother myself, or packed the children into the car and taken them to whichever nursery could accommodate them. I'd done it before, but then there had been no father. If Mr Storey had politely asked for help – had, metaphorically, said please – would I have hurried over to dress the children and get them breakfast on my way out to Chesford school?

I knew he had kind neighbours who would do anything for his wife. I wondered, would the man have the sense to say 'please' to them? Would he leave the house and drive into Coventry, leaving the children alone? Just to be on the safe side, I rang the NSPCC inspector before leaving home. He promised to look in on the family during the morning. If the father was there and getting on with it, he might be glad of support. If, on the other hand, the children were alone, they would be removed to a residential home and a summons served on Mr Storey. In any case I would be informed of the children's whereabouts from the inspector, or from my own office. If, as I hoped, they were placed in a local foster home, I would be visiting them as a matter of course, and could reassure their mother that all was well with them when I visited her in hospital.

There was a small one-teacher primary school by the Catholic church in Chesford as well as the main village school higher up the hill. In 1947 the idea of bussing children into towns at the age of eleven had not been thought of, and the village children grew up and were educated in their own community. Some of the Catholic children of Chesford would go on to the RC secondary school in Leamington, but most spent their school years under the wise, strict and loving authority of Miss Hodgkin.

This slight lady in her invariable grey flannel suits, with blouses in summer and hand-knitted jumpers in winter, was a respected and much-loved figure in the village. She had taught the mothers and fathers of many of the children now under her rule, and had known the little five year olds we were examining that morning as infants and toddlers. Her young assistant had been one of her own pupils, and he helped to inculcate into a new generation the headmistress's basic teaching on good manners, consideration for others, truthfulness and hygiene, as well as a good grounding in 'the three Rs'. There was no illiteracy in Chesford. Even the children from the camp were soon incorporated into Miss Hodgkin's system and adapted to her teaching, both educational and moral. It was a joy to see the respect and love with which strapping country lads of fourteen or more would jump to obey an order, or accept reproof for a misdemeanour, from a small woman who barely reached their broad shoulders.

The medical inspection was soon completed. All the mothers were there to undress their offspring, saving valuable time, and I left Dr Lang and Miss Hodgkin with their cup of coffee, to do some visits in the village. I left reluctantly, as Father Abbot had called in to discuss the problems of an eleven-year-old girl from the camp who would be moving from the Catholic school to Miss Hodgkin's the following term. Kathleen's younger brother had been born with a congenitally diseased hip (a 'continental hip' as his mother informed me with a certain pride). The little boy claimed a large share of his mother's care, time and love, and not much was left over for the elder girl, who was a slave to her brother, fetching and carrying for him, while her toys, her hoped-for outings and her wishes were all sacrificed to his demands and needs. Her deep resentment showed itself in her behaviour at school, in her demand for the attention she lacked at home, her greed, her selfishness and her grabbing at every opportunity to assert her will on others. It was a natural reaction which the school had understood, but the time had come when adjustments would have to be made to enable the child to develop into a properly balanced person – and who better to undertake the task than Miss Hodgkin?

'The parents, being good Catholics, wanted Kathleen to go to Leamington,' the priest told us, 'but I felt the child had a better chance here.'

He grinned. 'No doubt I'll be excommunicated for this. I should be persuading my parents to send their children to a Catholic school, not the other way round!'

Miss Hodgkin smiled at him. 'I don't think the faith of any child in your parish is in much danger, Father Abbot.'

I had to leave them and drive over the brow of the hill to call on Mrs Lord. She was expecting her second baby and had missed the last two antenatal classes, and I had to find out what was keeping her away. Was she ill? Or perhaps her three year old was unwell? Mrs Lord looked embarrassed.

'I keep meaning to come, then something seems to crop up. You know how it is.'

'You're keeping well?

'Well enough, Miss.'

'And everything's arranged for the birth?'

Her first confinement had been a very easy one, and she was looking forward to having her second baby at home.

'I've decided to have it in hospital.'

'But why? Has your doctor advised it?'

'No, Miss. Doctor's not worried.'

'Why then? I thought you were so happy about having this one here.'

'I was, but I don't want that woman in the house. I don't like the idea of strangers in my house, handling my things, and that.'

41

Mrs Lord was very house proud. She had some good furniture, and nice china, some quite valuable pieces. She had been in service before her marriage, and it showed. It showed in her feeling for what was good, in the well-kept garden, the polished brass on the door, the loving and knowledgeable care lavished on her home, and the never-failing neatness and freshness of her own appearance and that of her little girl.

I was puzzling over her statement.

'But *what* woman? I thought your neighbour, Mrs Dogood, was going to help out.'

'That's what I'd planned, and my husband had arranged to take a week off work, but then the midwife said I'd have to have that woman, a home help I think she called her, and I didn't fancy the idea. So I'll go to hospital, and my mum will have Julie.'

'But Mrs Lord, you don't have to have anyone. This is your home, and you're the one to say who comes into it and who doesn't.'

'But the midwife said I must have that home-help woman if I stayed at home for the baby.'

Those years of service in other people's houses, years of taking orders, still showed in her attitude towards those she continued to look on as her 'betters'. The midwife, concerned that her mothers should be well cared for during the ten days after their confinement, would not have foreseen a situation when any suggestion of one in authority was accepted as an order.

'I think, Mrs Lord, that the midwife was *offering* you the services of a home help, not realising you had made other arrangements. Some people haven't got such helpful neighbours as you.'

Her face brightened.

'I wouldn't *have* to have one then?'

'No. You wouldn't have to have anyone, or anything. It's a free country, and no one can make you do anything you don't want in your own home.'

Mrs Lord smiled happily.

'Oh, thank you, Miss! Then I'll stay here and have Mrs Dogood, like we planned.'

'You do that. Would you like me to let Miss Smart know?'

'That's kind of you, Miss, but I hadn't actually booked at the hospital. I was going to mention it next week when I go for my check-up.'

'You can tell her about Mrs Dogood, and that your husband will be at home. She'll be delighted that you've planned it all so well. Besides, it leaves a home help free for someone else. They are very much in demand.'

As my next visit was in Lapfold, I decided to call on Miss Smart on the way. She listened with interest to the story of Mrs Lord's little quandary.

'The trouble with that one is that she's spent too many years saying "yes ma'am" "no ma'am" to that Lady Merlin up at the hall.'

'I met "that Lady Merlin" at Chesford clinic last week.'

'How did you get on?'

'We didn't.'

Miss Smart gave a whoop of laughter.

'I bet you didn't! I wish I'd been a fly on the wall.'

'You wouldn't have liked it. The atmosphere would have cut your wings off.'

I had to raise my voice as the comfortable blue-clad bottom disappeared into the kitchen, and it was hard to distinguish the human chuckles from the gurgles of water being poured into the teapot.

'How do you get on with her?' I asked as we settled ourselves by the tea table.

'She thinks she owns me because she opens her garden once a year for the District Nurses Association, which makes me a sort of good cause, like SSAFA. You know she's the local representative of SSAFA?'

'I didn't. I wouldn't like to go to her cap in hand and be assessed down that long nose of hers.'

'Actually, she's extremely good. Her father was a colonel; husband's a retired brigadier. The army's her life, and being what she is, if any of the service families are in need she won't take no for an answer, not from anyone.'

I nodded. I could understand that.

'Good for her. I go along with that. Sons in the army?'

'No sons. She must have been bitterly disappointed. She put her daughters into Girl Guide uniform as soon as she could, and had them parading and saluting. One was a Wren during the war, another in the ATS, which compensated a bit.'

'Kind of Hitler to oblige her. Talking of uniforms, have you seen the twins recently?'

She looked startled.

'They're not in uniform, for heaven's sake?'

'They *are* uniform.'

She shook her head at me, twinkling.

'I saw them the day after you didn't see them.'

'You heard?'

'The whole village has been laughing about it ever since. You'll find Lapfold's taken you to its heart. Every door will be open to you.'

I groaned.

'But what an image to start out with.'

'A human one. Someone who cares about animals and flowers. A good image in a country village.'

I was reassured. I had been brought up in a village. I should have known about the grapevine.

'The twins?'

'They're fine. She'll be bringing them to the clinic next week. It is Lapfold, isn't it?'

'It is, and I hope it is a happier set-up than the Chesford one.'

'Don't worry. Mrs Roche-Anderson and Lady Merlin couldn't be more different. Actually, Mrs R-A's got more breeding in her little finger than her ladyship has in the whole of her great bulk. Her grandfather was a peer.'

She was collecting the teacups. Her voice was quiet. Diffident.

'I wonder . . . would you mind if I looked in at the clinic? Just for a few minutes? So many of my babies will be there.'

I didn't correct her. They had only been mine for such a very short time.

'Of course, Miss Smart. It would be lovely to see you there any time.'

I was moving to the door. As she opened it, she asked, 'Where are you off to now?'

'Mrs Perkins. Know her?'

It had been a hospital confinement, so the question was not as stupid as it sounded. The midwife shook her head.

'I've never met them. They're newcomers to the village and don't mix much. Good luck, anyhow!'

The Perkins family lived in an attractive old cottage lying back from the main street. Mrs Perkins had not attended our antenatal classes, so this was to be my first meeting with her. There was always a slight element of adventure when ringing the doorbell on a first visit, wondering who and what lay the other side of the door, and what sort of reception one would be given. I was not prepared for this one. Mr Perkins opened the door. For a moment his huge frame blocked the entrance, then he came out, shutting the door firmly behind him.

'What do you want?'

His red hair stood up on his head like the hackles of an angry dog, the red moustache bristled with indignation, muscular red arms, bare to the elbow, were folded across his massive chest. I hoped I appeared braver than I felt.

'I'm the health visitor. I've called to see your wife and the new baby.'

'Why?'

'I thought, perhaps, being a first baby, I might be able to help her.'

'She wants no help, not from you or anyone. This is

my house, and I'm having no one coming here telling my wife what to do with my child.'

An Englishman's home is his castle, and there he stood, lord of the castle, embodying, in his aggressive stance, all the castle's defences – the moat, the drawbridge, and a whole regiment of archers on the battlements. It was glorious. After my previous encounters that morning it was so refreshing I could have hugged him. In fact, I laughed from sheer joy at finding a man who held himself responsible for his own family.

'Well said, Mr Perkins! You're so right, so absolutely right.'

He looked astonished. Obviously, he had not anticipated my reaction. Anger, perhaps, indignation, or an abject retreat, but not pleasure. I saw he was nonplussed and pressed home my attack.

'May I come in, please? I promise I won't give any orders, not even offer advice unless asked for it, but I would love to see your baby.'

Suddenly he grinned. Unfolding his arms, he opened the door and stood aside. The castle had fallen.

Ten minutes later we were all three round the kitchen table drinking tea and talking about many things, about mothers, about babies and their needs, both ears under the red thatch of hair listening attentively for any word from me that could be construed as 'giving advice'. His intelligent and charming wife was obviously enjoying the game, and very subtly conveyed to me that her knowledge of childcare was considerable and sound. As Mr Perkins saw me off at the door, I asked, 'May I call again sometime?'

'Anytime. You'll always be welcome . . . as a friend.'

I was indeed always welcome in their cottage and would be hailed in the street by the red-headed giant as he drove by in his van. Ten years, two houses and four children later the three of us would still sit round the kitchen table drinking tea, and not one word of advice had been given or needed. The Lord of the Castle was still the undisputed master in his own home!

5

The Boy Who Stayed In Bed

I didn't wait for the clinic before seeing my twins. If Mrs Roche-Anderson was working there she would be too busy to discuss any problems she might have, and kind Dr Lang had promised to be there early so that the little girls could be weighed and checked over before the other mothers arrived.

The babies were in the garden that afternoon; so were the puppies, and, as was to be expected, so were the roses, and nobody seemed to be having any problems, not even the little hand-reared runt who was holding his own in the rough and tumble of puppy play. It was nearly feed time and the twins were awake, watching the birds chasing each other in the branches of the beech tree in whose shade they were lying. Mrs Roche-Anderson picked up Patricia, kissing and cuddling her. Phillida held out her arms.

'May I?' I asked

'Of course, Miss Corbally. Help yourself.'

So I helped myself, and the tiny hand stroked my cheek and pulled my hair as we carried the hungry pair into the house. I noticed that my little bundle was dressed in pink, her sister in white.

'Good idea,' I said, 'they are so alike, it does distinguish one from t'other.'

'That's not really why.' She started feeding Patricia while I changed Phillida's nappy. 'I am determined they shall be individuals, not just "the twins" but two distinct people, so I'll try to emphasise the difference, not the likeness. I plan different clothes and different hairstyles.'

A novel approach. She could have the right idea. Perhaps there was too much emphasis on the identical-ness of twins, too little thought for their separate identities.

The babies were, of course, differently dressed when they came to the clinic three days later.

Lapfold clinic was sheer bliss. It was held in the village hall, a well-lit, centrally heated building. The gay coloured bowls were an improvement on the chipped enamel ones at Chesford. There were toys to distract the toddlers while I conferred with mums and babies – a doll's house, an old teddy bear, a small rocking horse and a huge box of bricks and dolls and model cars. An assortment of biscuits was served with the tea, and the mothers could, and did, relax and enjoy a quiet chat at tables covered with bright checked cloths. At my first visit Mrs Roche-Anderson had introduced me to the tea lady and the food lady and the general dogsbody lady who had no particular function, but just liked to be there, helping generally. The helpers prepared the room and put out the teacups while I undressed Phillida and Mrs Roche-Anderson prepared Patricia for weighing and the doctor's examination. She was a little heavier than her sister – six and a half pounds to Phillida's six – but both looked in perfect condition, firm and compact without an ounce of surplus fat.

Dr Lang arrived as I lifted Phillida off the scales and we carried them through, cocooned in shawls, for her inspection. I thought I detected a slight reluctance in handing me Patricia to dress while Phillida was being examined, but decided I must have imagined it as I carried her out to the pram, where her sister was soon tucked in beside her. Then the mob arrived, and from then on it was non-stop. Everyone seemed to come early and no one wanted to leave. When the babies had been weighed the mothers stayed on to talk, to play with the toddlers, to admire everyone else's babies. I was caught up in the warmth and friendliness, and introduced by the mothers I knew to those I hadn't yet visited. Mothers were greeted by their Christian names by the food lady, who had known most of them all their lives. Miss Smart's arrival was greeted with shouts of joy, and she insisted on relieving me at the scales to enjoy my cup of tea in comfort at a table beside her. The twins' corner of the tearoom was a great attraction and congratulations were showered on their proud mother.

We had difficulty in restraining three-year-old Justin from picking them up when his mother came in for his orange juice. He was not used to restraint. 'No' was a word he seldom heard, but he forgave me.

'Come and have tea with us,' we urged.

'Yes, do,' said his mother as she joined us.

So he did.

Like all the inhabitants of Lapfold, I had a very soft spot for Justin, the vicar's grandson. Mrs Hughes was a bit of an invalid and the vicar, although in many ways an admirable man, was more at home with his parishioners in the village pub, or with his cronies on the golf course, or on the playing field captaining the very able Lapfold cricket team, than providing companionship for an ailing woman. Their son-in-law, Mr Ward, worked at the Shire Hall in Warwick, and when a small house near the vicarage became available Justin's parents bought it, so that the sick woman could have her daughter, and her daughter's son, to relieve her loneliness and do the many little services for her which her reverend husband was too busy rendering similar services to his parishioners to have time for.

Justin – pampered, spoilt and indulged by parents, grandparents and neighbours – was, surprisingly, a sunny-natured, friendly and completely likeable little boy. I had the greatest sympathy for my colleague in Warwick whose job it had been to steer a fortunately healthy infant through the perilous waters of all the latest, craziest ideas on childcare which the Wards swallowed whole from every relevant book or article they could lay their hands on.

The house was filled with books, pamphlets and magazine articles by paediatricians, psychologists, psychiatrists, theorists of every sort and kind, from Dr Spock to Freud. The result, to date, was a healthy, happy little boy, and a slightly harassed young mother who

was beginning to realise that some theories are coun-
terproductive to the smooth running of a home and
the maintenance of a happy marriage.

Although my visiting was concentrated mainly on
small babies in their vulnerable first year of life, I had
an overall responsibility for the welfare of every child
in my district. I looked in on all under-fives from time
to time to make sure that everything was going well,
that they were developing normally, and showing no
early signs of any abnormality in speech, sight, hearing
or any other function. I visited Justin more often than
most, partly because, having certain reservations as to
the wisdom of his mother's theories, I felt the child
could be, to a degree, 'at risk' regarding his psychological and moral development, but also because I found
the visits enjoyable. It was stimulating to be in the
company of this eager, chatty little boy and his very
intelligent young mother, who loved to discuss her
ideas with me, although well aware that I was not in
agreement with many of them.

'But if you never refuse him anything, isn't he likely
to grow up utterly selfish and demanding?'

'Frustrating children is so damaging to them
psychologically.'

She would get a book off the shelf, or leaf through
the pages of a magazine to show me the writings of
some eminent crank, who probably wouldn't know the
difference between a child and a dandelion.

'Society is governed by rules,' I protested. 'Wouldn't
it be kinder to start getting him used to them now . . .
just a very few?'

'No rules!' A stabbing finger would emphasise her point. 'Absolutely no rules. Children should be allowed to develop their personality freely.'

As my little friend climbed onto my knee to show me his latest book, I thought how fortunate it was for everyone that it happened to be such a delightful personality that was developing so freely. But for how long? How soon would the policy of complete freedom and total indulgence begin to adversely affect this seemingly unspoilable child?

'Aren't you afraid that if you bring him up to have everything he wants, the day will come when he'll take what he isn't given?'

That made her look thoughtful. I enlarged on the theme.

'Thieves and rapists, it's the same story. "I want, so I must have" and be damned to everyone else. Is that what you really want for Justin?'

An expensive model car was thrust into my hand.

'Mummy bought me this yesterday.'

'Justin, it's beautiful! But I didn't know you had a birthday this month.'

He looked surprised.

'I didn't have a birthday. I just saw it in the shop.'

I glanced at his mother. She had the grace to lower her eyes momentarily. 'He wanted it so much . . .' she murmured.

'I want, so I must have.' I smiled at her. 'Do think about it, Mrs Ward. He's only got one life and what he makes of it will depend, to a great extent, on how you bring him up.'

I felt that I really had started her thinking, so didn't leave it many weeks before following up my advantage. After a busy morning I was driving near her house on my way home for lunch, so I called in. Mrs Ward was preparing a meal in the kitchen. There was no sign of my friend Justin.

'He's in bed,' she told me.

'I'm sorry. What's the matter with him?'

She shrugged her shoulders, a small gesture of defeat that was alien to her.

'There's nothing the matter with him. He just didn't want to get up this morning.'

I kept silent. I heard in her voice that the moment of crisis was not far off. Motioning me to a chair by the kitchen table, she slumped down opposite me.

'He just didn't want to get up, and I'd planned a morning's shopping. If he doesn't move soon I don't see myself getting to the shops this afternoon. It's just not funny.'

'I never did think it was funny.'

She gave a shamefaced little grin.

'I know. You've never said much, but I've always sensed your disapproval of the way we're bringing him up.'

'It's not for me to disapprove. Justin's your child, and you're entitled to rear him according to your own principles, only . . .'

I paused.

'Only what?'

Her eyes were asking me for help. Pleading with me to save her from what she now recognised as a growing threat to her home, her marriage, her sanity, even to her child, without demanding total surrender of all she had believed in.

I smiled encouragingly.

'Only, do be consistent. Justin isn't the only person around here with rights. He is one third of your family and is entitled to a third share of rights and privileges, no more. You and your husband also have rights which Justin must recognise.'

She nodded.

'That seems fair, but what can I do about it? What can I do now, for instance?' She held up her hand as I opened my mouth to answer. 'I know what you're going to say. I know what you'd do. You'd get him out of bed, wouldn't you, get his clothes on, put him in the car and go to the shop?'

'You bet your life I would!'

She shook her head.

'It wouldn't be fair. It's never fair to take advantage of our superior strength.'

'I know, and I wasn't going to suggest it. I have a far better idea. Stay in bed tomorrow morning.'

'Me? Stay in bed? But what would happen to Justin's breakfast?'

'The same thing that happened to your shopping: it just wouldn't happen at all.'

A slow gleam came into her eyes.

'Fair dos. You didn't feel like getting up yesterday. I don't feel like it today.'

She grinned. 'I like it.'

'Will you be strong-minded enough to go through with it until he gets the message?'

'You bet I will! You bet your life I will!'

Anxious to know what had happened, I called back the following week. Grandad was just leaving the house as I drove up. He came over and opened the door of my car.

'Well, if it isn't the miracle worker herself! I don't know how you've done it, but you've certainly put the fear of God into that young grandson of mine.'

I raised my eyebrows.

'The fear of God? I hope not.'

The vicar smiled.

'You're right. Perhaps that's too strong a word, but you've certainly changed things around here.'

He laughed suddenly.

'Talking about the fear of God . . . did you hear about the bishop arriving at the gates of Heaven, and being kept standing around while a gorgeous young girl was let in before him? Understandably indignant, he asked St Peter why a young girl was given precedence over a high-ranking churchman.

''Well . . .' said St Peter, 'It's like this. That girl we've just admitted has been driving around the countryside in a red sports car. She and that car have put the fear of God into more people in one week than you've done in your whole life!'''

I laughed. I could have capped his delightful story with other, equally funny St Peter episodes, but I couldn't wait to see what the fear of God had done to our little Justin.

I found Mrs Ward jubilant. Over a cup of tea she told me about it; how Justin, full of energy after his long rest, had come bursting into her room at eight o'clock demanding his breakfast, returning to the attack at frequent intervals until, by eleven o'clock, her heart was melted by his tearful pleading. Half an hour later, over a brunch of bacon and sausages at the kitchen table, Justin helped his mother to draw up a charter of human rights which was to operate in the future in their home, for the benefit and happiness and convenience of every member of the family. Proudly she drew her charming little boy into the circle of her arm.

'His daddy was so surprised yesterday when Justin insisted on letting him choose the first cake at tea-time. It was Daddy's turn, you see.'

I felt there was some hope that Justin would grow up into a respectable citizen. I would gladly have lingered with those two delightful people, but I had to hurry home as my own little three year old was coming to spend the weekend with us. Actually Marcus was my nephew, but he had been visiting us so frequently since my elder brother's divorce – which happened when the child was not yet two years old – that Eileen and I had come to regard him as our very own. He lived with his mother, but his father had frequent access, and, in the early days, would bring his little son home to our mother when an SOS would be sent to me to go and cope with nappies, sock-washing, nose-wiping and the many jobs that surround small humans, while his father relaxed and his granny worshipped. As a result of these weekends, Marcus and I were already friends when he strode over the threshold of 149 on his sturdy two-year-old legs and took possession of our home and of our hearts.

Living with his mother in a London flat, Marcus was enchanted by our spacious garden, and chortled with joy as he marched up and down the narrow path of the garden, gently caressing the tiny plants growing beside it. He was always gentle with his hands. It is not every child that I would let loose among my precious flowers, but Marcus could be trusted not to bruise or break the most delicate stems. We early noticed the sureness and deftness of his movements. He was never a fumbler or a dropper or a breaker, and by the time he was four years old he would love to stand on a stool (he was too small to reach the sink) and wash up even our most precious glass and china, and he knew how it should be done. On one occasion, being in rather a hurry, Eileen was firmly reprimanded for taking a dripping saucer straight from his hand to dry it.

'No. You must let it drain first,' he told her.

We wondered about his future. With such sureness of touch, a surgeon, perhaps? Or an engineer? The second guess was right.

After that first visit, Marcus adopted 149 as his second home, and Pat invariably brought his little boy to Kenilworth for the weekends when he was allowed to borrow him. His ex-wife Diana was generous in this matter, even sparing her adored child for an occasional Christmas with his father's family. Of course, some weekends were still spent with Granny, but I was not so readily available as a nursemaid, now that I had my own home, so it was simpler for him to come to us. When Pat collected his son on Friday afternoon, the excited child would ask, in his deep throaty voice, 'Where we going? Aunt Molly and Eileen?' His excitement would increase as they drove through Kenilworth, passing the castle and through the ford. Pat would accelerate and shrieks of joy would greet the splash that surged over the car and sprayed the windows. We were always told of the delights of the SPLASH as our small guest tumbled out of the car and into our arms. In those first breathless moments of greeting we had to hear everything of note that had happened since his last visit, and that Friday afternoon was no exception. He had recently been on a visit to his uncle and aunt in France, and told us all about the flight, his first.

'It was the most exciting thing I've done in the last three years,' the little three year old announced solemnly.

6

The Camp

It was partly the demands of the large garden, and partly Eileen's worry over what she considered an unfair division of labour, that made us start asking around in case somebody knew somebody who had heard of somebody who would come and clean for us, leaving me my Saturday mornings free. Our enquiries resulted in a visit from Mrs Wilson, who was one of the best things that ever happened to us. An excellent worker, completely reliable, her kindness, thoughtfulness and dry sense of humour combined to create a friendly relationship which was to last many years, until her husband's illness forced her to give up work.

During her years in our employment, we often laughed together over her first interview with Eileen and me. We had never engaged anyone before. We had, of course, been responsible for staff, for probationer nurses, for orderlies and ward maids, but we didn't employ them nor pay their salaries. This was different. Mrs Wilson, if we liked each other (and we did) was going to work for *us*; she would be our 'staff'. On her first morning, arriving punctually at 9 a.m., she told me how she had looked back that day as she walked away up the drive, and had seen us through the open window, dancing with joy, telling one another, with gurgles of laughter, 'We've got a staff!' She had told her husband that she felt she was going to enjoy working at 149.

It was fortunate that our 'staff' arrived in good time. I seldom left the house before 9.15, allowing time for emergency phone calls from the office, or from any mother needing an urgent visit, so there was time for a quick look round the house, the locating of brooms, dusters, etc. and, of course, the tea caddy for the mid-morning cuppa. I would be home for lunch and would probably see Mrs Wilson before she left to check that all had gone smoothly. I planned to spend the afternoon at the camp at Chesford.

After five years, the camp dwellers had more or less been assimilated into the life of the village. A new generation of children had been born in Chesford who had no memories of Coventry, and the older children were losing their fear of the wide open spaces, learning country lore and country manners, identifying birds and trees and wild flowers, recognising the difference between mushrooms and toadstools, edible blackberries and deadly nightshade, shutting gates behind them as they plucked up courage to walk through a field of cows or sheep, and touching their caps to the gentry in the village street. Some never did lose their fear of cows, never acclimatised to rural life and drifted back to Coventry as soon as they left school. Some women, in the early days, had complained of the silence, missing the constant hum of traffic. Others complained of the noise, of being woken by a cockerel from a nearby farm, their sleep disturbed by the hooting of a barn owl, the lowing of a cow which had lost her calf, the barking of a dog – even, unbelievably, the singing of a nightingale. Gradually they adjusted, and were drawn into the life of Chesford, joining the WI, learning to make jam, to bake bread, to skin a rabbit and pluck a fowl.

Although Lady Merlin, as a member of the District Council, had vigorously opposed the siting of the camp in 'her' village, she had to accept the *fait accompli*, even inviting 'the foreigners' to the annual harvest lunch in her barn. She had to concede that many of the camp children were brighter and quicker and better workers than the cottagers, but it was almost a physical hurt to her, at the school prizegiving, to hand some of the highest awards to the Coventry children, many of whom, under Miss Hodgkin's excellent tuition, went on to grammar schools in their native city. Perhaps the lucky children were the slower learners who, in a big town school, could not have received the individual and painstaking care available at the village school, and might, in different circumstances, have grown up illiterate.

The wide range of ability and accomplishment among the camp children reflected the wide range in their living conditions. Many people might think that a hut is a hut, until they looked inside, as I so frequently did. Some were dark, dirty, sparsely furnished with broken-down odds and ends; neglected slums. Others were gay and bright, charmingly furnished homes, clean and shining with carefully tended little gardens. There was as much variety in the hutted homes as there was among the housewives who ran them. They were always a bone of contention between me and my friend, the housing manager. Man-like, he tended to take pity on the slum dwellers, and was apt to offer them the council houses as they became vacant.

'They're living like pigs,' he would argue. 'We can't leave them in such appalling conditions.'

'They make their own conditions,' I pointed out. 'These women would turn a new house into a slum within months. Give your houses to those who deserve them, the house-proud women who can transform a hut into a palace.'

I won my point, and the council houses were allocated as a reward for good housekeeping, until the bad house-keepers realised that unless they made an effort to put their homes in order, they had no hope of leaving the camp. In desperation they brought out their brooms and dusters and scrubbing brushes, polished the windows to let in the light, saved their coupons for curtain material, and rummaged around to replace the wooden crates and orange boxes which had served as tables and seats. All such efforts received every encouragement, and persever-ance would be rewarded by an upgrading on the housing list for long-standing tenants of the huts.

On the whole, the camp dwellers were a friendly community and would help one another in any diffi-culty. Close friendships would develop among neighbours, which would suddenly be broken over some trivial disagreement, only to be resumed equally suddenly.

Bosom friends, often to be found in each other's huts when I visited, would, one day, not be speaking to each other, but, on my next visit, be again inseparable. Living under difficult and cramped conditions, tempers would flare easily, but no quarrel seemed to last long.

It is natural to assume that anyone living in a hut is short of money. This could be true if they had a choice, but in the 1950s people lived in huts because there were not enough houses to go round. Their income had nothing to do with it. On the contrary, the rents of the huts being low, many of their occupants were better off in terms of 'disposable income' than those paying higher rents in council houses. I was not yet very experienced in social work when I was conned by Mrs Black into promising to find her a layette for her third baby. She was not one of the better housewives, and her hut, although reasonably clean, was poorly furnished. In my enthusiasm, I was even looking out for a second-hand pram to replace the tatty vehicle that had carried her two previous babies, groceries, firewood, and any other cargo that required four wheels.

Mrs Black's neighbour, Mrs Crane, was invariably with her when I called. She was going to look after her friend when the baby came, and seemed a little envious of the clothes I was hoping to find in the Women's Voluntary Service (WVS) store or from young mothers among my own friends and relations. No one had helped her when her babies arrived, she grumbled. I had got some knitting wool from the Red Cross, but Mrs Black was not making much progress, and the vest she had started never seemed to grow. She hadn't time for knitting, she told me, with the hut to look after, and the children, and the cooking and washing and all. I took most of the wool home for my friend and I to knit up in the evenings.

I was still waiting for the nappies and nightgowns and little frocks from the WVS when, calling in one afternoon, I found Mrs Black very low-spirited. Could I find someone to help her out when the baby came?

'But I thought Mrs Crane was coming in to help you?'

'She was, but we've fallen out. I'm not speaking to her, let alone having her in my home.'

'But I thought you were such friends. What's gone wrong between you?'

'She won't come out with me any more. It's that husband of hers, wants her to go with him now their eldest can be left with the kids. We used to go to the pictures together, twice a week, regular, and have a bit of supper in the town.'

'Twice a week?'

'Yes, regular. It made a bit of a change.'

I was doing a quick mental calculation of the cost of even the cheapest seats, twice a week, and a 'bit of supper'. What a soft, gullible fool I'd been! I wasn't really worried about the help, there were still ten weeks for the neighbours to patch up their quarrel, and I knew Mrs Crane wouldn't let her down. The layette was different.

'I haven't been able to get the things from the WVS yet. It's a difficult time; with coupons, people hang onto their baby clothes in case another comes along.'

She looked sulky.

'I'm counting on them things. I can't afford to rig out a new baby.'

'I think you can, Mrs Black. With the money you'll be saving from your little outings with Mrs Crane you'll be able to get everything you need. If you'd been content to go out only once a week all these months you'd have saved enough by now for the pram as well.'

She looked sullen, trapped, no doubt cursing herself for not keeping her mouth shut.

'We've finished the vests, Mrs Black. I'll be out here next week and will bring them over. There's enough wool left for three matinee coats and a few bootees. I'll let you have it back now that you've more time in the evenings.'

As in many closed communities, the neighbours at the camp minded one another's business, nosily perhaps, but caringly. The gossips at least ensured that any real trouble would reach the ears of the concerned member of the community who would help where they could, or call in assistance from outside, not infrequently from me. That is how I heard, via Lady Merlin, that the Crawley children were being left alone in the evenings while their parents were out drinking.

One of the girls from the camp was working at Chesford Hall, and the 'little creature', as her employer described Rita, was pumped regularly as to 'what was going on in that dump'. Her ladyship took it for granted that people who lived in huts, for whatever reason, were only half-human, and 'those sort of people' must be living lawless and immoral lives. She was delighted to receive any scrap of evidence to give weight to her considered opinion of 'those pathetic creatures', and if little Rita could win herself a rare smile from her stern mistress by providing such evidence, who could blame her.

I was summoned to the Hall. My Lady was seated at her desk when I was shown in. She glanced up, then continued reading the letter in her hand as I crossed the deep pile carpet. For a moment I stood in front of the desk.

'Good morning, Lady Merlin.'

She looked up.

'Good morning, nurse.'

She put the letter aside, clearing the desk for battle.

'I've sent for you, nurse, because I'm very displeased.'

I moved a Chippendale chair near to the desk and sat down.

'What about, Lady Merlin?'

'About the shocking goings-on at the camp. Children being neglected.'

She lowered her eyes in some surprise to my seated form. I waited.

'I have heard from the most reliable authority that that slattern, Mrs Crawley, goes out drinking at night leaving those brats of hers alone in the hut.'

I had been let in by 'the most reliable authority' – looking scared stiff, poor girl. She may have worked at the Hall, but she had to live in the camp, and it was not an environment that encouraged tittle-tattle.

'I'm appalled, nurse. Did you know about this?'

'No, but I'm glad you've told me.'

She shook her stately head in pained bewilderment.

'But I don't understand. How could you not have known? That's what people like you are for, isn't it – to protect helpless children from those sort of creatures?'

I was too fascinated to be angry or indignant. She was tapping the desk with her gold pen, the same pen that I remembered poised above the clinic record cards.

'Well?'

I pulled myself together. This wasn't really meant to be a monologue.

'Now I know about it, I'll investigate.'

'Investigate, indeed!' She sniffed derisively. 'There's nothing to investigate. You've heard the facts.'

'But not from Mrs Crawley.'

'What nonsense! It's none of her business. She's the culprit, isn't she? The children must be taken away. I could probably use my influence to get them a place in Dr Barnado's.'

She paused for my gratitude to pour over her. As none was forthcoming, she stood up. The interview was ended; the sentence pronounced.

'You'll see to it then?'

I replaced the chair by the wall.

'As I said, Lady Merlin, I shall visit Mrs Crawley and see what she has to say before I decide anything.'

'Before *you* decide?'

She had gone red in the face with anger.

'Yes, the decision will be mine, in what I see to be the best interests of the children, and I will not be bullied or hectored into taking any action against my own judgement.'

I was due to see Mrs Crawley anyhow. Her eldest was nearly ready for school. Now, I am very much in favour of parents enjoying an evening out together from time to time, and many of the camp mothers took turns to babysit for each other to make this possible. Casually, I asked Mrs Crawley whether she and her husband were able to arrange an occasional evening free of their children. She bridled and coloured up.

'The neighbours have been talking.'

It was a statement, not a question. She was on the defensive, trying to justify to herself, rather than to me, what she knew to be wrong.

'I know I shouldn't leave the kids, but I make sure they're asleep.'

She was looking straight at me, defiant and challenging, but a sudden lowering of the eyelids made me wonder what means she took to ensure the deep sleep of her lively children. Aspirin? Gin? Her eyes met mine again.

'I make sure to leave nothing around, no matches or knives or poisons or anything that could harm them, but I have to go with him.'

'Why, Mrs Crawley?' I asked gently.

'I know my old man. If I'm not with him, he'll take up with some woman in the pub. It's happened before and nearly broke us up.' Unconsciously she had clasped her hands, and her voice, quieter now, was pleading for understanding.

'If I stay home with the kids I risk losing my man, then where'd they be, without their dad? What am I to do?'

There's a French proverb very dear to my heart: *Tout savoir c'est tout pardoner.* 'To know all is to forgive all.' If the neighbours, so quick to condemn, knew what I had just heard, how helpful they would be. They knew what marriage was all about. They'd had their own husband problems. They would understand and give sympathy instead of blame to this hard-pressed mother. They would rally round her instead of threatening her with the 'Cruelty Man'. I could not betray her confidence, nor could I suggest that she should lower the dual flags of pride and loyalty that flew so bravely over the huts where the poorest and most troubled families lived. I could, and did, suggest a babysitter at least twice a week, and the wise, kindly Scotswoman, whose eldest girl was willing to share the evenings with her mother, needed no hint from me to volunteer her own solution to the problem.

'I'll ask my Jock to go along with Tom Crawley of an evening when the lass is at home with the bairns.'

How much damage can be caused by jumping to conclusions or by hasty judgements. Our own blissful domestic arrangements could well have been shattered by just such a judgement.

❧

Under Mrs Wilson's expert hands our house began to shine, and it was heaven to come in at lunchtime on 'Mrs Wilson's mornings' to a warm fire. Other days I didn't light the fire until I had finished work, and lunchtime was cold and cheerless and hurried, filled with chores I had got up too late to do in the morning, and often shopping to be fitted in. There is a saying: 'Every working woman needs a wife!' Mrs Wilson's mornings were such luxury for me, and she wanted to do extra jobs for us, like cleaning windows and washing paint, so we suggested a second morning, an extra two hours. We agreed to pay her for six hours, which she could divide between the two mornings to suit her convenience.

'We'll pay you for six hours and you can do what you like,' I told her. Never to be forgotten words, which were to erupt in a saga of misunderstanding, embarrassment and laughter.

It was the next 'Mrs Wilson's morning', a Friday, when I met her in the drive on her way home. The conversation went something like this:

Me: 'What have you been doing this morning?'

Mrs W: 'I had a nice half hour in the garden, and glanced through your new magazines. I did do a bit of dusting.'

Me: 'It was kind of you to do the dusting.'

Mrs W: 'Well, we did agree, didn't we, that you would pay me for six hours, and I could do what I liked.'

We parted with grins of mutual understanding, and, chuckling, I went into my warm shining home, fragrant with the scent of burning wood and furniture polish. Gratefully enjoying a hot lunch, I was unaware of the furore that was taking place on the other side of the fence. Unknown to us, Charlie had been in his front garden and had overheard our conversation. His indignation knew no bounds. That dreadful woman was taking advantage of his angels. We were too good, too

72

kind. Something would have to be done to protect us. What he proposed to do, I shudder to think. Fortunately, I met him in the local post office the following morning, relating, with tears in his eyes, the story of Mrs Wilson's perfidy to the postmistress and her customers. What a laugh we all had when I explained that it was all just one big leg-pull. After that, if I ever wanted to get a laugh out of Mrs Wilson, I had only to ask her: 'What have you been doing this morning?'

7

Mothers and Daughters

One of the chief reasons for making our home in Warwickshire was to be near my mother as she grew older and needed support. Before her heart attack in 1948, she had been in reasonably good health, leading an active life, walking miles over the countryside with her whippet, and driving around in her little Austin visiting her many friends. It had been a mild attack, and I nursed her at home for a short time before bringing her to convalesce with us at Kenilworth. With maternal pride she announced to the friends who came to see her at 149, 'Molly is really a very good nurse.'

Smiling, they reminded her that her daughter had, in fact, been trained as a nurse! Some mothers can never realise that there comes a time when their children are children no more. My brothers were very senior officers in their respective services, the Royal Ulster Rifles and the RAF, when we attended a memorial service for an uncle in Westminster Abbey. Meeting our mother outside the main entrance, she exclaimed, to our delight, 'How grown-up you boys look in your uniform!' Such are mothers, and such mothers can pose a problem if and when it becomes necessary for one of 'the children' to take control. Fortunately, my own mother was mentally alert and knew exactly what she wanted. She just liked to feel I was there and available at the end of a telephone. After her illness I advised her to slow up, to have an electric fire instead of carrying coal and logs, to curtail her walks.

'Let's get this straight,' she said. 'I intend to go on as I have always done and take my chances. I would rather live for two years than exist for ten.'

I went along with her choice. I sympathised with it and remembered it often while dealing with other mothers and their daughters. In fact, my mother 'lived' another nine years, and died a month before her eightieth birthday, quietly and peacefully, after coming in from a long walk with her dog in the lanes and fields she loved.

Mrs Hennessey was the first 'mother' problem that came my way.

Miss Hennessey sounded desperate on the phone. Could I meet her somewhere? For lunch perhaps? I could, and we fixed a rendezvous at a small coffee shop not far from the big, new hotel where she worked as assistant manageress. I had not yet met Miss Hennessey, although I'd been visiting her elderly mother on and off for nearly six months, in the untidy, over-furnished, and charming five-bedroomed house where she lived alone with her budgie. After her husband's death, five years previously, she had had a companion living with her, and my visits started after that lady had left to share a home with her own widowed sister. On the edge of Coventry, domestic help was almost impossible to find and Mrs Hennessey was well above the financial bracket for a home help, even if we had one available. Even so, the big house, although cluttered, was clean and well cared for, and the old lady fed well, although she admitted that, after a lifetime of servants, she was hardly able to boil an egg. She conceded that Alicia was a good daughter, but, until we met over lunch, I had no idea how good.

I recognised Miss Hennessey from a photograph on her mother's piano; a tall, handsome, capable-looking woman with dark hair, softly waved and caught into a bun in the nape of her neck. She looked tired and anxious, almost distraught, and I sensed that her controlled manner was a cover for a state of nervous exhaustion.

When a light meal of egg salad and home-made rolls had been ordered, she leant towards me across the table.

'I don't know what I'm going to do about my mother.'

I had heard those words before, and was to hear them many times again.

'What's the problem, Miss Hennessey?'

'She's draining me. Ever since Miss Weller left, she's on the telephone at all hours. It's not enough that I go in every morning and get her breakfast and clean through. I shop for her and get her lunch, but she still rings up . . . several times a day. She's lost something, or wants something, or has forgotten something, or just suddenly feels lonely and frightened. I've a responsible, demanding job. I can't just down tools and rush over to her every time she rings. We have receptions in the evenings, dinner parties, dances. I have to be around.'

I could visualise it. A lonely old lady, the telephone her only link with the outside world, and her daughter so conveniently working in her office with a telephone on her desk. That was what one paid companions for, to find things, to remember things, and since Miss Weller had left there was the telephone.

'I can't find my reading glasses.'

'I've mislaid my address book.'

'I've forgotten which grocer stocks the china tea you recommended.'

'I forgot to turn the oven on and I've nothing for lunch.'

By the time the second cups of coffee arrived the picture was quite clear.

'I can't go on like this, I'll lose my job. The manager's very understanding, but there have been mistakes recently through my worrying about mother, and he's had to cope with things because I've not been there when people have rung up.'

The dark eyes looked desperate.

'When did you last have a holiday?' I asked.

'Not since Miss Weller left, not a real holiday. I just go home and look after Mother.'

'You need a real holiday, two whole weeks right away from the hotel and your mother and everything.'

My companion smiled grimly. 'Don't tempt me. She couldn't manage without me, not for one day, let alone two weeks.'

'Have you ever discussed her giving up the house and going into a private home where she'd be looked after?'

Miss Hennessey looked genuinely shocked. 'I couldn't suggest such a thing! I'm not the sort of person to put my mother away because she's old.'

I smiled. 'I'm not talking about a workhouse, or a geriatric ward. There are a few delightful private homes in the town, one I particularly like run by a married nurse who really cherishes her guests. Perhaps your mother would go there for a couple of weeks, while you're away, and see how she likes it?'

Hope dawned in the brown eyes. 'I'll suggest it. It certainly would be wonderful to get a break. I'm due for a holiday next month.'

I wrote down Mrs Gould's address and gave it to her. 'Why not go and look at it. I'll ring Mrs Gould; she'll be expecting you.'

Neither of us were surprised when Mrs Hennessey refused to move, even for a week. Her daughter was resigned to spending yet another holiday looking after her, although the old lady urged her to go away.

'She needs a break,' she told me at my next visit. 'I'll be all right. Do I look as if I need to go into a home?'

Relaxed, well fed, well dressed, in her clean comfortable drawing room, she certainly did not appear to need any other accommodation. But I knew her daughter had reached breaking point. Her health as well as her job was at stake. Neighbours were good, but the old lady's constant demands, even on them, were beginning to pall. They were not prepared to carry the full load if her daughter went away. Poor Mrs Hennessey, deluded by her comfort and well-being, was blissfully unaware of her total dependence on others. She had never yet lacked anything necessary to her comfort and saw no reason why she ever should – even if her daughter went away, even if the neighbours just happened to take their holidays at the same time.

It took all my powers of persuasion to talk Miss Hennessey into booking a holiday with a friend of hers in a seaside town not too far away, just in case our plan failed to work. Predictably, when she told the neighbours, they discovered that the same dates would suit them very well for their own holidays, or they would be having guests to stay. They were very sorry. Any other time they would, of course, have been delighted to help the old lady in any way.

A room was reserved at Mrs Gould's for two weeks, with the option of a permanent booking. Miss Hennessey stocked her mother's larder, filled the fridge with pre-cooked dishes, and drove down to the sea. For two days all was well. I was the finder of missing objects, the looker-upper of telephone numbers, but most of the day the telephone lay idle. There was no one at the other end. By the third day the old lady was confused. She seemed unable to find a thing, to make any decisions. She was beginning to feel the effect of a lifetime of total dependence on her husband, her companion, her daughter. Hurt by the lost look in her eyes, I suggested driving her over to see Mrs Gould. She shook her head.

'I'm all right. I'm managing very nicely. Alicia thinks I can't manage without her, but I can.'

I rang her up that evening. I knew from her voice that she had been crying. The next day I took her, unresisting and deeply relieved, accompanied by her budgie, to be welcomed with warmth and infinite kindness by Mrs Gould and her fellow residents. She never returned to her home. When Miss Hennessey came back from her holiday she found her mother happily settled into her new life, stimulated by the companionship of the other guests, secure in the unobtrusive vigilance of her hostess. The charming bed-sitter was refurnished with her own belongings, but there were less of them to be lost, less places to lose them in, fewer decisions to take. Like all Mrs Gould's guests, she became younger as her worries fell from her, she became more active with her new friends to do things with, to go for walks and coach trips, to enjoy concerts together, or a quiet evening of bridge.

I first met Mrs Gould when the Carson family were in danger of breaking up. Mr Carson spent every evening at the local pub, the teenage children were rebellious and uncontrollable, and Mrs Carson was on the edge of a breakdown. Why? Because Mrs Carson's parents had moved in with the family when they decided to sell their house fifteen years previously. It had worked well at first. Inbuilt babysitters are a boon to a married couple, and they worked their stint in the house and garden, while their financial contribution helped with the mortgage. Unfortunately, with age and ill health, they had become difficult, querulous and bitter. They kept more and more to their room, demanded more and more attention. Family holidays had stopped, because the old couple could not be left alone in the house. When they did leave their room it was to complain and find fault; with Mr Carson for not helping his wife more, with the children for being too noisy, with their daughter for a badly cooked or over-due meal. In a three-bedroomed house they occupied one of the large rooms, leaving the two girls to sleep and study and enjoy what fun they could in one small room. No wireless was allowed, no jazzy records. There was no room for guests to stay, and even friends, invited in for a meal, would need to be shielded from unpleas-antness or downright rudeness, from one or other of the grandparents.

There was nothing for it. If the little family was to stay together the old people would have to go. Mrs Carson wept copiously when I suggested it.

'I've had them all these years, how can I turn them out now? I've always despised people who refuse to provide a home for their old parents, and I was deter-mined I would do so.'

I tried to make her understand what she was doing to her own family.

'You've done your duty by your parents, far more than most daughters would have done, but your first duty is to your husband and children, and they're being damaged, so are you. You'll be really ill if this situation goes on.'

'But I *can't* put them away. They're my *parents*.'

'You can't keep them here. There's no shame in "putting them away", as you put it, provided we find somewhere where they'll be well looked after and happy. Are they really happy here?'

She paused to think. It was patently obvious to me that they were far from happy. How could they be? Over the years small tiffs had escalated into bitter quarrels, little misunderstandings had festered, and hatred was creeping in. How could they be happy? How could anyone be happy? Six human beings were living together in mutual antagonism and misery to satisfy one woman's sense of duty, to pander to her pride in being one of those righteous daughters who provided a home for her aged parents.

'Why don't you take your family away for a holiday and try and find each other again?'

'What would happen to my parents?'

'Leave that to me. I'll find somewhere for them.'

'Suppose they won't go?'

'I think they will.'

I guessed right. They were overjoyed at the idea of a change, of escape, even temporary, from an atmosphere of hatred for which they knew themselves to be partly responsible but felt unable to dispel.

'We don't mean to upset them, but, when one's tired, and not feeling too grand, and the kids start kicking up a row, one speaks more sharply than one means to, then Robbie gets on his high horse and goes banging out of the house, and Janet scolds us, and the girls sulk.'

They had a bit of a nest egg put by. They had hoped to leave a tidy bit to their grandchildren, but, as things were, they felt the girls would prefer their room now to their money later. They would be able to afford Mrs Gould's fees, and she expected to have a large room vacant within the next few months.

Independent, wanted, cherished, no longer aware of being a burden or a nuisance, the old couple mellowed and were soon transformed into loving and much-loved parents and grandparents, whose visits to the family home were occasions of joy to all.

There wasn't always such a satisfactory solution to this ever-increasing problem of ageing parents, but I will never cease to regret the betrayal and deception that led to the death of one particularly sweet old lady.

Mrs Nathan shared a small semi-detached cottage with her elder sister, also a widow. Her daughter lived in Warwick and visited them often. She was devoted to her mother, but found her old aunt increasingly trying as she became more and more infirm. When they came into my orbit, the aunt was virtually bedridden, stone deaf, and totally dependent on her sister. The daughter, Mrs Hanford, felt the burden was too much for her mother, who was well over eighty herself, and eventually managed to get her aunt admitted to a geriatric ward. What she had not understood was the deep love that existed between the old sisters – the companionship of the presence of a loved one in the cottage, the communication of touches and smiles and the joy of service, of being needed.

There is a touching story told of a small boy seen by a stranger carrying a smaller brother on his back up a hill. 'Isn't that a heavy burden for you?' asked the stranger. 'He's not a burden,' replied the small boy. 'He's my brother.'

Mrs Nathan's sister was no burden to her and her going was traumatic. The silence and emptiness of the cottage became unbearable and she would wander for miles over the countryside, dropping in on neighbours for a chat. She was a sweet old lady, with a puckish sense of humour and was dearly loved, but her frequent and interminable visits became an embarrassment. She loved being taken for drives, and would turn up at a house, excited and expectant, asking where they were taking her that afternoon. No one wanted to hurt her, but one can't always drop everything and cancel plans to give a lonely old lady the pleasure of a drive through the countryside.

Although physically strong and active, her mind was deteriorating. She became forgetful and absent-minded. I would find clothes smouldering by the electric fire, and gas taps left on, unlit, in the kitchen. Understandably, her neighbours were worried and expressed their concern to Mrs Hanford, who was now visiting her mother more frequently. Apart from her intense loneliness, the old lady was happy pottering around her beloved home and garden, which were immaculately maintained, visiting her neighbours, and walking through the fields and woods she loved, but the neighbours were not happy. The risk of fire was a very real one, and their lives were being disrupted by the frequent ringing of their bells, and the pleading eyes in the lined old face.

'I'm so lonely,' she would murmur, and it was good-bye to their peaceful evening, their afternoon in the garden, or the morning's shopping in Leamington.

Every summer the Hanfords spent a month touring on the continent, and it was clear that the neighbours could no longer accept responsibility for Mrs Nathan in their absence. The answer seemed to be a temporary stay in an old people's home they knew of. They discussed it with me, and I agreed that it seemed a sensible plan, if they could persuade Mrs Nathan to leave her cottage. Mrs Hanford hoped that her mother would adapt to life in the home and stay on there, but I very much doubted it. It was in a town, and Mrs Nathan was a countrywoman who needed to breathe country air and walk on grass and woodland paths, to sit under trees and listen to the birdsong, but, for a few weeks, I agreed that it might be an acceptable solution. I should never have agreed, not to a home. I should have combed the villages for temporary accommodation in a private house. If I could have found a better solution, her daughter would have gladly accepted it, but I didn't look for one.

The Hanfords were leaving very early on Saturday morning and called for Mrs Nathan on Friday afternoon. Excited at the thought of a drive, the unsuspecting old lady got into the car with her son-in-law, while her daughter hastily packed a suitcase. As they drove off, Mrs Nathan waved to her neighbour. 'I'll see you this evening and tell you all about it,' she said. That was the last the neighbours saw of her.

They left her at the home, where she waited, puzzled, for them to come and fetch her. Suppertime arrived, and they hadn't come, then bedtime, and she was taken to her room. Frightened, disorientated, she wandered round the building trying to get out, trying to get home. Hoping to calm her, the matron gave her a drug, which, as such drugs can occasionally do, had an adverse effect, and the gentle, courteous old lady went berserk, striking the nurse who was trying to get her to bed. The doctor was sent for, a psychiatrist called in, and by midnight Mrs Nathan was under heavy sedation in a mental hospital. They phoned her family early next morning, but they had already left.

When I visited her in Hatton hospital I could have wept. She was restrained in her chair. She wandered, they told me, got out into the grounds. Of course she wandered. She was seeking the fields she knew, the home she loved, the sister lying inert in a nearby hospital. Her eyes were swollen and red from crying, and as I stooped to kiss her she whispered, 'I knew you'd come. Take me home now.'

I went straight to the almoner's office. Miss Waldron was sympathetic. She had tried every possible avenue to locate the Hanfords, to no avail. No way could a decision be made about the old lady's future without consulting her daughter. In her present disturbed state it was unlikely that any home would accept her, and she was in no state to return home on her own. In spite of the caring support offered by Father Abbot and the village it was too late for them to help. She was too ill; too disturbed. The hospital could not discharge her to community care.

Father Abbot visited her frequently, giving what comfort he could, but sadly and helplessly we watched the old lady's flesh fall away. She didn't eat. She had no heart for living. Soon this strong, wiry countrywoman, who so recently could out-walk most people in her village, was shuffling down the ward, supported on a nurse's arm. Within three weeks she was dead.

What did Mrs Nathan die from? Shock? A broken heart? Perhaps homesickness can be numbered among the lethal diseases of our time.

8

The Restoration

It was a Saturday afternoon in May. Eileen was busy planting out seedlings in the rockery – with difficulty, as Solow was stretched out across her feet trying to take an afternoon nap in the sun, and grunting in protest each time her 'bed-legs' moved to the next planting area. The rockery was Eileen's domain. She loved housework, cleaning, polishing, and even dusting. I disliked it in all its forms, so she ruled in the house and I ruled in the garden, as I was happy with all forms of gardening, some of which Eileen was not over keen about. As I gladly helped with the housework, she would help in the garden, which was rather too big for one woman to manage. She found the work more bearable, even enjoyable, within her own particular sphere of activity where she could plan and plant and create. I was in the rose garden spraying the fresh green and coppery leaves when Eileen called to me.

'I've thought a thunk,' she said.

My tummy turned over. Eileen's 'thunks' could mean anything from a new idea for lunch to a drinks party, a weekend at the sea, or a major alteration to the house. She had dislodged Solow and was standing up.

'Bring it over here,' I invited.

Eileen and her thunk crossed the lawn and I put down the spray and joined her on the bench under the apple tree.

'I think we should increase our staff.'

'What have you in mind, a parlour maid?'

We laughed. The idea of a parlour maid was a joke between us since a rich elderly aunt had sent me a parcel of gifts for the house which included dainty coffee-coloured caps and aprons.

'No! One woman on the staff is enough. I was thinking we should employ a man.'

'A butler? A chauffeur?'

An earthy trowel tapped me on my bare arm, dislodging a weed which fell into my lap.

'Don't be a chump! A gardener. This garden is too big. Why have a garden and no time to enjoy it?'

We sat, relaxed, the thunk between us, Solow curled up at our feet. The thunk looked quite attractive, but . . . it was *my* garden. Could it stay mine with a gardener?

'We could have a small border, and grow vegetables,' I suggested.

Vegetables were not my favourite kind of gardening. Eileen nodded.

'The money we'd save would help pay his wages.'

'It would be fun picking our own vegetables.'

The thunk was looking better and better.

'He mustn't touch the roses,' I murmured. 'They're private.'

Eileen had removed the weed from my lap. She threw it into the nearest rose bed.

'Do you hear that, you lot? You're private and untouchable.' She turned back to me. 'Thunk OK?'

I nodded. 'Thunk OK.'

So Beez came into our lives.

'Old Beez' was a typical worker of the soil: slow, plodding, tough. Never hurried, he wasted no time, nor did he waste words. He came to us one day a week, working other days in other gardens. He dug and planted our vegetable garden, started it off with healthy young seedlings: cabbages, sprouts, lettuces and beans. When asked what we owed him for the plants, his reply was cryptic.

'Same as what I gave for 'em.'

'What did you give for them, Mr Beasley?' we asked.

'Nowt.'

I repeat. He worked in other gardens.

I was keener on gardening than Eileen, and a fraction more knowledgeable. Also I would see Beez more often, as I was often home before he finished work. If Eileen got home early enough to see him and discuss the garden, making suggestions, he would nod his grey head under the cloth cap towards the house. ''Er says . . .' and Eileen would come in, laughing, to tell ''Er' of his reaction. Anyone who has employed a gardener of the old school will know that ''Er' didn't say very much. Old Beez knew his job, and there was nothing a beginner like me could tell him. He preferred vegetables, but looked after the shrubs, even the flower border, although he thought we had a lot of 'newfangled ideas' that he didn't entirely approve of. In his book lupins were blue, so were Michaelmas daisies, but he was rather impressed by the variety of colours we cultivated.

Dear old Beez! Dour, stolid, faithful – he never let us down, until, in his later years, a weak chest caught up with him and a grandchild would be sent down with a message to tell us that our gardener could not come as he was in bed with bronchitis. When we called to see him, the lined weather-beaten old face would light up with pleasure. That was all the thanks we needed, all the thanks we got. He would never express in words, not even with a smile, the very real affection we knew he had for his 'ladies'. His wife told us of it, and was effusive in her thanks for every visit. Among the high-lights of our Christmases at 149 were the cards from Old Beez, always snow scenes shining with sparkle and glitter. Even now, at Christmas-time, there seems to be a gap on the mantelpiece where the sparkling 'Beez cards' held pride of place. We have always regretted that we did not know about his last illness and were not present at his funeral. He had already become too old and frail to work, and his humble little wife had not wanted to bother us.

Beez worked in the Smalleys' garden among others, and when they lunched with us I sometimes wondered if they were the original providers of the sweet home-grown peas, beans, sprouts and lettuce that they were eating with such relish. It was on one such occasion that Leonard asked me, 'Are you involved at all with old Ma Pimms?'

I shook my head. Of course, I knew old Ma Pimms – who didn't? I saw her occasionally when visiting on the council estate, staggering down Byron Avenue at closing time.

'Molly wouldn't be involved,' said Claire. 'Ma Pimms is not a child, not disabled, probably not even a geriatric.'

'Geriatric?' I chuckled. 'Awful word. My mother was tickled pink when I told her she was a geriatric. She can never remember the word, and when she feels her age, refers to herself as a genasprin.'

Leonard's eyes twinkled. 'Well, geriatric or genasprin, I think Ginny qualifies. She isn't as old as she looks, but I don't think she'll see sixty again.'

'Ginny? Is that really her name?'

'No,' said Claire. 'It's her occupation, everyone calls her Ginny.'

I turned to Leonard. 'Do you think I could help?'

Eileen jabbed a finger in my direction. 'You're not getting involved. You've quite enough lame ducks on your plate as it is, professionally and otherwise.' She turned to her sister. 'It's that wretched young priest. He seems to attract problems like a magnet, then dumps them onto old Moll here.'

Leonard's smile was affectionate. 'He's a great fellow, young Father Pat, better value than any psychiatrist.'

'I know all that,' Eileen sounded impatient, 'but if only he wouldn't use Molly so much. Then there's old Jake, you know what an old softie he is. If he's worried about any of his customers, you can guess who he tells.'

'Molly?'

'Of course, Molly. Why can't he look after his own lame ducks?'

'Dogs,' said Claire.

Eileen looked at her.

'Dogs,' she repeated. 'Lame dogs.'

'Ducks,' said Eileen.

'Dogs,' said Claire.

Leonard winked at me. After the fourth 'ducks', I kicked Eileen to remind her Claire was our guest.

'What the hell! Dogs or ducks, they're lame anyhow. I'm going to found a society, the SPM. Society for the Protection of Molly. I'll get Charlie to join, and Jake. That will keep him off her back.'

'Father Pat?' Claire was smiling the amused half-smile she reserved for her 'little sister'. 'Not a hope. You, Leonard, as her doctor, should be chairman.'

'In that case,' Leonard turned to me, 'as chairman of the SPM I order you not to get involved with Ma Ginny Pimms.'

'You can't,' I said. 'I'm not a member of the SPM.'

As it happened, I did get involved.

A phone call from the housing manager stopped me as I was on the point of leaving the house. It was about a Mrs Pimms on the council estate.

'Unless she comes up with the rent we're going to have to evict. She's months in arrears.'

It was their custom to warn us of an impending eviction order relating to families or old-age pensioners, in case there might be a genuine case of hardship, or a good reason, such as illness or pregnancy, for exercising mercy and deferring the sentence.

'I'll look into it,' I said. 'I'm sure there's a good reason why she can't pay.'

There was a snort the other end.

'We know the reason. She's drinking the rent money.'

'Tell me more.'

He filled me in with the not very salubrious picture of sixty-six-year-old Mrs Pimms, a childless widow. She lived alone in a three-bedroomed council house which, over the fifteen years since her husband's death, had been getting progressively shabbier and dirtier. The widow had similarly become progressively shabbier and dirtier, had lost all pride and self-respect, and was a familiar figure in the local pubs, where she spent much of her time. She was also the butt of her neighbours' scorn as she staggered along the street, dirty, shabby and down-at-heel, singing in a high falsetto voice.

'If you want to catch her in, get there before opening time,' I was advised.

The housing manager was quite honest about the situation. He wanted an excuse to put her out, as he needed the house for a family. A new block of flats had recently been completed, and the policy was to offer this very pleasant accommodation to the single occupiers of the three-bedroomed houses, which could then become available to families on the waiting list. Not that there was any question of offering a new flat to Mrs Pimms.

'She'd make a slum of it in no time. We've an empty cottage in Maple Terrace which we can move her into.'

'That dump?'

Maple Terrace, due for demolition, was recognised as the place the council liked to dump all their 'problems'. The non-payers, the drunks, the unmarried mothers, the shiftless, the unemployed, they were all to be found in Maple Terrace, or on the caravan site up Red Lane.

I timed the visit for eleven o'clock. Any later, she would have been on her way to the pub; any earlier she would, no doubt, have been sleeping off the previous night's intake. It was good timing. The door was opened by a little woman in a greasy, torn jumper of faded blue, an old tweed skirt, crumpled and stained, and a man's old, torn carpet slippers. The silvery white hair was matted and unkempt. Bleary, pink-gaping holes were exposed in an uncertain smile of welcome.

'Good morning, Mrs Pimms. I'm your health visitor. I wonder if I may come in and have a chat about your rent problems? Perhaps I can help.'

The door was thrown open. The housing manager was right, she had no vestige of pride, or else she was totally unaware of the depth of squalor and degradation in which she was living. A bed, covered with a filthy blanket, was in the sitting room. At least it eliminated the risk of falling down the stairs while 'under the influence'. Piles of old newspapers cluttered every available space. Years of dust had settled on every piece of furniture, and the place reeked of sour food, stale drink and unwashed humanity. Mrs Pimms showed no trace of shame. She was dancing with joy at having a visitor in her home, and the trim girlish figure tripped across the filthy carpet with amazing grace.

Would I have a cup of tea? I hadn't been through to the kitchen, but I could imagine it, yet how cruel it would be to dampen the happiness of the eager little sprite. Perhaps this was the first moment of happiness she had known for years, the first kind approach that had been made to her for a very long time.

The tea was stewed, the milk was tinned. I dared not look too closely at the chipped white cup into which it was poured. While I occupied the only uncluttered chair she sat on the bed, jumping up from time to time to execute a little jig, or to fetch a photograph or an old letter to show me, while she told me all about her past life and the happiness she had known with her adored husband. She had been a cabaret dancer before she married, and had retained her agility and grace. I wondered when she had last talked to anyone, really talked, in that pleasant soft voice, interspersed with the most engaging chuckles. As she rambled on, I began to see her as she once was. Photographs revealed a pretty woman in smart tailored suits and fresh cotton dresses. I admired her dress sense. I noticed some good pieces of furniture under the layers of dust. I told her how I envied the pure white wings of hair above her temples.

'Many women pay their hairdressers a fortune to get just that effect.' She stood by the mirror, gazing into it with her bloodshot eyes, thoughtfully fingering the greasy matted hair. We found an old money box among the clutter, and she promised to put by the rent money, and try to save, week by week, to pay off the arrears.

The housing manager was human. I was able to talk him into waiting.

'Give me a month. If there's no improvement then, and no rent paid, she's yours.'

He laughed. 'You won't change her. No one can change that old tippler.'

'Has anyone tried?' I asked.

He shrugged his shoulders. 'One month, then, but after that . . . OUT.'

'If she does pay, even a little,' I begged, 'and if she makes some attempt to tidy things up, however slight, you must promise to give her more time.'

Time, the great healer. How much time would she need to climb up from the depths of degradation into which she had sunk, to climb back to respectability and self-respect, to forget the taunts of her neighbours, the snubs and humiliations to which she had been subjected? Her neighbours were my families. It soon got round the street that Mrs Pimms was under my care, and that I expected her to be treated by them with kindness, compassion and respect. Above all with respect.

It was less than a week before I called again. I could have shouted with joy as the door opened to reveal a sleekly groomed head of hair, the white wings shining against the silver-grey waves. The eyes were still pink-rimmed, but they danced at me out of a clean face. Much of the clutter had been removed from the furniture I had admired, and the graceful lines and beautiful graining could now be seen. I caressed the starved wood, recommending a good polish that was not too costly. Having enjoyed freshly brewed tea from an unchipped cup, I dared to look at the kitchen, and was overjoyed when her chattering stopped and she looked shamefacedly at the pile of empty bottles, her little face brightening at my suggestion that she might trade them in for money which would pay for the furniture polish. Upstairs the rooms were full of junk, broken furniture, moth-eaten clothing and soiled bed linen. I could see some of the clothes had once been good, and, as I recognised the suits and dresses from the old photographs, the scene was set for more pathetic reminiscences. I asked her whether, with her taste for nice clothes, she would mind accepting a few garments from the WVS – undies and a few woollies, perhaps a coat, just to tide her over until she had paid off her rent. I gave her a note for the clothing store, and hurried round to ask them, in spite of her appearance and reputation, not to unload any rubbish on her, but to fit her out with the best they had in the store.

I visited regularly, week by week, praising, admiring, encouraging, and each new visit revealed some small improvement in the condition of the house and its occupant. Each visit was received with touching joy, expressed in little dances, sometimes a song. The moving of the bed upstairs was the signal for a gift of bed linen and blankets, which I had obtained from the Red Cross, and she pirouetted so gaily round the bedroom, now cleared of its junk, that I thought we would never get the bed made up.

With Father Pat's enthusiastic support, I enlisted the help of local church workers, and of kindly neighbours, to swell the one-woman admiration society, and the old lady glowed and expanded in the warmth of their approval and friendship, she who for so long had been rejected and despised. Gradually her pride and self-respect returned to her. For the first time I was glad of the middle-aged spread that was catching up on me, and my contemporaries, as the WVS handouts and jumble sale purchases were replaced by well-cut suits and dresses from our wardrobes. From a local charity I begged the money to buy her a new coat, and wished the committee could have witnessed her excitement as she chose the first new, unworn garment that she had owned for nearly twenty years.

A visit to the dentist improved the appearance of her wide, generous smile; the pink rims disappeared from her soft blue eyes. She felt that my clothes would not feel at home in a pub, so her drinking, now rare, became confined to a small hotel nearby.

Soon a more subtle change took place. There would be flowers in the house when I called. Little gifts appeared on the table, chocolates or small ornaments. There was a new confidence in her manner, a glowing happiness. Shyly she told me about Bill – the Australian waiter she had met at the hotel – a few years her junior, but lonely, and glad to spend his free time in the company of the kind, gentle little woman. She was humbly surprised that any man should seek her company. I stood her in front of the mirror and made her take a long look at her pretty, piquant face, her glorious hair, now completely white, her neat well-dressed figure. She had become a woman any man might admire, and her house was now a home whose hospitality anyone would welcome. Bill treated her like a queen, and his chivalrous kindness, his respect and deep affection helped to complete her rehabilitation.

In time the rent arrears were paid off. The housing manager, deeply impressed by the transformation of her home and her person, offered her one of the new flats, an offer which set the seal of approval on her new-found respectability. For a long time Mrs Pimms had coveted one of those flats, the tenancy of which had seemed an unattainable dream. Now that the dream was within her reach, there was an obstacle. Bill still worked at the hotel, but had moved in with 'his Nellie' as a lodger. In a three-bedroomed house, with the rent coming in regularly, the council had turned a blind eye, but the housing manager told me that a male lodger in a one-bedroomed flat was out of the question.

We talked it over, the three of us, Nellie and Bill, Nellie and I, and Bill and I. There was an obvious solution, but they both felt it seemed silly to marry at their age. Now, faced with the alternative of losing either the flat or Bill's companionship, Nellie decided that, silly or not, married they would be ... and married they were.

I was a witness at their wedding and an honoured guest at the reception in their new flat, in which the sparkling glass and silver and the sheen of the highly polished furniture were outshone only by the sparkling radiance of the little bride.

9

Landlords

Ialways saw the necessity for tied cottages, usually rented by farmers to farmhands, but I never liked them. They had a nasty habit of producing babies in midwinter, and I came to associate them with long, cold, wet treks across muddy fields, clambering over fences, elbowing cows away from gates, avoiding bulls and rams and other lethal animals. Most tied cottages could only be approached up narrow lanes, but during a hard winter these would be made impassable by rutted snow.

Miss Smart had warned me of an expected birth at a farm cottage outside Chesford village. 'I don't like it,' she admitted. 'It's so far off the beaten track. If anything goes wrong we couldn't get the ambulance near.' She drew a brief sketch of the cottage, down a narrow lane and across two fields. 'The husband's out working all day, and there's no one to call on if she needs help. Besides, there's the time element for me, visiting every day for ten days.'

I was studying the sketch. 'Where's the nearest cottage?'

She indicated with her pencil a spot further down the lane. 'And they're an old couple, they really need help themselves. No home help would go out that far.'

I visualised an autumn and winter visiting that baby. It would be bound to have problems; all my far-flung babies seemed to have problems.

'Have you suggested to her having it in hospital?'

'Yes, but she's scared of hospitals. Her mother died in one when she was a child and her dad blamed the hospital. I wonder . . . would *you* have a go at her?'

'If you like. But what can I do that you can't?'

'Nothing, my friend! But two people saying the same thing might carry twice as much weight.'

I grinned. 'Twice nothing is still nothing, but I'll have a try. If it's a nice afternoon I'll look in on her after the Chesford clinic tomorrow.'

I was surprised by her next question.

'How would you explain a baby that normally loves its bath suddenly beginning to scream at the sight of the water? Have you ever come across it?'

'No,' I said thoughtfully, 'but I can understand it.'

'How? I mean, why should it?'

'Dreams. I think they are responsible for a lot of unexplained behaviour in small children. The poor little mite had probably been half-drowned in a nightmare.'

'Dreams? I'd never thought of that. Babies do dream, of course, but I hadn't connected it.'

She smiled as if she had shed a small load of worry.

'So, what does the mother do?'

'I'd suggest she waited for a few weeks, just "topping and tailing", then try again.'

A strange question, I thought, as I drove home. If it was one of our babies she surely would have told me. Perhaps a relation? Or friend?

The death knoll of Chesford clinic was sounded the next day – by a tin of National Dried Milk. We had struggled through one year in a state of armed truce. The babies were weighed and examined and immunised and received their quota of vitamins and milk. National Dried Milk was not my favourite baby food, it was too fat-making, but it was difficult for some of the mothers to get to a chemist, and the government milk coupons were a great saving on the budgets of farm labourers' wives.

All was going smoothly until Mrs Lord came to the scales. Her baby had been born at home, to her great joy, and her kind neighbour Mrs Dogood had helped out, so no home help had needed to cross her threshold. Now she seemed distressed.

'I've left my milk coupons at home.'

Lady Merlin looked up, and snapped at her. 'You silly girl. You'll have to go and get them, won't you?'

Mrs Lord glanced at the clock. 'I don't think I could, Madam. The clinic would be closed before I got back.'

I smiled at her. 'Don't even think about it. I'll be passing your house later this afternoon and I'll collect the coupons. You take the milk.'

'But . . .' Madam was spluttering with rage. 'We have rules. No coupons, no milk.'

Mrs Lord had gone white. I took her hand and walked with her to the food table. The other mothers watched.

The Mouse watched through the kitchen door. I knew Dr Lang was listening. The food lady placed a protective hand on her tins. I was aware that Lady Merlin had left her seat and was standing behind us.

'This is outrageous! The books will be upset. The money won't tally.'

I turned to look at her and was shocked by the fury in the narrowed eyes.

'Babies need milk, Lady Merlin, and welfare centres are about babies, not accounts and statistics.'

I took two tins from the table and handed them to Mrs Lord.

'Put them in the pram, and I'll look in after four for the coupons.' I turned to the food lady. 'I'll ring the stores and tell them I'll be dropping the coupons in early tomorrow. Don't worry.'

My hand touched hers briefly as I picked up another tin and followed Mrs Lord out of the clinic.

This could not go on. We both knew it. Lady Merlin was not a quitter, and stayed at her post until the clinic closed. Then she stood up.

'I think, nurse, that it is time you found someone else to run this clinic for you.'

Our eyes met.

'I'm sorry, Lady Merlin, and I am truly grateful for all you have done, but we just don't seem to see eye to eye. The babies are what really matter.'

Dr Lang and I went to see the MOH and it was decided to close Chesford clinic as the attendance was so poor and the village was on the bus route to Lapfold, where the clinic would, in future, be held fortnightly.

Before returning to Warwick I called in at the farm cottage. It was a nice thatched cottage with a well-kept garden, but I was surprised at the response to my knock. A timid voice whispered through the keyhole.

'Who is it?'

When I declared my identity I heard a key turning and a bolt being drawn back. A scared little face confronted me, tears still wet on the pale cheeks.

'Mrs Horam. Whatever is the matter?'

'It's the landlord. He's just left.'

It appeared that her husband had given up his job as a cowman and gone to work in Warwick. The farmer, quite naturally, wanted the cottage for his successor and Mr Horam was doing all he could to find accommodation in Warwick. The landlord kept calling on Mrs Horam when her husband was out, insisting that they should leave immediately and threatening eviction. The little woman was terrified.

'He says he's coming tomorrow morning, and if we're not gone, he'll put all our furniture out in the field, and me as well.'

She burst into tears, sobs tearing her swollen body. The baby was due in less than three months.

'Has he been to court?'

'I don't know. I didn't ask. He was ranting on so.'

'Has he spoken to your husband?'

She shook her head.

'He always comes when I'm on my own.' She looked round the little room. 'We haven't much, but it's ours, and if they put it all outside, and it's raining . . . and where will we go?'

I put an arm round her heaving shoulders. 'He can't put you out, not without a court order.'

'But how can I stop him, all on my own?'

'You won't be on your own. What time do you expect him?'

'About half past ten, he said, and he's bringing another man with him.'

'I'll be here, Mrs Horam.'

I was there, just after ten, and waited in the little front room until I heard a knock on the back door and the men's voices in the kitchen.

'Still here, Mrs Horam? Lucky for you it's not raining.'

As I came through into the kitchen two large men were already carrying a table towards the door.

'I think you'd better put that down.'

They stopped and stared at me.

'Who the blazes are you?'

'I'm Mrs Horam's health visitor. Being pregnant, the lady is under my care. She has told me how you have been bullying and harassing her while her husband is out and it's got to stop. It's bad for her, in her condition.'

They had put down the table. The larger man, who I guessed was the landlord, decided to bluff.

'I need this cottage for my new cowman. I've the right to evict the Horams.'

'Have you an order from the court?'

He hesitated. I went on.

'Of course you haven't. I know, and you know, that no court would sanction the eviction of a woman within three months of childbirth, nor for at least three months afterwards. Mrs Horam knows it too. She knows you can't touch her without an eviction order. She also knows there is a law against harassment to protect people from bullies like you.'

He was beaten, and he knew it. There is nothing quite so deflated as a deflated bully. The two men slunk out of the cottage, not to return until it had been vacated the following month when, at my insistence, the council found the Horams a house in Warwick, where the baby was born. I was glad the midwife and I were both saved from that particular safari. I was also glad that the new cowman got his cottage.

The Horams were unfortunate in living on one of the farms in Chesford that did not belong to Lady Merlin. Such a situation would never have arisen with a tenant of hers, however unsatisfactory. She owned nearly half the cottages in the village, and two prospering farms, and she kept all her property in excellent repair. Her policy to put bathrooms into all her cottages was temporarily in abeyance, due to the difficulty of getting permits for any unnecessary building projects in the post-war period.

She had the same protective possessiveness towards her tenants that she had for her service families, made sure they were well cared for when they were ill, remembered the children's birthdays with some little gift, and, in times of hardship, would not be too insistent about the rents. In exchange she expected her property to be well looked after, the gardens cultivated. She demanded diligence from the men who worked on her farms or in her grounds and an almost feudal respect and defer-ence. It would not have surprised me if she had insisted on all her male tenants and employees growing fore-locks to pull when they met her. An excellent landlord, she was respected, appreciated and looked up to, but loved only by the very few who had been privileged to glimpse the essential goodness, kindness and generos-ity behind the harsh façade.

Now, I am a firm believer in the right of an owner to sell or rent their property to anyone they wish. My memories go back to the days before the iniquitous tenancy laws of today, under which families are homeless while excellent potential homes stand empty because their owners dare not lease them on a tempo-rary basis, even under contract, lest it should prove impossible to recover possession. In those days the law was on the side of the owner, and rightly so. People have a right to own property and, owning it, the right to dispose of it as they wish. Yet there were occasions when I could not range myself on the side of the owner or the law.

The Barretts occupied a very pleasant cottage adjoin-ing the farm where Tom Barrett had worked for four or five years. The owner, Mr Brook, was the manager of a prosperous business in Coventry and left the manage-ment of the farm to his agent, taking very little personal interest in it, or in the men who worked it. His stock had been depleted by an outbreak of foot-and-mouth disease and some of the men had become redundant, including Tom, whose cottage had been earmarked for Mr Brook's son, who had recently got married. It was to be enlarged and modernised for the young couple, and the builder was due to start work within the next few weeks.

I found a very worried Mrs Barrett on my first visit to her second baby. Tom was out looking for a job, but all the farms in the area had suffered from the epidemic and were cutting down on labour.

I was due to return two weeks later, but a telephone call early the following week brought me hurrying to the farm. Mr Brook was trying to force the couple out so that the builder could get started. He refused to accept rent from them, and his latest move was to cut off the supply of electricity, gas, and water. Apart from the three-week-old baby there was a two-year-old boy, and we were already in the season of chilly autumn evenings, cold winds and rain. Unbelievably, a request for a kettle of boiling water to make up the baby's bottle had been refused in the farm kitchen. Madam had given her orders, and it was as much as the cook's job was worth to disobey them. Tom had bought two large thermoses, and trudged, twice a day, across the fields to the next cottage to have them filled. He looked desperate.

'We can't go on living like this, but where can we go?'

Where indeed? But autumn was moving inexorably into winter, and how could the little family exist without heat or water? He showed me their kettle, blackened and ruined from the smoke of the fire he had built in the back yard. At least it provided an occasional cup of tea, and hot soup for the little boy.

I crossed the yard and rang the bell of the farmhouse. Mrs Brook received me in the study, where she was busy dealing with correspondence regarding SSAFA, of which she was the local secretary. My anger must have showed in my face, as she looked slightly startled as she offered me a chair. Coffee was suggested and refused. I came straight to the point. She insisted that her husband was within his rights. He was breaking no law.

'No government law, perhaps, Mrs Brook, but there are other laws above the law of the land, the law of God, of common humanity. There's a small baby in that cottage.'

She had the grace to lower her eyes.

'I know, and I'm sorry about it, but if the builder can't get in this month we may have to wait a long time before he's available again.'

'Is it so important? I mean, you have a big house here. Your son and his wife will have a roof over their heads.'

She looked pained.

'It's not a good thing, young couples living with parents. It never works. You should know that, Miss Corbally.'

Indeed I knew it. How often had I seen the near-breakdown of a marriage through the continued proximity of mother and daughter-in-law, the husband/son torn by divided loyalties, the interference with the management of the children. Many a time had I begged the housing manager to jump the queue with some such couple before their relationship was damaged beyond hope of repair. I agreed with Mrs Brook.

'But this house is big enough. You needn't be in each other's pockets, and Tom might find another job sooner than we think. In the meantime that little family must not be made to suffer. I'm asking you to restore all services to the cottage immediately.'

She looked surprised.

'You have no right.'

'I have every right. I'm responsible for the health and welfare of those children, and I consider, under the circumstances, that both are at risk.'

Mrs Brook stood up.

'Very well. I'll speak to my husband, but I can't promise anything. The decision must be his.'

'You speak to him, Mrs Brook. I'm coming back tomorrow, and I expect to find the cottage supplied with gas, electricity and water.'

She paused, her hand on the door handle.

'And if not?'

'If not, Mrs Brook, the NSPCC inspector will be calling on your husband, in his office.'

She gasped.

'Not in his office? Not in uniform?'

'In uniform, Mrs Brook, in his office.'

'But it would be too embarrassing, in front of all his staff.'

Mr Brook was a vain man, with an inflated sense of his own importance, and a public image that he hoped, one day, would win him a seat on the council. I was not surprised, the following morning, to find that all services had been restored to the cottage. Tom was unable to get another farm job, but found a position as groom in a hunting stable, with a flat above the stables, in a neighbouring village. The young Brooks took possession of their modernised cottage in plenty of time before the birth of their first baby could have raised the problem of an interfering grandmother. I often visited them there, and was always courteously received by Mrs Brook whenever I had cause to enlist her help on behalf of any service families on my district.

I didn't often need to call in the NSPCC inspector, although I kept him up my sleeve. It wasn't really fair to use the inspector as a bogeyman, as he was the kindest, gentlest person imaginable, but the presence of the 'Cruelty Man' on the doorstep of a house would disgrace that family forever in the eyes of their neighbours.

I had frequently warned Mrs Moffat about leaving her small children alone in the house while she was out at work. She had five children, ranging in age from two and a half to eight. The three eldest were at school – 'latchkey children' who collected the babies from a neighbour on the way home, and grabbed themselves scratch tea whilst waiting for their mum to come home. When winter came the house would be cold, and I was afraid of what might happen if Paul, the eldest, tried to light a fire or cook a hot meal for the family. On the third occasion that a neighbour reported to me that the children were on their own, I called in the evening to warn the parents that, if it ever happened again, I would have no alternative but to report the matter to the NSPCC. Mr Moffat was indifferent. I suspected that he kept his wife short of housekeeping money, but there were other jobs which would allow her to get home to light the fire and prepare a meal before the children finished school. She promised to look for one, and we parted friends. We'd always been friends, since the elder children had been toddlers, and I knew her to be a warm-hearted and loving mother who spent the extra money she earned on clothes and treats for the children. I really thought she had got the message this time, and was disappointed and deeply distressed to receive a telephone call during lunch, at the time of the school half-term holiday.

'Mrs Moffat's out at work, and the children are on their own. I wouldn't have bothered you, but there's smoke coming from the chimney, so they must have lit a fire.'

I just had time to drive over to the council estate before the afternoon clinic. Paul opened the door to me. He had dealt with the cold lunch Mum had left, and put the babies down to sleep. The elder ones were sitting round the fire with their drawing and painting books, and what a fire! It roared up the chimney, as I had feared, unguarded. Having slacked it down a bit, I found the fireguard in the kitchen and put it in position, then went to a callbox and rang up the NSPCC inspector. I explained my predicament, with a clinic holding me up until after four, and he promised to come straight over and stay with the children until I was free, or until the mother returned home.

Soon after four I was knocking on the door again. Mrs Moffat opened it, looking rather shaken.

'Oh, Miss Corbally, do you know what's happened? The Cruelty Man's been. He was here when I got home.'

'I know, Mrs Moffat. I asked him to come.'

'You?' She shook her head in disbelief. 'You asked him to come? I thought you were my friend.'

'That's why I asked him. I'm too much of a friend to allow you to go on running the risk of having your children burnt to death.'

She lowered her eyes.

'He told me. Terrible things he told me. Showed me pictures of the poor little mites in hospital, all bandaged up.' She smiled suddenly. 'You did quite right, Miss Corbally. I've been very silly. Those poor little children, they could have been mine, like he said.'

She opened the door wide. 'The tea's still fresh in the pot. Come along in.'

The inspector returned later that evening to have a talk with Mr Moffat about increasing the housekeeping allowance, so that his wife would not need a full-time job, and from then onwards the little Moffats found a warm house and a hot meal waiting for them when they came out of school.

10

The Man Who Was Overpaid

I was surprised to find Mr Steele at home on a week-day. I had called to see Mrs Steele about their youngest child, Henry, who was four and a half. At that age I liked to see the children to ensure that there were no small defects that needed to be remedied before starting school, and no disabilities developing that would require a special school. It took time to secure a place in these schools for the deaf, the partially sighted, the asthmatic or children with learning difficulties, and it also took time and patience to persuade most parents to let their children go to these establishments, particularly when the child would need to board there. Not infrequently, all such efforts would be in vain, and all but the most severely disabled would have to take their chance, and a slim chance it was, at the local school. On one occasion, perseverance on my part and on the headmaster's resulted in a deaf boy, in the same street as the Steeles, being admitted to a school for deaf children at the age of nine. A bright child, he soon caught up on the time he had lost, with all the special aids at his disposal, only to be withdrawn by his disgruntled parents after the second term, because 'They were teaching 'im nothing but heducation'. Had they hoped the deaf boy could be taught to hear?

There was no such problem with Henry Steele, and his mother had already got his name down for the excellent infant school on the estate where his elder sister, Patsy, was in her last term, while nine-year-old Geoffrey was doing well at the adjacent junior school. It was while we were discussing the booster injection against diphtheria, now due, that I noticed Mr Steele, at the bottom of the garden.

'I see your husband's at home. They're not out on strike again, are they?'

The Standard Motor Company, in Coventry, where many of the Dodsworth men were employed, was notorious for the frequency of its strikes. She shook her head.

'No. He won't go to work.'

'Is he ill?'

'He's fit enough. Look at him, digging out there. Just doesn't want to go to work.'

'Is he drawing the dole?'

'Can't. He's not unemployed, not while he's still on their books.'

'But what about money?'

'That's what I want to know. That's what I keep asking him.'

'What does he say?'

'Won't talk about it.'

'But how are you managing?'

'I've a bit put by. One has to put by with the men

being called out every five minutes, you never know what you can be sure of, but that won't last for ever.'

Of course it wouldn't last, with three children to feed, and the rent to pay, and probably hire purchase on the furniture and cooker. Most families on the council estate bought their goods on the 'never-never'.

I was visiting a baby in the street the following week, and called at the Steeles' house to see what was happening. Mr Steele opened the door. I feigned surprise.

'I'm sorry to see you at home, Mr Steele. Not another strike, I hope, or aren't you well?'

He welcomed me in, calling to his wife to put a kettle on.

'I'm well enough.'

'Another dispute then?'

Mrs Steele came in with the teacups.

'He's walked out. Chucked in his job.'

'Left the Standard? But why, Mr Steele?'

'They pay too much. Since that last strike they've been paying far too much. It's against my principles to take that sort of money for the job I do.'

I thought he must be joking.

'You don't mean you've left your job because you think they're paying too *much*?'

'That's right. It doesn't seem honest, somehow, taking all that money.'

I swallowed hard, and was glad of the strong cup of tea Mrs Steele poured for me.

'That seems a bit hard on your family. Good money means good living and nice clothes and holidays.'

'We'll get along.'

'Have you another job in mind?'

'No. I'm not bothering.'

'But Mr Steele, you can't just not work, not with a wife and three children to look after. You can't draw the dole for ever, not when jobs are available.'

'Who said I was drawing the dole?'

'But you're entitled to it while you're unemployed.'

'I don't agree. If I choose not to work why should I live on other people's charity?'

This conversation was becoming like something out of *Alice in Wonderland*.

'But you must have money from somewhere. There's the rent to pay, and food to buy. How can your wife feed you all if you give her no money?'

He smiled at his wife, passing his cup across the table to be refilled.

'There's food enough.'

'Won't be for much longer,' she said, as she passed his cup back to her husband. Her eyes met mine, and she shook her head, her lips set in a hopeless expression. We walked to the gate together.

'I don't think your husband's well, Mrs Steele. I think he should see his doctor. Would he go to the surgery, do you think?'

She shrugged her shoulders.

'I'll ask him.'

'Could you have a word with Dr Bell first? Tell him how things are. With a doctor's certificate he'd get sick pay while he's having treatment.'

She looked so worried, poor woman. I held her hand for a moment before getting into the car.

'Come and see me at the clinic. We can't really talk here when your husband's around.'

She came to the clinic, her face drawn with worry, her eyes red-rimmed. Mr Steele had refused to go to the surgery, and, when the doctor called at the house, he disappeared through the back door. Dr Bell was sympathetic, but until he saw his patient there was nothing he could do. The money was running out.

'I'd get a job, but I don't like to leave Henry with him. He gets so moody, and talks a lot of rubbish. He's not like himself at all. The kids are scared of him.'

'I know Mrs Thomas is wanting extra help in the shop. I could get Henry into the day nursery until the end of this term. Would that help?'

She nodded.

'I don't like to leave him, not the way he is, but I must get money from somewhere, enough for food. I don't know what we're going to do for the rent money.'

As the doctor was leaving, I brought my visitor into the privacy of the inner room, where my ever-watchful and kind-hearted helpers followed us up with a tray of tea. It was not unusual for distressed and desperate women, and sometimes men, to seek me out at the clinic. As the door closed, I poured out a cup for Mrs Steele, who was on the verge of tears.

'I'll see the housing manager about the rent. Don't worry, I won't let him put you out. Why not pop round and see Mrs Thomas on the way home? The nursery will be closed now, but I'll ring first thing in the morning, and they'll be expecting Henry.'

Mrs Steele wiped her eyes. I was concerned with an immediate solution to an immediate problem, but she had lain awake night after night churning over every aspect of this crisis.

'But what about the holidays? What happens to the kids then? They wouldn't stay with their dad, not the way he is, not without me in the house.'

'I hope, before the schools break up, that he'll be in hospital, and well on the way to recovery.' I could see she didn't share my optimism.

'You have a married sister in Leamington, haven't you? Would she have them during the holidays? If not, there are children's holiday homes. I could probably get them into one of those.'

The tea and the conversation did her good, and Mrs Steele left the clinic with more hope than when she entered it, to collect her two elder children and, with luck, secure a job at Mrs Thomas's drapers shop.

Within the week Mrs Thomas was on the phone to me. Mrs Steele had arrived for work that morning with a black eye and badly shaken. Could I call round to see her? I went immediately. There were bruises on her arms as well, and I insisted that she should see her doctor without delay, before the bruising faded. Mrs Thomas agreed to release her for the morning, and I drove her straight to the surgery where the doctor examined her thoroughly, recording her injuries for future evidence. He called me into the consulting room.

'I'm prescribing tranquillisers for Mr Steele. Mrs Steele could slip them into his food, or his tea.'

I shook my head.

'After this attack I don't consider it safe for Mrs Steele or the children to stay in the house with him. That man is very sick, Doctor, he's not responsible.'

'I know, but what can I do if I can't get to see him?' He turned to Mrs Steele. 'What will you do?'

She looked at me. The poor woman was in a state of shock, unable to see her way out of the crisis or to make any clear decision. I answered for her.

'I'm taking Mrs Steele to the Citizens Advice Bureau. Their lawyer will be there this morning.'

The lawyer was helpful and sympathetic. The safety of Mrs Steele and the children was the first priority, with money as a close second. The solution to both, in his view, would be to apply for a separation order. The court would then assess a reasonable maintenance allowance, which she would receive through the National Assistance Board; it would be their headache to recover the money from her husband.

'But I can't leave him when he's ill,' she sobbed. 'How will he manage?'

'If you stay you risk another attack, perhaps serious injury, which might put you into hospital, and your husband into prison.'

It was arranged that the solicitor would bring her case to the Magistrates' Court without delay, and meanwhile she and the children would go to her sister in Leamington. Over lunch I pointed out to her the long-term advantage of this course of action.

'Left on his own without food, and without money to buy any, he will soon be ready to see Dr Bell. If he does hold out long enough, he'll end up in court for non-payment of the maintenance, and the court will have the power to commit him for treatment in hospital.'

She looked stricken.

'You mean at Graylingwell?'

'Graylingwell or the Warneford? Does it matter so much? They're both hospitals.'

'But if the neighbours get to know they'll think he's mad. We'll never live it down.'

'Mrs Steele, your husband's mentally sick, as you well know. It's not his fault. It's an illness, like pneumonia is an illness, and the hospital will cure him. When he comes out he'll be as sane as you or I. There won't be anything "to live down", as you put it.'

'But the kids. They'll never feel the same towards their dad, after seeing him like this, moody and silly.'

'It will work out, don't worry.'

I hoped it would. The erosion of a child's respect for their father can be damaging to a future relationship. Fortunately, the one incidence of violence had occurred in the privacy of the bedroom while the children were asleep. It was imperative that they should be got away before another such incident could occur in front of them.

After lunch we contacted the schools and the day nursery, arranging for the children to be collected by me when they came out, then I took Mrs Steele home to pack their things and her own. I found Mr Steele quite cheerful, and he greeted his wife affectionately, showing great concern about her damaged face. Obviously, he had completely forgotten how she had received her injuries. He had found enough money in the house to take himself out to the pub for a snack lunch, and while his wife was upstairs packing, he talked to me happily and with great seriousness about his plans for a magnificent youth centre he was going to donate to the town. He was too absorbed in the sketches he was showing me to notice when his wife came down and slipped quietly out through the back door with two large suitcases.

I sat with Mrs Steele when the case came up in court. There was no difficulty. The separation order was allowed on the grounds of assault and failure to maintain his family, and a regular allowance was ordered to be paid. The presiding JP, a friend of mine and a local councillor, rang me up that evening. She was very concerned about Mrs Steele and her children.

'I wish we'd had more information from Dr Bell about the husband.'

'He can't get to see the man, so can't really give an opinion, not to a court.'

'What do you think is the trouble? Is the man bats?'

'Definitely. This violence is completely out of character, and he's been depressed and moody for weeks.'

'Was he sacked from his job?'

'No. He left it because they were paying him too much.'

'Too much?' She chuckled. 'That alone makes the man certifiable! If he won't see his doctor do you think he'd come to see me?'

'That's an idea. He might.' I remembered my last conversation with the patient. 'As a councillor, would you be interested in a super youth centre for the town?'

'Very interested. What's that got to do with it?'

'He's planning to have one built. At his expense, of course.'

'Splendid. I'll ask him round to tell me about it. David Bell can meet us here with his psychiatrist friend and we'll get the poor devil certified and into Graylingwell.'

Mrs Steele returned home with the children, and the income from the maintenance money and from her job enabled her to start paying off the accumulated arrears of rent. At first she visited her husband regularly in hospital, but the visits distressed her. She found him resentful and abusive, blaming her for his incarceration, and he would have attacked her if the ever-watchful nurses had not intervened. After that she was advised to stay away as her visits only upset him.

She was resigned to a long separation, and she and the children were adapting to their new way of life and recovering from the trauma of their father's illness, when he escaped from Graylingwell . . .

I learnt of the escape quite by chance, when I rang up to book a taxi for the following Saturday. Jack, the taxi driver, who was a friend of mine, told me, in the course of our conversation, that he had just brought Mr Steele home. He'd had a call from Warwick to pick him up there. I was horrified, and so was Jack when I explained that his client had escaped from the mental hospital, and that his wife and children could be in danger if they walked into the house while he was there. It was just after three thirty. Mrs Steele stopped work at three, and would already have collected Henry and be on her way home. She might already have arrived.

Jack offered to drive round to the house at once, on the pretext of confirming his next booking, which was to take Mr Steele to meet his friends at the George and Dragon at 6 p.m. Meanwhile, I hurried over to the nursery, following Mrs Steele's route home, and intercepted her just before they turned into their own street. While she took Henry to a neighbour's house, I drove back to collect the elder children from their schools and take them to join their mother, then I went to see Jack. He had found Mr Steele quite calm and happy, enjoying a very adequate tea, which had been, no doubt, intended for the children. The 6 p.m. booking had been confirmed, so I rang the hospital to put them in the picture, and they arranged to send out an ambulance and two male nurses to pick up their patient at the pub. Poor, good-hearted Jack was very upset at the thought of betraying his client, and agreed to co-operate only when I explained that the man was ill and needed treatment.

It was many months after that episode before the hospital advised Mrs Steele that her husband was sufficiently recovered to wish to see her, and from then on he improved rapidly, being able to spend an occasional day at home, then a weekend, then, eventually, returning to his family and his job. I kept in close touch with Mrs Steele during those early months while he was still under the supervision of the hospital, and was delighted to hear that they had resumed their warm, loving relationship, and that the children were thrilled to have their daddy home. They seemed to have quite forgotten the silly stranger of whom they had been so afraid.

Fortunately, the Steele crisis occurred the day before the twins' second birthday party, and, having stayed around until I knew the patient was safely back in hospital, I felt justified in knocking off early the next day, in time to change into one of my prettiest dresses and drive over to Lapfold. Most of the guests were already there, including, of course, Miss Smart, in uniform as she was leaving early for her evening rounds. Dr Lang looked charming. She was always impeccably dressed, hair soigné, hands beautifully manicured, but she had dressed up for this occasion, and the result was a delight. We all felt it was an occasion. The birthday of any premature baby is an achievement, that of twins doubly so. These two little beauties had survived two years free from any ailment, not even a cold. Mrs Roche-Anderson had used her own considerable common sense, Dr Gibbens's book, *The Care of Young Babies* and no other, and any guidance or advice from me that I felt was needed.

We all shared the mother's pride as the little girls, in different but equally pretty party frocks, moved among their guests, Patricia on her mother's arm, Phillida on her father's. Had they been dressed the same they would be almost indistinguishable, level pegging in weight and general development, but to us who knew them well the little faces were carrying the early imprints of the different personalities. Patricia, gentle, placid, accepting, a serene happy child. Phillida the boss, volatile, extrovert, gurgling with laughter or screaming with rage, hitting her sister one minute, caressing her the next.

The small hostesses were helping their parents cut the cakes – one cake each, we were celebrating two birthdays – when Lady Merlin arrived. She had been held up at a committee meeting. There were mutual friends for her to greet – she and Mrs Roche-Anderson moved in the same social circle – but she evidenced slight surprise at meeting 'the nurse' at a social gathering. I saw her puzzled glance in my direction. I knew the feeling . . . such a familiar face, but whose? It was quite a while before she placed me. A group was wandering round the garden after tea, and I was discussing the roses with a fellow guest when Lady Merlin came up and joined in the conversation. She was a very keen and knowledgeable gardener, and we got on famously until my companion had to leave.

'Goodbye, Miss Corbally. Don't forget our little cocktail party next Saturday.'

'I'll look forward to that. Bye.'

We were alone.

'Have you seen the herb garden?' I asked. 'It's worth visiting.'

On the way I told her the story of my herb stew. She laughed delightedly. We sat for a few minutes on a rustic bench by the goldfish pond.

'I hear you've closed Chesford clinic.'

'Yes, Lady Merlin. We felt it wouldn't have been the same without you. After all, you'd been in on it since the beginning. Anyhow, there weren't all that many babies attending.'

Her voice was quiet. Her hand touched mine briefly.

'Thank you, Miss Corbally.'

11

Never Deceive A Child

'Moll, can I ask your advice?' It was teatime at the nurse's cottage, and I had been glancing through a pile of magazines while Helen brewed.

'What is it this time? Another baby been dreaming?'

'No. It's this.'

She took a paper from a pile on her desk and handed it to me.

Dear Nurse Jane,

My elder girl has recently started school, and the headmistress tells me she is stealing, helping herself to the other children's toys and sweets and pencils, even their scarves and gloves. What should I do? The headmistress suggests I take her to a child psychologist.

Worried Mother

P.S. Our girls have always shared everything at home, even clothes.

I grinned.

'So, you're Nurse Jane of *Mothers' Monthly*. I've been looking at the letters and your answers. Good sound stuff, I thought.'

'This is rather a poser. I don't like the idea of a psychologist.'

'Unthinkable. It's simple really. The child has always shared everything, so she goes on sharing in school.'

'What advice should I give her worried mother?'

'Stop sharing. I'd suggest keeping her girls' clothes and toys apart – give each her own drawer, her own toy cupboard and book shelf, and never allow borrowing without the owner's permission.'

'That makes sense. May I use it in my reply?'

'Of course, any time.'

I helped myself to a sandwich.

'Sharing everything in common might have been all right in the early Christian community, but it doesn't work out in our modern world.'

Helen had brought the letters to a table and was looking through them.

'Here's another. "My little girl doesn't seem to trust me. Everything I say has to be confirmed by someone else before she believes me."'

'I wonder how often she has deceived that child. She'll just have to stop telling lies, won't she?' I stood up. 'Talking about lies, do you know the Brownings? That's a mother who is heading for big trouble.'

Joy Browning was true to her name, a happy, outgoing little girl, an adored only child. If I had one fault to find with Mrs Browning's loving care of her child it was her over-protectiveness of the lively four year old. Joy would soon be at school and would have to face the realities of life and take her chances in the rough and tumble of the school playground. She came to the clinic for her booster injection against diphtheria, totally unprepared.

'You go with Miss Corbally,' said Mrs Browning. 'The doctor just wants to have a look at you.'

'You're not coming in with her?'

'No, I couldn't bear to see it.'

Joy had already gone in and was chatting with Dr Lang as she prepared the syringe. I pushed up the loose sleeve of the child's jumper.

'Just a little prick, Joy.'

She pulled away from me. 'Mummy said the doctor was going to look at me. She didn't say I'd have a prick. Will it hurt?'

I drew her gently back and swabbed the arm.

'Only a very little, like a prick with a needle when you're sewing.'

'That's all right.'

She smiled at Dr Lang and didn't even wince as the injection was expertly given. Mrs Browning was almost in a state of shock when Joy bounced back to her, proudly displaying the jelly baby with which she had been compensated.

'You didn't tell me I was going to be pricked,' the child reproached her mother as she was being buttoned into her expensive tweed coat.

'I didn't want you to be frightened, darling.'

'You should never deceive a child, Mrs Browning,' I said quietly as she ushered her little girl towards the door. If only she had taken the advice to heart.

When I was informed that Joy had been discharged from hospital after a tonsillectomy, I arranged a routine visit to the house.

The Brownings lived next door to the Hughes family, as I was told by the postmistress. There was no longer any need for instructions from her or her customers about white gates, green doors or flowering trees, just 'opposite the nurse's cottage' or 'three doors up from the twins', or, as in this case, 'next door to Justin'. Justin was now at school. Like most children in Lapford, of all classes, he would be attending the village school until he was eleven, old enough to send away from home to a prep school en route for a public school. Mrs Hughes, in spite of her way-out ideas, or perhaps because of them, had brought her son up in an atmosphere of total honesty, and she found it difficult to go along with her neighbour's over-protectiveness of Joy from facing unpleasant truths. Actually, Joy was aware of more unpleasant truths than her mother realised, as she spent a great deal of time in the company of the horror-loving little boy next door. He was just arriving home from school when I pulled up at the Hughes' house, and ran over to my car to tell me happily, and in great detail, about the very dead rabbit they had found in the woods at the weekend.

Joy was waiting at the door to greet me and lead me into the house, but, when Mrs Browning reached out to draw the child towards her so that I could look at her throat, Joy stepped back, sat herself in a chair out of her mother's reach, and opened her mouth for my inspection. She then ran from the room, and I heard her walking slowly up the stairs. There were tears in her mother's eyes.

'She's always like that now. She won't come near me, won't let me touch her.'

Certainly Joy's behaviour was quite out of character. She had always been such an affectionate little person. I moved to sit beside Mrs Browning.

'Tell me about it. When did she change? Why?'

'Since the operation. When I brought her to the hospital she was her usual self, clinging to my hand, and happy and excited about the doll I told her we were going to buy. Then, when I went to fetch her home, she pulled away from me when I tried to kiss her, wouldn't take my hand. She's been like this ever since.'

The words ended in a sob.

'But you said she was happy, so she wasn't afraid of going to the hospital?'

'She didn't know.'

I remembered the injection.

'Mrs Browning, you don't mean you didn't tell Joy about the operation?'

The answer was jerked out between sobs.

'I didn't want to frighten her. I told her we were going to buy a new doll and we'd call on the way to see a little friend in the hospital. I took her to the ward and she was talking to the Sister – you know how she talks to people – so I just disappeared.'

I said nothing. I didn't dare speak, as such words as rose to my lips would have been no help to this unhappy mother – 'Imbecile! Idiot! Unfit to have a child!' She dried her eyes before continuing the tragic story.

'The new doll was here when she got home, a beautiful doll. She threw it to the floor and stamped on it. She has hardly spoken a word to me since, and refuses, absolutely, to go anywhere with me unless my mother or a neighbour comes with us.'

'You can't really blame her, Mrs Browning. How can she trust you after being so cruelly deceived?'

Fortunately, Joy's loving, wise and understanding father was able, in the course of time, to break down the barrier of mistrust and resentment between his little girl and her mother, but things were never quite the same again between them.

❧

Children need to know where they stand. If they are to feel secure they must be able to depend on grown-ups for truth and honesty and consistency. No promise made to a child should ever be broken, nor, for that matter, should a threat. Children expect to be punished for being naughty; it puts things right for them, rubs the slate clean, but it is supremely important that they should be clear in their little minds as to what is naughty. A small child is unable to cope with the sort of situation I have so often seen when what is fun one day, like playing with water or banging a drum, is naughty the next day, because Mummy has a headache, or received a worrying letter that morning, or has burnt the cake. Such inconsistencies would lead to the appalling confessions of failure that

Dr Lang and I would occasionally hear, with mingled pity and anger, from mothers of five- and six-year-old children at school medical inspections.

'I can't do anything with him!'

We heard it, inevitably, from Mrs Patch.

As an infant, Billy Patch was never allowed to cry, and I always found him in her arms when I called, never resting quietly, or even noisily, in his cot or pram. I advised her not to pick him up the minute he cried, or he would never give her any peace. At eighteen months he still got his own way by tears and screaming.

'If you don't assert yourself soon this child will be quite impossible by the time he's three,' I warned her.

Visiting there soon after Billy's third birthday I found her a nervous wreck, exhausted by disturbed nights, her once charming little house neglected, muddy foot-marks on the carpet and chair covers, broken crockery on the kitchen shelves. I was not surprised by her reply to my enquiry about her little son.

'He's impossible!'

I begged her to insist on some sort of discipline while Billy was still young enough to train. She promised to take him in hand, but, as I feared, her good resolutions were undermined by the violent rages of the small tyrant. He behaved himself at school (he had no option; he was at Chapford School) thus proving that he could be taught to do as he was told. The depth of his mother's subjugation was abundantly clear when Billy's immunisation was discussed.

'The booster dose against diphtheria is due now, Mrs Patch. You'll want him to have it,' suggested Dr Lang.

Mrs Patch turned to the five-year-old boy.

'Do you want it, darling?'

'No,' said Billy, predictably.

'No thank you, Doctor,' said Billy's mother.

When Billy had returned to his classroom Dr Lang and I tried to make her understand the criminal stupidity of her behaviour. Once again I warned her.

'If you don't get that boy of yours under control now, Mrs Patch, he'll be in the juvenile court before he's twelve.'

And he was.

I was often asked about punishment. When possible I advised that it should bear some relation to the offence. Damage, in justice, demands restitution, and the docking of pocket money to this end can be a salutary deterrent. I feel these principles could work at all ages, and sometimes regret that the attitude of our benevolent Home Office towards criminals is not unlike that of Jack Wilson's parents.

Jack was mischievous almost to the point of viciousness. I had received complaints from St Austin's School that the eleven-year-old boy was intimidating the younger children, who, if they unwittingly annoyed him, would suffer damaged books, broken pens and slashed coats. I called at the house to talk to his mother, and see if anything in his home background or family relationships could account for his behaviour. I found, as I had been told I would, a pleasant, likeable, well-mannered boy. I remembered him from the school medical inspection as grossly overweight, and our conversation confirmed what I had suspected, that he

135

was extremely sensitive about his appearance and thought the other children were making fun of him. His mother told me that, only the other week, he had overheard their neighbour refer to him as 'that fat boy'. The neighbour had come home from a holiday yesterday to find all her roses dug up and left to wither in the hot July sun.

'His dad has promised him a bicycle so that he can get away on his own.'

Rehabilitation, fair enough. But what about restitution?

'But what about the neighbour's roses?'

'My husband's seeing about them.'

'Your husband didn't dig them up, Mrs Wilson, Jack did, so surely it's his responsibility to replace them, not his father's.'

'He's only a lad. He hasn't got the money.'

'He would have, if you gave him the money you plan to spend on his bike. That would pay for the roses, and any left over he could take to school to replace the books and pens and other belongings he's damaged.'

Jack looked sullen. I resolved not to park my car anywhere near his house until he was safely back at school!

'How do you feel about that, Jack?' I asked. 'Don't you think it's fair?'

In my experience, most children have a great sense of fairness. They can stand a great deal from grown-ups, but 'it's not fair' is the ultimate complaint. We looked at each other for a few seconds, then he nodded slowly.

'I suppose so, but I think it's rotten.'

'It's pretty rotten losing a whole bed of roses. If you behave rottenly you deserve to be treated rottenly, don't you Jack?'

He lowered his eyes.

'S'pose so,' he mumbled.

I then talked to his mother about his food. I begged her to be firm with him and to stick rigidly to the diet the doctor had given him. For my part, I would ensure the co-operation of the school.

'Weigh yourself every week, Jack, and when you've lost the first stone,' I turned to his mother with a questioning smile, 'perhaps your parents might think you've earned that new bicycle.'

His eyes brightened.

'Would you, Mum?'

She nodded.

'I'll speak to your dad, but you must be a good boy and not keep at me for cakes and sweets. You know how soft I am!'

We both laughed with her.

'I'll be looking in from time to time to see your weight chart,' I promised. 'Meanwhile take plenty of exercise. Walking is really better than cycling at his stage, and perhaps your neighbour could find work for a strong boy in her garden once you've planted her new roses.'

Who was I to blame Jack's mum for being soft? Hadn't Eileen and I spent the last two evenings preparing for the visit of our darling Marcus, now five years old? We knew all his favourite food and made sure he got it. Meals were no problem, not even in the first thrill of arrival, when we had his favourite tea prepared for him. His mother's London flat was not very big, so we kept the toys and books we bought for him at 149, which saved her the trouble of packing such amenities when he came to us.

On this occasion a new clockwork train set was laid out in the drawing room, complete with stations and bridges, and our newly acquired black and white kitten, Whisky, was the focus of his attention from the moment he arrived. He was too absorbed in Whisky's antics to realise he had been kept out of the drawing room until after tea, and was still clutching the kitten in his arms when he saw the train. We had already promised his favourite television programme after tea, so switched it on. After we had washed up, I peeped into the drawing room. A wide-eyed little boy was sitting on the floor, tense with ecstatic happiness, the kitten curled up in his arms, one small hand laid adoringly on the engine of his new train, his laughing eyes watching the adventures of Muffin the Mule on the TV screen.

There was so much fun, so much happiness, so much love to be packed into two short days. He had always accepted that toys and books were to be left with us, but we were a bit worried about the railway. Could he bear to be parted from it? With a philosophy beyond his five years he reassured us. 'Mummy's flat isn't big enough for my railway. I'd better leave it here.' Each time he came to us he found his beloved railway had grown new rails, new coaches, new signals, bridges or stations.

Who was I to blame anyone for being soft with a little boy?

12

The Woman Who Didn't
Hold With Vitamins

❦

The summer was over and the first cold winds of autumn were browning the leaves and bringing the winter woollies out of storage. At my Dodsworth clinic, as I lifted the babies off the scales and handed them back to their mothers, I murmured to each one in turn, 'Remember to get your cod liver oil or Adexolin before you leave. It's time to start giving it again.'

Mothers of the new summer babies were further advised, 'Eight drops of Adexolin, or a teaspoon of cod liver oil.'

'In the bottle?'

'No. Oil floats, so when you tip the bottle up to feed him, it wouldn't go down into the teat. I'd give it in a spoon, just before the feed.'

A nose wrinkled. 'Nasty, smelly stuff.'

I smiled in sympathy. 'If you make that sort of face when you give it you'll put him right off. He's old enough to sense your revulsion. Perhaps you'd be better with Adexolin drops.'

'The babies don't like cod liver oil, do they?'

'Not at first, but they soon get used to it. It's a good idea to give it in the bath for the first week or so, then what is spat out can be easily wiped off without marking their clothes and making them smell.'

Mrs Cooper held out her arms as I finished weighing her Alfie.

'A six-point gain this month. Very nice. He's just trebled his birth weight, which is as it should be.'

The active little boy was trying to stand up on the scales – a difficult feat, as they swayed and wobbled as he struggled and kicked. Between us we managed to rescue him and anchor him safely in his mother's arms.

'Would you like the doctor to give him a check-up now he's a year old?'

'Is that usual?'

'It's up to you. It's all part of the clinic service.'

I hesitated, Alfie's record card poised over the doctor's pile. 'I suppose it will do no harm . . . but there's nought wrong with our Alfie.'

'I'm sure there isn't, so why not let doctor tell you what a splendid baby he is?'

She followed me through to the doctor's waiting room as I handed the card to my colleague who was helping with the injections. On my way back to the weighing room I paused to remind Mrs Cooper, 'Don't forget about the cod liver oil on the way out. Or did you give him Adexolin last winter?'

'Neither. I don't hold with these vitamins. He gets all he needs from the good fresh food on the farm.'

'He'll be walking soon, Mrs Cooper, he really does

need vitamin D to strengthen his bones. You wouldn't want him to grow bandy, would you?'

'Bandy? Not him. Look at those lovely little legs on him.'

Certainly his limbs were straight and strong, he had eight healthy teeth, and a light touch on his head satisfied me that the fontanelle was closing satisfactorily. So much for my theories. But I still believed in them, and continued to remind each mother to collect her vitamin A and D before leaving, until Mrs Cooper passed through on her way back from the doctor.

'Everything all right, Mrs Cooper?' I enquired.

''Course it is. Doctor says our Alfie's a perfect baby.' She was looking at me, but her voice was raised so that all the mothers could hear, 'And he's never had no vitamins, nor never shall.'

The winter of 1952 hit us with all the weather it could muster. The fogs started in late October, blanketing the countryside for weeks, making a nightmare of every drive to the villages. Dr Lang and I shared a car to the clinics and schools. It was less nerve-racking than being on one's own for mile after mile of impenetrable blackness, and one of us could get out and listen at road junctions, signalling with a torch when, hopefully, it was safe to cross. Mothers were urged to keep their babies indoors, which put more pressure on me to visit them, as they could not be brought to the clinics, which opened only for the sale of milk and vitamins, and for consultations with Dr Lang or myself.

There was a brief respite in December, then the snow came. It lay thick on the ground, piled up in drifts, and froze hard on the roads in the wake of the snow-plough. Kenilworth was bad enough. I walked everywhere, warning mothers to keep their prams off the roads, even if the going was easier than on the uncleared pavements, as they would have no chance against a skidding car. Everywhere one saw legs in plaster and arms in slings, invariably the right arms. If only people would carry parcels, bags, etc. in the right hand in slippery conditions, leaving their left hands free to take the impact of a fall (unless, of course, they are left-handed).

My expeditions to the villages were horrific. Loading the car with tins of milk and baby foods, bottles of orange juice, packets of Adexolin, a spade, an old blanket, wellingtons, and a thermos of hot coffee (just in case), I would set out in trepidation, alone. If it was a whole day trip, Charlie would keep an eye on Solow and give her a run. Conditions were too hazardous to risk taking the little low dog. Food centres were set up in the villages so no one had too far to walk. Milk and vitamins were available at Chesford School so that mothers, when delivering their elder children, could collect supplies for themselves or their neighbours.

The big boys and girls were enchanted to act as 'milk roundsmen', pulling home-made sledges made by them in the carpentry class. At Lapfold, Mrs Roche-Anderson turned one of her guest rooms into a storeroom, which she kept stocked from the chemists in Warwick and Leamington with spare nappies and feeding bottles as well as the necessary food, supplied by me. Basic medicines could be obtained at the nurse's cottage, and I brought over supplies each time I came to the village. Helen struggled valiantly round her district, sometimes on a bicycle, more often on foot.

'If only,' she sighed, 'the sap wouldn't rise in the spring, or the gestation period could be shorter.'

'Like three months?' I suggested.

She nodded. I shook my head.

'What can a countryman do with the long dark evenings in autumn?'

Helen shrugged her shoulders.

'We can't win.'

But we were winning. It was a tremendous help having Helen on the spot but I still had to get around to my small new babies, especially the delicate and premature ones who were at risk in the extreme cold of that winter. Having made it to the village to deliver the milk supplies, I would venture up the narrow lanes, either deep in uncleared snow, or rutted by the farm vehicles – ruts so deep that my little Austin would be straddled helplessly in the middle. By the time the car had been lifted back onto the road, pulled out of a ditch and rescued from a snowdrift, I decided it was easier, and less bother to the friendly farmers, to leave my car in the village street and walk from there.

Not so much easier as less difficult, and quicker in the long run. I often met the postman in the middle of the morning, whistling as he cycled carefully down a lane. I would sometimes be tempted by his offer to deliver a packet of milk and vitamins to a distant farm or cottage with the mail, but I felt the mother just might have a problem, especially when the telephone lines were down, so instead I would save him a journey by delivering the letters.

At last the snow stopped, the sun came out, and the countryside was covered with slush and water from the melting snow and the rising rivers and canals. Then even that misery passed, and it was spring. That spring Alfie Cooper had a baby sister. I was always grateful when residents of remote farm cottages had the good sense to have their babies in the spring, thus sparing their health visitor from trudging across fields or up rutted farm tracks in rain and sleet and snow and biting east winds.

It was a pleasure striding out across the open pasture that early April morning, keeping Solow well to heel as we passed the grazing sheep. Once over the railway bridge she ran ahead of me on the narrow path that skirted the cornfield. I knew the Coopers had no dog, and my little dachshund was trained to sit quietly outside the back door while I was in the cottage. The fields were visible from the windows, and Mrs Cooper was waiting for me at the gate, eager to show me her very small daughter. Alfie was asleep upstairs. The baby was waking him at night, I was told, and he needed the extra sleep, so Mrs Cooper would appreciate it if I didn't go up, in case it woke him. I'd see him at the clinic, anyhow, when she brought little Rosie for her milk. The new baby had been put onto a bottle almost immediately, which was surprising, as Alfie had been breastfed with no difficulty for six months. I thought Mrs Cooper seemed a bit strained and taut, but put it down to the recent confinement, and the disappointment about feeding, although I did wonder was it perhaps the tenseness that had interfered with the milk supply, and not the other way round?

Everything appeared to be all right. Her husband was fit and in a secure job, he got on well with the farmer, and ran no risk of being sacked and losing his tied cottage. Her mother lived nearby and was helping out with the work for the first few weeks. There was nothing wrong with the baby, and Alfie, I was assured, was 'getting along nicely!' Then why the tenseness? I wasn't altogether happy as Solow and I returned past the sprouting corn and across the meadow, where, the sheep having moved away from our track, the patient little dog was allowed to scamper freely back to the car, her long ears flapping, her short legs covering the ground at an amazing speed.

Mrs Cooper turned up at the clinic the following week with Rosie, but not Alfie. 'His nan has taken him out for the afternoon,' she explained. Every clinic day seemed to coincide with her mother's sudden wish to take her little grandson out for the afternoon. I didn't remember Mrs Nest showing such devotion when Alfie was a baby.

My next visit to the cottage was a Monday morning.

'His nan has him at her place Mondays,' I was told. 'It gets him from under my feet while I do the washing.'

My next visit was a baking day, and again Alfie was 'out from under her feet' with his grandmother.

One afternoon in early June, when we were packing up the clinic, Mrs Russell called to me from the sales table.

'We had quite a shindy with Mrs Cooper. She was demanding her cod liver oil, although I explained that we didn't issue it in the summer.'

I thought I must have heard wrong.

'Did you say Mrs Cooper?'

'Yes. She was most insistent. I told her about it being the sunshine vitamin, and how a double dose in summer would be bad for the baby.'

I smiled.

'Good for you! You've learnt your lesson well.'

'I've heard you explaining it often enough, I know it by heart. She is a difficult woman. We had quite a time with her. In the end she said she'd get it from a chemist.'

She must have done just that. Next time I saw Rosie she had a nasty rash and Mrs Cooper told me she was being sick, which was unusual for her. Apart from the rash, her fair skin was slightly blistered from over-exposure to the sun, and I recognised the rash and the sickness as a typical reaction to an overdose of vitamin D from a combination of sunshine and cod liver oil. I could only advise against the bottled vitamins during the summer, but knew I was wasting my time. What could have changed her deep-rooted opposition to vitamins into this fanatical enthusiasm for them? Predictably, Alfie was not at home. Mrs Cooper was full of regrets. Had she known I was coming she would have kept him with her, but 'His nan does enjoy his company.'

Suddenly I knew that I had to see Alfie, and soon.

The following Monday I called on Mrs West. She seemed surprised to see me.

'I'm on my way to your daughter, but thought I'd look in as I was passing, to see Alfie.'

'But why call here?'

'I understood you always have him on Mondays, to leave his mother free to get on with the washing.'

'Have him here? Not me. I've my own wash to do.'

She gave me a penetrating look.

'What do you think of our Alfie?'

'I haven't seen him for some time.'

'Not seen him? But you've been up to the cottage to see the baby.'

'I've been unlucky. Every time I call there, Alfie seems to be with you.'

'With me? He never has.' Her eyes narrowed. 'I think our Nell's been having you on, my dear. He's at home, with her, where he's always been.' She walked to the gate with me. 'Our Nell will be in the back this morning. The window looks right across the fields.'

Our eyes met. I nodded to show I had understood.

I left the car at the end of the lane, preferring the long walk up the rutted track to a broken axle. Crossing the farmyard, I opened the little green gate, carefully shutting it behind me as I saw the children on the lawn. I was glad to see the pram was under an old apple tree, and Rosie's dose of vitamin D was filtering through the leaves. Alfie, now well into his second year, was playing on the grass beside her. I was distressed to see that he was very much overweight. As the gate clicked, he got to his feet, calling to his mother, and stumbling towards the cottage. I gasped in dismay as I saw the extent of his deformity. The bent, rickety legs could hardly support the heavy body. I

147

moved quickly as they gave way under him, but his mother reached him first and caught him up into her arms. As her eyes met mine, her face suddenly crumpled.

'Now you see how he is,' she sobbed. 'I should have told you long since, but I was so ashamed.'

Alfie, frightened by his mother's tears, had started to howl, and I steered them both into the kitchen before Rosie awoke and joined the chorus.

'Now calm down, Mrs Cooper, don't upset yourself. Would a cup of tea help?'

She nodded mutely. I put on the kettle.

'And a biscuit for Alfie?'

I knew where the tin was kept. She hung her head.

'He can't eat biscuits, can't manage to chew them.'

I might have known. She showed me his teeth, rotten, discoloured, and probably painful.

'I'm so ashamed. You did tell me, but I wouldn't listen, thought I knew better. Now look at him.'

I knew my way round her kitchen, and soon had the cups on the table and the tea brewed. Mrs Cooper dried her eyes and put Alfie on the floor, where his weak legs buckled under him and he subsided cheerfully beside her chair.

'I'm glad you've seen him. I wanted to tell you, but I was so ashamed.'

'He was here all the time, wasn't he?'

She nodded.

'When I saw you coming over the field I'd fetch him in and shut him in the bedroom till after you'd gone. I couldn't bear you to see him, not like he is, not after what you told me.'

Her hand was still shaking, so I took the pot from her and poured out the tea.

'We mustn't lose any more time, Mrs Cooper. Can you take him to your doctor tomorrow?'

'I could go in the evening, when Bill comes home. He'd run us over. It is rickets, isn't it?'

'I'm afraid it looks like it.'

'That's bad, rickets is.'

'Bad, yes, but not hopeless. He's still very small, and the bones aren't set. They should be able to put him right in the hospital.'

A ray of hope lit up the tear-smudged face.

'He won't always be a cripple then?'

'He shouldn't be, but it will take time. He'll be a long time in hospital.'

A hand stole down to caress the fair head cushioned against her knee.

'Then the sooner he goes in the sooner we'll get him home. I'll get Bill to take us along to the doctor this evening.' She gave me a rueful smile. 'I'm glad you've seen him. Sneaking up on me like that!'

'I'm glad too, Mrs Cooper. I only regret that I didn't sneak up on you a little sooner.'

Alfie was nearly a year in hospital, with his legs in plaster. He lost all his baby teeth, but his legs grew straight and strong, and by the time he went to school he was running and jumping with the best. Every winter after that, each member of the Cooper family was given a daily dose of the 'Sunshine Vitamin'.

It was the spring of Rosie's birth that I received another summons to the Hall. Her ladyship was displeased again, outraged. She had called on the young wife of a soldier serving in Germany and found, to her horror, that the girl was pregnant.

'Filthy little slut! They've only been married a few months.'

'It couldn't be her husband's?'

'Not possible. He's been in Berlin since Christmas.'

'Oh dear, what a mess!'

This time I'd been offered a chair and Rita had brought in a tray of coffee and biscuits.

'Outrageous behaviour,' said my hostess, 'sleeping around while her husband's serving overseas.'

She poured coffee from the silver jug.

'Well, Miss Corbally, what can be done?'

'Could you bring him home?'

'Pass the baby off as his? It's too late, she's already three months pregnant. No baby could be that premature.'

She handed me the biscuits.

'What will you do?' I asked. 'Write to his CO?'

'I suppose he'll have to be told, unless . . .' she paused. 'Could we get her away somewhere, before it becomes too obvious?'

'Until she's had the baby?'

'Yes, I could find somewhere. There are places for girls like her.'

'How long will he be in Germany?'

She shrugged.

'Probably two years. He might be due for leave, which would be awkward, but I could square that with the colonel. He'd back us up. I know him well, friend of my husband's.'

'I could arrange for the baby to be adopted if that's what she'd like.'

'Has she a choice? It's no picnic for our occupation force. He can do without being greeted with another man's baby when he comes home.'

She refilled my cup.

'That's settled then.'

'Oh no!'

She nearly dropped the cup.

'No? What do you mean, no?'

'We can't make that sort of decision with other people's lives. I think the husband has a right to know, unless the girl asks us to keep it from him, in which case we have a plan to offer her, but the decision must be hers. It's her baby, even if . . .'

I paused, cup in hand. At the back of my mind a memory stirred, a letter in a magazine, 'Dear Nurse Jane'.

'I wonder . . .'

'What?'

I gulped down the coffee and stood up.

'Leave this with me. I'll see the girl this afternoon and give you a ring. I've got an idea.'

She had got to her feet and accompanied me to the door.

'I hope it's a good idea.'

'So do I. Thanks for the coffee. I'll be in touch.'

I drove straight to the nurse's cottage. Helen was just going out.

'This is urgent. You answered a letter recently from a young army wife, expecting a baby. Her husband was in Berlin. Remember?'

'Yes, I remember. The husband had hitched a lift home with the RAF for twenty-four hours, strictly against regulations.'

'That's the one. He daren't admit paternity for fear of a court martial, so where did she stand? Her reputation apart, what about the child's allowance? That was the gist of it wasn't it?'

'Yes,' she chuckled. 'An absurd situation, if ever I heard one. I advised her to get in touch with her health visitor, who could call in the help of SSAFA.'

'I think I am her health visitor. Can you check the address?'

My hunch was confirmed by the bright-eyed happy young wife, thrilled about her baby, proud that her husband had risked so much to spend even a few hours with her.

'That SSAFA lady, she's a bit fierce, isn't she?'

'She thought you'd been a very naughty girl, and, on the face of it, you can't blame her.'

'I didn't dare tell her.'

'I think Lady Merlin should know. She's a very caring person really and she has a vast amount of strings she can pull.'

She hesitated.

'If it won't get my husband into trouble. We can manage without the money, but I don't want him in trouble.'

'I think I can promise that.'

I rang Lady Merlin after tea. She was delighted and her laughter was good to hear.

'He's a lad after Brian's own heart! That's his colonel. I'll get him to send the boy home when the baby's due.' She laughed again. 'Brian's going to love this!'

13

Cynthia

I called on Mrs Roche-Anderson as the twins were approaching their third birthday. We watched them from the window playing happily on the lawn with Smudge.

'They're great company, the three of them,' I commented.

'Yes. It sounds silly, but I almost resent it. They're so horribly self-sufficient, I sometimes feel an outsider.'

She moved away from the window.

'It seems awful, but I feel really jealous when Patricia prefers her sister's company to mine.'

'And vice versa? When Phillida prefers to be with Patricia?'

There was a pause. She flopped onto the sofa, patting the seat in invitation to me to join her.

'No. That's my trouble. I adore Patricia . . . but I've no feeling for Phillida at all. I don't love her. I never have.' She was concentrating on her hands, tightly clasped on her lap. I was silent, watching her. She looked up.

'Are you shocked?'

I shook my head, reaching out to unclench her hands and take one in my own.

'No, my dear, not shocked, not even surprised. You had a bad time at her birth, and she was a difficult feeder, both of which are rather off-putting. If there had been only her you'd have got over it, you would have had to love her, but you had Patricia to love, so, subconsciously, your rejection of Phillida took root.'

'You knew?'

'I've wondered. I'm glad you told me. It's not an easy thing to admit.'

Her face crumpled. My arm went round her shoulders.

'I've felt so awful about it, so guilty. I felt like a sort of unnatural monster that couldn't love her own child.'

I hugged her, letting her cry quietly against my shoulder.

'You've been a wonderful mother to both of them. Phillida's a happy, healthy, well-adjusted little girl, which proves she doesn't know you don't love her.'

She was drying her eyes. My arm was still round her. I went on.

'Do you know why she doesn't know?'

She shook her head, and blew her nose loudly.

'Because, my dear, love isn't all about feelings and emotions. Deep down, in your real innermost self, you do love your little girl.'

'But . . .'

I put a finger on her lips as she protested.

'Yes, you do. For nearly three years she has shared with your beloved Patricia the same care, the same food, the same clothes, the same fun, the same correcting, the same cherishing. In my book all that adds up to a great deal of loving.'

Her eyes were wide, the tears still glistened on the long lashes.

'I never thought ... but if only I could feel something for her, something warmer than resentment and irritation.'

I did some hard thinking while the kettle boiled, and was ready with a suggestion when she returned with the tea tray.

'There's a playgroup opening in the village next month. Would it be an idea to use it? Start breaking up their complete dependence on each other? You could send Patricia, perhaps, for two mornings and Phillida for two, that would give you some time each week alone with each of them. No rival for Patricia's company, no other child but Phillida to cuddle.'

She thought it over, watching her children from the window as I sipped my tea. When she turned back to me her smile was dazzling.

'It could work! I feel it's going to work, that things will be different now.'

As she helped me into my coat she kissed me lightly on the cheek.

'Thank you, Miss Corbally. Thank you for listening and understanding.' She gave a small sigh. 'I'm so lucky, having my two beautiful girls. When I think of people who long for children and can't have them, people like the Russells.'

I paused at the doorway.

'I'd no idea. Mrs Russell always struck me as such a happy person.'

'She's not. Not deep down.'

'But the clinic? If she feels that strongly how can she bear being among all those babies, selling milk to all those happy mothers?'

'Joan's that sort of person. She knew we needed help and she was available, so she came along. As she says, not having children of her own leaves her free to help those who have.'

I was seeing Mrs Russell in a new light. I'd always liked her, but had wondered whether she was simply a woman who preferred to spend her time and money on herself and her home to rearing a family. Her husband was a stockbroker in Birmingham. There was plenty of money there. It showed in her expensive tailor-made suits, in the Jaguar parked outside the village hall on clinic afternoons. I had no doubt it showed in the long, low rose-covered house of golden Cotswold stone that overlooked the pond. I could only guess at the richness of the furnishings, the valuable pictures, the beautiful collections of glass and china. I hadn't been inside the house, not then, but I was soon to do so.

After fifteen years of marriage, of hope, disappointment, then despair, Mrs Russell became pregnant, to everyone's surprise and delight. She was welcomed at the antenatal classes by girls young enough to be her own daughters, and was maturely conscientious about her diet and exercises, getting as excited as a child over her shopping expeditions to Mothercare and the preparation and decoration of the nursery, with her husband's help.

Not surprisingly, Cynthia was a caesarean birth and it was nearly three weeks after the event that I drove out to Lapfold to share in the joy of this so long desired and eagerly awaited little girl. Mrs Russell was in a seventh heaven of ecstatic motherhood and I was immediately brought up to the nursery. She was trembling with excitement as she opened the door of the whitewashed little room with its frieze of Disney characters and led me towards the cradle, so lovingly decorated with flounces and ribbons and covered with an exquisitely embroidered quilt. She stood back, glowing with pride as I bent over the sleeping baby. It was a little while before I raised my head. While I made appropriate noises of rapture and appreciation, I was struggling to fight back the tears stinging behind my eyes, to control the surprise and worry that I must not show: Cynthia had Down's Syndrome.

Mrs Russell brought her precious baby to the clinic every month, and I visited her frequently, closely watching her development, alert for any sign or hint that her mother suspected that everything was not quite perfect with her adored little daughter. She was attending the hospital at regular intervals for consultations with the paediatrician, who gave her no indication that anything was amiss. It is probable that he was under the impression that she had already been told of her child's condition, and the baby's physical progress was satisfactory.

Cynthia did all the right things at the right time, smiled, laughed and made the right noises, rolled over, cut her first tooth, and was even sitting up before she was seven months old. Her diet was being carefully watched, cereals and starchy foods being avoided, as children with Down's Syndrome tend to become fat and flabby. Mrs Russell was encouraged to stimulate her baby by talking to her and playing with her, not that she needed my encouragement. Her world revolved round Cynthia. Friends and relations came to see her, grandparents visited, a christening party was given in her honour. I wondered, had nobody noticed? Had nothing been said? Just before her first birthday, Mrs Russell had brought Cynthia for her routine check-up at the clinic. Dr Lang called me into her rooms.

'Mrs Russell's been asking some leading questions. I think she's beginning to suspect something.'

We'd all been waiting for this moment, and dreading it.

'Do you think she has any idea what's wrong?'

'No. But she's wondering why Cynthia has to go on seeing the paediatrician.'

'I know. She's asked me that. I told her it was probably because of the caesarean birth.'

Dr Lang nodded.

'I muffled a bit, said it was probably her age and not being able to have another, making Cynthia a rather special baby.'

'She's certainly that. What do we do now?'

'Apparently her doctor's never seen the baby. I've advised her to ask him about that hernia.'

Quite a few babies, and nearly all children with Down's Syndrome are born with an umbilical hernia, which usually resolves itself in the first eighteen months, but it was a good excuse to give the GP a chance to deal with the situation. I rang Dr Stevens the following evening.

'Did Mrs Russell bring her baby to the surgery this morning?'

'She did. It's a nasty hernia. If it's no better in six months we'll have to think about operating.'

'But did you tell her?'

'About the operation? Yes. She's quite happy about it.' He sounded peeved.

'I don't mean the hernia. That was just an excuse to send her to you. I mean, about the baby having Down's Syndrome.'

I heard him draw in his breath.

'Good heavens! Doesn't she know? Surely she's been told at the hospital?'

'No one seems to have told her, but we feel she's beginning to suspect something.'

'What about Dr Lang? She's been seeing the baby regularly, I understand, and Mrs Russell has great faith in her. I hardly know the woman.'

He had a point there. It might come better from someone she knew well.

'I'm seeing her tomorrow. I'll tell her what you suggest.'

Dr Lang was reluctant. The clinic was too public a place for such a revelation. I agreed, yet it was important that Mrs Russell should be told the truth about her baby soon. There were two other children with Down's Syndrome in the neighbourhood, in Leamington and Warwick, both boys, aged four and eight. The older boy's physical and mental development was slow, and he displayed the typical facial characteristics. The younger was a cheerful little fellow, but he was not talking yet, and his gait was clumsy. Sooner or later Mrs Russell would meet one of the boys, and their mothers would see Cynthia, and inevitably recognise that she had Down's Syndrome. There were kinder ways of breaking the news than a casual encounter in the street, and sooner or later, as the condition developed, the crooning and 'dear little thing' of the local pram-stoppers would become 'poor little thing' and Mrs Russell would be perplexed by the sympathy and pity in their eyes. Such a shock would be best sustained in the privacy of her own home and with the immediate support of her husband. It was not Dr Lang's province to visit the homes of other doctors' patients. That left me.

When an unpleasant job has to be done I believe in getting it over with, so I drove out to Lapfold that evening, timing my arrival for about half past six, when Mr Russell would be home from his office and Cynthia would be in bed. Mrs Russell was surprised to see me, but greeted me warmly and brought me in to meet her husband. She offered me a chair.

'What brings you out so late, Miss Corbally?'

'I wanted to talk to you both about Cynthia.'

She smiled fondly.

'I was telling my husband how pleased Dr Lang was with her.'

Had she no idea what I'd come about? Mr Russell was watching me warily. There was no gentle way of doing what I had come to do.

'Cynthia's physical development is excellent, in fact quite remarkable . . . under the circumstances.'

'You mean, being a caesarean birth?'

'Not only that.' I took a deep breath. 'Mrs Russell, Mr Russell, we feel the time has come when you have to be told that your little girl has Down's Syndrome.'

Mrs Russell looked stunned. Her husband, standing beside her, put a protective arm round her shoulders and clasped the hand reaching out towards him. I realised that what I had said was not news to him and wondered how long he had known. I talked on, giving the stricken mother time to regain her composure.

'There are different levels of the syndrome, and we have every reason to suppose that Cynthia will do well. She may always need extra help, but she should be able to go to school, to read and write, and could be really good at practical things. I've known quite a few children with Down's Syndrome, and they are the most endearing, affectionate and lovable children. In spite of her condition, perhaps even because of it, Cynthia will bring you much happiness, and give you an immense amount of love.'

I paused. Gently, Mr Russell withdrew his hand.

'I think we could all do with a drink.'

As he moved across to the sideboard, I knelt by Mrs Russell's chair and took her cold hand in mine.

'I'm sorry, but you had to know.'

She blinked, and focused her eyes on me.

'How long have you known?'

'Always. Since I first saw Cynthia.'

'And you said nothing.'

'Should I have done? Do you feel I've let you down? Cheated you?'

Mr Russell, crossing the room with two glasses of sherry, shook his head.

'No. Joan has had a year of indescribable happiness. I'm glad no one took that away from her.'

I took the glass he held out to me.

'Did you know, Mr Russell?'

'I wondered. Not being with her all the time, I suppose I noticed more.'

He fetched himself a glass of whisky, and I sat on the sofa beside his wife. She squeezed my hand.

'I'm glad it was you who told us.'

Mr Russell rejoined us.

'Good of you to come out all this way, after a day's work. It can't be easy for you, this sort of thing. We appreciate it.'

He raised his glass, hesitated.

'To Cynthia,' I said, 'and many happy years for you both with your sweet little girl.'

I was glad of the drink. My hand was shaking almost as much as Mrs Russell's. Having delivered my difficult message my presence was superfluous, so I excused myself. Mr Russell saw me to the door.

'Thank you,' he said as he shook my hand, and I knew he meant it.

'It's not going to be easy for Joan. You'll help her, won't you?'

'Of course I'll help her – all the way.'

I had already read up every available book on Down's Syndrome, and had collected information on an association for parents of children born with the condition. The first hurdle to be overcome was acceptance. Her daughter's condition was a fact that Mrs Russell had to face up to and live with. The second, and more difficult hurdle, was to face other people with the fact, to walk out proudly with her little daughter, to meet people's embarrassment with honesty, to make it quite clear that her beloved little daughter was no embarrassment to her.

Cynthia continued to develop normally. She was walking at eighteen months, and walking well. Her speech was a bit thick and nasal, but understandable, and her vocabulary extensive by any standards. Mrs Russell understood why I had stressed the importance of talking to her from the very beginning. She began to read to her, to play games with her, to do exercise with her daily to tone up the rather flabby muscles. On my recommendation she bought toys which would encourage co-ordination of eyes and hands, and train the little fingers not to drop, or spill, or bungle. She taught her nursery rhymes, she let her loose with crayons and paints, she treated her like any other child, and Cynthia responded. She was a merry little girl, loving and demonstrative, only rarely indulging in fits of temper, and easily coaxed out of them. I urged Mrs Russell not to let the child's disability become an excuse for bad behaviour, and as the Russells' standards of discipline and good manners were high, so were Cynthia's.

Children with Down's Syndrome easily put on weight, so the diet was closely watched, and each winter a course of Scott's Emulsion helped to ward off the coughs and colds to which such children seem particularly prone. I visited the Russells frequently, and Cynthia would jump up and down with excitement when she saw my car draw up outside the house, and would fling herself into my arms before I crossed the threshold. I had barely time to greet her mother before I was taken by the hand to see her latest accomplishment – a drawing or a simple jigsaw puzzle, or I was installed in a chair to hear the newest nursery rhyme. If she made a mistake, she would explode into gurgles of laughter – so much more pleasant than the tears which a more self-conscious child might have shed under similar circumstances.

I persuaded Mrs Russell to join the association for parents of children with Down's Syndrome, and she derived so much help and encouragement from their meetings and their excellent publications that she began to take an active part in the work of the association. She took Cynthia to visit a nearby home for children with learning difficulties, planning, later on, to let the child spend a few weeks there every year, so, if she was ever left alone, she would be among friends and in familiar surroundings.

The headmaster of the village school was happy to accept Cynthia into the infant class, and, when I visited the school, my little friend would run to greet me, claiming me as her very own 'Miss Corbay', and introducing me to the teacher and the other children. I had to be shown her work which, in the early years, compared favourably with that of her classmates. She learnt to read simple books, to write, and do easy sums. She enjoyed painting and Plasticine, and singing and listening to stories and she could run and jump and skip with her companions. She enjoyed tremendously the company of the other children, who accepted her without question as just another child.

When I left the Midlands to live and work in Sussex one of my greatest regrets was saying goodbye to Cynthia.

Should Mrs Russell have been told earlier about her baby's condition? Do parents have a right to know? Of course they do. But a woman who has just given birth is in no fit state for the shock of such knowledge. To tell too much too soon can give rise to feelings of guilt and shame, to rejection of the baby and the stillbirth of maternal love. I have always been glad that some oversight, a failure of communication, or just the imaginative and humane decision to say nothing, allowed Mrs Russell to enjoy twelve months of blissful happiness with her little girl; twelve precious months to allow the growth of a deep and indestructible love between her and Cynthia.

14

A Polio Epidemic

❧

Since the introduction of polio vaccination in the 1960s, the crippling disease once known as 'infantile paralysis', fortunately, rarely occurs in this country. I well remember the discovery of the vaccine and also the years before its discovery, when active young people would be struck down, to live out the rest of their lives in wheelchairs or iron lungs.

It was soon after the precious vaccine had come to our clinics, but before wholesale vaccination in infancy had become established, that an outbreak of polio struck Kenilworth. The infection had come from Birmingham, via Coventry, where so many of the local men were employed. We contacted all our schools. Notices were put up in clinics and surgeries and appeared in the local papers. We visited as many families as we could, and more than seemed humanly possible. The message was vital.

'At the first sign of illness, fever, stiff neck or aching limbs, go straight to bed and send for your doctor. Do not walk or indulge in any physical activity.'

When a well-known swimmer had become paralysed after entering a competition when suffering from 'a slight cold', all sporting events were cancelled, and the swimming baths closed. Young people were particularly vulnerable. What normal young man or woman would give up an afternoon's sport or let down their team because of a cold? Yet the symptoms were so alike: a slight temperature, aching limbs, nothing so serious that a healthy youngster couldn't throw off with a couple of aspirin and the stimulus of competition in a much-loved sport. If the despised cold was, in fact, the early onset of poliomyelitis, the strenuous exercise of the affected muscles could damage them beyond repair. To be on the safe side we advised the schools to cancel PT and all competitive games. A child feeling below par would be less likely to overindulge in ordinary playground activities. Headmasters were asked to notify the health visitors of any children who seemed so unwell that they had to be sent home, and all such messages were followed up with visits to their parents.

The pressure of these visits, on top of our routine work, was such that we often worked late, and evening surgery had already started when, on my way to see an eight-year-old boy sent home from school that afternoon, I passed him with his mother, on the way to the doctor. He looked flushed and unhappy and was walking with a slight limp. His mother was trying to urge him on. As I stopped the car, I heard her say, 'Hurry along, our Tom. Your dad will be home before long and wanting his dinner.'

I got out of the car and had a closer look at 'our Tom'. I could see he was glad of an excuse to stop walking. I noticed that he was standing with all his weight on his right leg. His mother looked impatient.

'We're in a bit of a hurry. I want to get to the doctor early, and be back home for his dad's dinner, but he's walking so slow.'

Her voice trailed off as I bent over the boy.

'Is your leg hurting you, Tom?'

'Yes, it aches bad, and I don't feel good.'

He didn't look good. His forehead felt hot, and his eyes were dull. The tears were not far away.

'He shouldn't be walking, Mrs Grant. If his leg hurts he shouldn't be using it at all. I'll run you home in the car, and I suggest you get Tom straight into bed while I ring the doctor and ask him to call.'

Mrs Grant grumbled a bit about making such a fuss about a bit of a cold. The leg, she said, was just 'growing pains', all kids got them, nothing to worry about. But she came with me and settled her son into bed with rough kindliness. She showed her true worth when Tom eventually came out of hospital, encouraging him to exercise his shrunken left leg, re-educating him to walk again with the help of the callipers and the built-up shoe which he was to wear for the rest of his life.

We opened special vaccination clinics and distributed the impregnated lumps of sugar in the schools. Women of all ages queued up in the afternoons, mothers bringing their small children to be protected from the dread disease. Twice a week the clinic opened from half past five until seven in the evening for the workers, and young women poured in from offices and shops and factories. There was only a trickle of men, and this alarmed us. I spoke to as many mothers as I could, urging them to remind their husbands about the evening clinics. The answers were all the same.

'He's tired and hungry when he comes home, just wants to put his feet up with his cup of tea (or mug of beer) and enjoy a good hot meal.'

I explained the risks their men were running, engaged on heavy work, taxing their muscles, and exposed daily to the polio virus.

'What is the point of protecting yourself and your children while the wage-earner is taking a chance of being crippled for life?'

They began to see sense in my argument.

'I'll tell him what you said, but if he won't go there's nothing I can do.'

'I think there is. You say your husband comes home hungry? Then let him wait for his meal until he's been to the clinic.'

A thoughtful nod of the head.

'But how'd I know he'd been there? The pub's nearer. He could drop in there for a quick one and I'd be none the wiser.'

That made sense. The clinic was centrally situated, but Kenilworth was spreading rapidly in all directions.

'I'll give them all notes and sign them, so you'll have the evidence. No note, no tea. What about it?'

The idea caught on. The women discussed it in the streets, in the shops and launderettes, and over the garden gates. 'No note, no tea,' became a password among the women of Kenilworth.

Some men were waiting at the clinic before we'd even opened. The early trickle became a flood. The men poured in, self-conscious and embarrassed, still in their working clothes on their way home. Others, less credulous, had been turned back at the door of their homes.

'No note, no tea.' The slogan passed from man to man. They laughed over it and joked, or grumbled and swore, according to their natures, but they came. They'd had a hard day's work and a sandwich lunch and they were hungry. Sheepishly they held out their hands for the signed notes, which I handed to each of them while they crunched the lumps of sugar, moist with the life-giving drops of vaccine.

'Let's have that note please, Miss. I want my tea.'

From time to time the Master of the House would attempt to bluff.

'I'd better have a note, in case they ask at work about this vaccination.'

I'd hand it to him, smiling, and he'd smile back, knowing well that I knew to whom the note would be delivered.

The epidemic passed, taking its toll in deaths and broken lives, in crippling and paralysis. Kenilworth escaped lightly. Perhaps our greatest concern during those anxious weeks was over an expectant mother struck down with the disease four months before her baby was due. No one could foresee, with any certainty, how serious the risk was of the baby being infected. Her weakened muscles necessitated a caesarean delivery, and I went to the hospital as soon as I heard of the operation. I didn't know what to expect. Would I find the baby in an oxygen tent? An iron lung? Would any of its tiny limbs, or all, be paralysed? It was just before feeding time, and I was taken to the nursery. As the yelling infant was put into my arms, I gave a great shout of joy, as the flailing arms and kicking feet thudded against my chest.

The mother made a slow but complete recovery, and there was no day so dark that would not be lightened for me by the sight of her little boy walking by her side, running and jumping on the school playground, competing in the local sports, and growing strong and straight and whole.

Although work was concentrated on the town I was not unaware of my responsibility towards the rural community. Dr Stevens had retired in 1956 and the practice had been taken over by a much younger man, keen and dedicated, as he was to prove during those hectic weeks. Aware of our commitments in Kenilworth, Dr John rang the MOH with an offer to run vaccination clinics at his evening surgery, an offer enthusiastically accepted, which left Dr Lang and myself to cover the Lapfold infant welfare centre and the schools. Mrs Roche-Anderson joined us in the doctor's room during a lull in the weighing at Lapfold. She brought two fresh cups of tea; the first ones were still where they'd been placed, cold and undrunk, but the queue was thinning now.

'You look worn out, both of you. Can I do anything to help?'

'You are helping, being here. What matters is to get everyone immunised.'

I opened another box of sugar lumps, measured the dosage onto each and gave them to the toddlers and mothers, while Dr Lang dropped the life-saving fluid on to the tongues of the protesting babies.

'It's a huge area,' I said. 'Do you know if people are getting to Dr John's surgery? Do they need transport from the outlying farms and cottages?'

Mrs Roche-Anderson smiled happily, thrusting the tea under our noses.

'I could arrange it. There's lots of people with cars would be glad to help. Leave it to us, we'll get them to the surgery.'

And they did. Down narrow lanes, up rutted farm tracks, the cars were out, their owners persuading, cajoling, bullying, but succeeding in getting the workers to the surgery – men and women, farmers, builders, teachers, commuters. Miss Smart told me about it.

'They were absolutely splendid, like sheepdogs rounding up their flock. I can understand Lady Merlin not taking no for an answer, does she ever? But Mrs R-A filled her car every time, and went back for another load. I don't know how she did it.'

'I do. She cares, and it got through to them.'

My friend looked exhausted. It had been a very busy time for her, helping at Dr John's vaccination clinics every evening after her day's work. When I was in the village I'd call in to check her lists against my own, to ensure that all our precious children were protected – Cynthia, Justin Ward, the Crawley children, Joy Browning, all of them. I'd missed Helen at the clinic that afternoon and called in on my way home. There

173

was no answer to my knock and the door was unlocked, so I walked in. My friend was fast asleep in an armchair, and I saw with a shock how she had aged in the last few weeks. Her hair was now heavily streaked with grey, and the once ruddy cheeks were sallow. She woke with a start and glanced at the clock.

'Good heavens, is it that time? The clinic must be over.'

She got up, bustling, clearing the table.

'I'm so sorry, I meant to come. I usually have a little sit down after lunch, and must have dozed off.'

'You needed the sleep. It's been a busy month.'

I helped her lay the tea tray, picked up the bowl of sugar.

'I feel I never want to look a lump of sugar in the face again.'

She laughed.

'Nor me. But what a good thing this didn't happen during rationing.'

'You're so right. All sugar was precious, but lump sugar was like gold. We'd saved some for a tea party. My brother was with us that weekend with his little son.'

I chuckled at the memory.

'The child ate it all?'

'No. We were talking, not noticing Marcus. I vaguely heard "plop" and a giggle, then again, and again, until I looked and caught the little imp red-handed, a sugar lump poised over one of the teacups. The bowl was nearly empty, and the tea! You can imagine what it tasted like.'

She laughed, then looked wistful. 'You're lucky, having brothers and nephews and a family. I was an only child. I have nobody close, not even cousins. It's sad to think when I die there'll be no one of my very own at the funeral.'

I grinned at her. 'Don't be morbid, talking about funerals, when we should be celebrating all those funerals that might have been taking place now and aren't, thanks to that polio vaccine.'

15

That Interfering Woman

❧

'It's four days since he had a dirty nappy,' she moaned.

'Try increasing the sugar in his feeds,' I suggested. 'There's more sugar in breast milk than in cow's milk, and he's probably missing it. Have you some Milpar in the house?'

'Yes. I never use anything else for the children.'

'Then I'd give him a dose now, and repeat it tonight if nothing's happened, just to get him going.'

'I'll do that. I'm so glad you called today. That young Dr John prescribed suppositories.'

I paused at the door. 'Did you send for the doctor?'

'Send for the doctor? Not me. I intended to ring you up later if he hadn't performed. This new doctor's calling to see all the babies.'

'Is he? And when did he see Paul?'

'He's only just left. You must have passed him in the lane. The prescription's still on the table. I'll not get them, of course.'

Suppositories, for a six-week-old baby! I know I should have told Mrs Good to carry out her doctor's

176

instructions. Our duty of loyalty to doctors was instilled into us from the earliest days of our nursing training, but I felt I also owed loyalty to the mothers who relied on me and to the babies whose health and well-being were entrusted to my care. However, I felt bound to make some sort of gesture.

'You really should have told me of the doctor's visit and what he said before asking my advice.'

Mrs Good smiled. We had known each other for some years now. Her eldest was nearly six.

'And if I had? Would you have said he was talking through his hat and told me about the sugar? Or would you have kept quiet and let me use those things on the poor little scrap, and have him all bound up again within the week?'

Our eyes met. We understood one another.

On that occasion the prescription was simply torn up and nothing said, but some mothers were not so discreet. Dr John's practice covered many of the villages where I visited. He was young, keen and not over-busy, and he rather fancied himself as a budding paediatrician. I had been working in those villages for nearly fifteen years. All the children in the local schools had been my babies, and many of the current little ones had elder brothers and sisters whose first years had been supervised by me in the monthly clinics and in their homes. My ideas on baby care, learnt from experience and well proven, were well known to all my mothers and passed on to friends and neighbours before their babies even arrived. It was not unusual for a brand-new mum to quote me to myself on my first visit to her. Regrettably, but understandably, many mothers quoted me to Dr John when he proffered advice which cut right across everything I had instilled into them.

'Miss Corbally doesn't hold with that National Dried Milk. Makes them too fat, she says.'

'I've never given teething powders to my babies. Miss Corbally doesn't like them.'

'Cod liver oil in June? Don't talk rubbish, Doctor. Miss Corbally won't have it in her clinic before the autumn.'

'Miss Corbally wouldn't approve . . .'

'Miss Corbally wouldn't agree . . .'

I was not surprised when I received a summons to the office of the MOH. Dr Brand had received a letter from Dr John, a very angry letter.

'I object strongly to your health visitor calling on my patients and advising them about the feeding and care of their babies.' Generously he added a postscript to his long list of complaints about *'that interfering woman'*:

To be fair, I must admit that Miss Corbally's advice is sound, but its very effectiveness is making it diffi-cult for me to establish a relationship of trust with the mothers who she is visiting.

I groaned. 'Oh dear! Poor Dr John. Have you answered his letter?'

'Yes.' Dr Brand paused, and for a moment I panicked. Men have a way of hanging together: men against women, doctors against nurses. It was obvious that Dr

John wanted me off his back. A younger, less experienced health visitor would leave the field clear for him.

'You're not going to take me off the district?'

The MOH looked surprised. 'Take you off the district?
Of course I'm not.'

I breathed a sigh of relief. 'Then what have you said
to him? What do you want me to do?'

'Carry on with your job.' His eyes twinkled. 'I've told
young Dr John that our health visitors are employed to
visit mothers and advise them on the feeding and care
of their babies, and that I'm gratified to learn that in his
opinion, you are doing your job so effectively.'

Dr Brand's letter did nothing towards placating Dr
John, who continued to visit perfectly healthy babies,
hoping in time to win the mothers over to his way of
thinking. We had a totally different approach to our
babies and their problems. He saw every problem as
something to be 'cured'. I had been trained in preventive medicine and delved deeper, looking for the cause
and, by eliminating that, curing the trouble and preventing its recurrence. His job was to heal the sick; mine was
to prevent sickness. Constipation, in his book, was a
disorder requiring suppositories and enemas; in mine it
was caused by an unbalanced diet, lack of sufficient
fluids, and, in older children, lack of sufficient exercise.

Things came to a head when Paul Jennings caught a
cold.

Paul was an idolised first baby. His only problem was
an overanxious mother. She was feeding him herself,
and her anxieties and tension communicated themselves to the baby at her breast, who cried in sympathy,

his frequent crying increasing the tension which, in turn, increased his crying. It was a classic case of the chicken and the egg. Had she not been so set on breast-feeding, I would have seriously considered weaning the baby to a bottle. My first tentative suggestion in this direction reduced her to floods of tears. To her such a step would be accepting that she had failed as a mother.

Having dried her tears, I visited frequently, supervised the feeding, satisfying myself that the supply of milk was plentiful, the baby was sucking well, was gaining weight and generally thriving. I encouraged Mrs Jennings to ring me up as soon as a problem arose, however small, and not allow it to build up. I advised her to invest in Dr Gibbens's *Care of Young Babies*, a handbook of childcare which, while practical and helpful, emphasised the fun and enjoyment of motherhood. 'Gibbens babies', as I called them, were happy babies of relaxed mothers, and I was determined that young Paul Jennings would be just such a one.

By the time Paul was four months old his mother had stopped worrying over him. She was still breast-feeding, supplementing with broth and vegetable purees. Firm and solid, with no surplus fat, he was gaining a steady four to five ounces a week and his skin had that flawless bloom which only breastfeeding can give. He was as perfect a baby as I had seen.

A week after Paul's check-up at the clinic his father came home from work with a cold, and the baby was soon snuffling and coughing. Mrs Jennings rang me up. She had tried a few drops of eucalyptus oil on his pillow, which she knew I recommended, but, as he still seemed distressed, I advised her to see her doctor, who would probably prescribe some drops to clear his nose and relieve his breathing. The following day I was in the village, so called to see how Paul was getting on. Dr John had prescribed the drops, which seemed to be helping, but, as she described her interview with the doctor, she became almost incoherent with anger. He had examined and weighed the baby, described her beautiful little son as 'puny', advised her to wean him immediately and fatten him up with National Dried Milk, and given her a prescription for pills to get rid of her milk. She was in tears when her husband came home that evening, and, when he heard her story, he picked up the telephone and rang the doctor. Mr Jennings was not a man to mince his words, and he made it quite clear to Dr John that the baby had been brought to his surgery to have his cold treated and for no other reason, that he and his wife were completely satisfied with the advice of feeding and general care that they received from me.

It was not difficult to imagine Dr John's reaction to such a conversation. I felt this situation could not continue any longer. It was causing embarrassment, confusion, and a certain amount of amusement among our mutual clients, and was doing no good to anybody: not to Dr John, not to me, and certainly not to the babies, and the babies' welfare was, after all, the prime reason for our visits. It was only our different ways of pursuing the same goal that caused the disagreement which was rapidly building up to a dangerous degree of mutual resentment and hostility. Something would have to be done before the situation deteriorated any further.

Eileen wanted to see her sister about some family matter, so I walked up the road with her to have a talk with Leonard. Unfortunately, he had had a bit of trouble with one of the previous health visitors in Kenilworth and was not overly keen on the breed. Claire, on the other hand, thought we were doing a good job of work. They had met Doctor John at a medical conference.

'Seems a nice enough young chap,' said Leonard. 'Perhaps a bit over keen and opinionated, but he'll settle down.'

'But what do I do during the settling-down period?'

Leonard smiled kindly. 'He is the doctor, you know. You haven't got his qualifications, have you?'

Claire bridled. She had been a nurse. 'Molly has qualifications and experience he hasn't got. Not all GPs are as knowledgeable about babies as you are.'

Eileen said nothing. She wouldn't take sides against me, nor against Leonard, in whom she had the utmost faith. Her silence, in such a situation, was surprising, as she had very definite opinions on all subjects and expressed them in an uncompromising 'don't you dare disagree with me' manner. Such conversations she called 'putting the world right' and enjoyed them enormously. Younger sisters often have a need to be self-assertive in later life, which was one of the reasons why Claire, knowing me to be also a younger sister, had not been too enthusiastic about us sharing a home. After ten years the partnership was still working happily. We had our arguments, perhaps less than most married couples. We had fewer major issues to argue about, like whether to have children or not, and, having got them, how to bring them up, which school to send them to, etc.

People still wondered how it worked, especially the men, who couldn't imagine how women could exist, let alone be happy, without male company.

'How can you give a party,' we were asked, 'without a man to look after the drinks?' They soon found out. We had to justify the extension of our house, and gave many parties: drinks parties, dinner parties, lunch parties, theatre parties – never, in our henhouse, hen parties. Another question. 'Don't you find it difficult to find two extra men to balance your parties?' Never bothered us. Our parties didn't 'balance'. Why should they? We invited our friends to eat and drink and talk, not to do anything for which an equal number of men and women might be necessary.

When Eileen did break into the conversation it was to stop her family from arguing among themselves as to the respective merits of doctors and nurses and health visitors.

'All this isn't helping Molly. This situation is really worrying her. What do you think she should do?'

Leonard would have let it drift.

'Carry on doing your job and keep out of his way.'

Claire recommended confrontation.

'Go and see him and talk it out. I think you'll find him quite human, just rather young.'

I didn't like the idea one little bit, but it seemed preferable to letting things go on as they were. Claire handed me the phone while Leonard looked up the number.

'Go on. Ring him.'

Mrs John answered the telephone.

'I'm afraid my husband is out. Can I help you?'

'I rather wanted to speak to the doctor personally. I'm the health visitor, Miss Corbally.'

I heard a sharp intake of breath. Surprise? Anger? Neither. It was, surprisingly, pleasure.

'Miss Corbally! I'm so glad you've rung. I was going to get in touch with you.'

About what? My response was non-committal.

'Yes, Mrs John?'

Her voice came through, warm and comfortable. I sensed that she had settled into a chair for a nice cosy chat.

'It's about the antenatal clinics at the hall. It is you who runs them, isn't it?'

It was indeed I who ran them. What had gone wrong there? What complaints could Dr John have received from his patients who attended? He probably considered their very presence there as a personal affront to himself.

'Yes, Mrs John . . .'

'I was wondering . . . are you fully booked? Or could I come along? I thought perhaps Thursday week. They are held on Thursdays, aren't they?'

'Yes, Mrs John. The first Thursday of every month.'

Why? Was this a new approach? Doctor's wife shows an interest in village activities? And, no doubt, reports back to her husband. It would be the Infant Welfare Clinic next, I supposed. How right I was!

'Will it be all right then? You have room for another in your class?'

'In my class, did you say?'

'But of course!' There was a gurgle of laughter. 'I'm so sorry, I forgot to say I'm expecting a baby. Silly of me.'

'I see, and I'm very glad for you. But are you sure you really want to attend my clinic? I mean, your husband is a doctor.'

She laughed softly. What a happy woman she sounded.

'My husband's a man, a medical man, granted, but still a man. I very much want to come to your clinic. May I?'

There was only one possible answer. I did not want Dr John's wife at any clinic of mine. I could imagine the cross-examination he would subject her to, the disparagement, the counter-advice. But all citizens are equal under the law, and Mrs John had as much right as any other expectant mother to all the services provided by the local authority.

'Of course you may, Mrs John. You'll be very welcome. Thursday week then, two thirty, at the village hall.'

The suppressed giggles of my companions exploded as I put the phone down.

'It isn't funny,' I said. 'This is an impossible situation.'

Claire put a soothing hand on my arm.

'It could be just the answer you're looking for. Don't worry. Mrs John is rather a sweetie. I think you'll like her.'

I enjoyed the opportunity provided by the antenatal clinics to get to know my mothers before their babies were born. The months of pregnancy are a very receptive period, and a warm relationship of trust and friendship would be forged between us which would prove most valuable later on in the often more stressful days of motherhood. After the midwife had put them through their exercises, and taught them about breath control and relaxation, they would lie on their blankets for a few minutes quietly while I brewed the tea. Some were so totally relaxed that they dropped off to sleep and had to be woken when the time came for the little group to gather round me with their cups of tea to discuss the many aspects of mother-craft. Sample layettes were displayed, baby feeding gone into, a life-sized doll was bathed and dressed, handled and winded by each in turn. Deeply aware that a human baby is more than just a young animal and has needs beyond food and shelter and clothing, I had added an extra subject to the set curriculum – 'The Whole Child' – which was received with enthusiastic discussion on the mental, psychological and spiritual needs of the small beings who were mind and soul as well as body.

Mrs John's enthusiasm and sheer animal excitement soon got the better of her early diffidence, and she joined eagerly in every discussion, plying me with questions, anxious to ensure that her first precious baby should have the very best care and should suffer in no way from her own lack of experience. Sometimes I wondered how the champion weaner of babies was reacting to his wife's determination to breastfeed his own baby. From my own conviction I gave advice, advocating feeding patterns I knew to be in complete contradiction to everything Dr John believed in. I owed it to the other mothers to give only what I knew to be sound advice.

One afternoon I was telling my little group about the services available to them and their babies, such as the Infant Welfare Clinic and my own visits to their homes. They seemed to find it comforting to know that someone would be around to tide them over the first worrying months of motherhood, and to guide them through each phase of their new job of bringing up a child.

'How soon do you call?'

'On the tenth day, when you come out of hospital or the midwife pays her last visit.'

'How often do you call?'

'As often as you need me. Each week in the first month, and probably monthly. If there's a problem, I'll be round every day until we've solved it.'

'You do visit every new baby, don't you?' Mrs John asked.

'Yes, Mrs John, I must visit every new baby initially. If further visits are not needed, or wanted, I don't call again.'

Perhaps I sounded sharper than I meant to. When the class was over Mrs John stayed behind and helped me to carry the teacups through to the kitchen.

'Was I wrong, Miss Corbally, or did I get the idea that you're not planning to visit me regularly when the baby comes?'

'Do you expect me to? After all, your husband is a doctor. It could be a bit awkward.'

'I don't see why.'

She sounded hurt, and there was an uncharacteristic droop to her shoulders as she put the cups on the draining board. I felt guilty. Her husband may be a doctor, he may be a thorn in my side, he may have tried to cause trouble for me with my boss, but this young girl was an expectant mother, one of my mothers, and no works or attitude of mine must detract, in any way, from the joyful anticipation of her baby's birth. As I took the cups from her, my hand rested for a moment on her arm.

'Would you like me to visit you regularly?'

Her eyes lit up.

'Oh yes! Yes please, Miss Corbally.'

I remembered the adage of my training days: 'Visit where you're needed whether you're wanted or not, and where you're wanted, whether you're needed or not.' It was certain that Mrs John wanted me, and, remembering the incident of the suppositories, I thought it quite possible that she might also need me.

When the birth notification arrived on my desk my heart sank. Delighted as I was to know that my friend Mrs John was safely delivered of a seven-pound baby boy, I dreaded the thought of calling at the doctor's house. Suppose he opened the door to me? What could I say? When the tenth day at last came round I found I had no appetite for breakfast. I welcomed the telephone calls that kept me at my desk a few precious minutes longer. As I drove out to the village I almost hoped for an accident, not a bad one, but just bad enough to put me out of action for a week or two, so that one of my unsuspecting colleagues could ring the doctor's door-bell, and write across the baby's record card 'Doctor's house. No further visits required'.

The Johns' house was just off the main village street at Lapford. Several cars were parked outside and in the short driveway. I drew up behind the last one, hoping that the cars augured a busy surgery that would keep father occupied until I had completed my business with mother and son. I read and reread the particulars of the birth, which I already knew by heart, until, realising that further procrastination might find me still in the house when surgery finished, I opened the car door and forced myself to get out and walk through the gate. Passing the surgery door, I tried to look invisible, acutely aware of my telltale navy-blue uniform. Gently I pressed the front doorbell, hoping against hope that it might be out of order and that I could withdraw after a decent interval and write thankfully on the card, 'Ineffective visit. No reply'. To my dismay I heard foot-steps in the hall and the door was opened by a sour-looking woman in a green overall.

'Surgery's next door, on the right,' she snapped.

I smiled, understanding the irritation of a morning's work being constantly interrupted by unobservant patients.

'It's Mrs John I've come to see.'

The sour woman looked surprised.

'Missus is busy upstairs, feedin' the baby. You'll have to come back later.'

I was edging through the door, hoping the harsh voice wouldn't penetrate the surgery door.

'I'm the health visitor. I don't think Mrs John would mind me seeing her feed, if you'd be kind enough to tell her I'm here.'

The Sour One snorted.

'The very idea! What would the missus be wanting with a health visitor anyways, with the master a doctor and that nurse in the house. As if a body hadn't enough to do without all this carry-on . . .'

A nurse? Perhaps this accounted for the sourness. The presence of a nurse in the house is frequently resented by domestic staff, as I knew from my experience of private nursing. If I knew a 'monthly' nurse was in attendance I usually postponed the first visit until the fourth week. Still, having got so far, I felt I must go through with this visit. I might never again find the courage to ring that doorbell.

'Mrs John asked me to call, so if you would tell me where the nursery is, I'll go up to her.'

As the Sour One shuffled off towards the stairs I knew she was hoping that the nurse would be more successful in rebuffing me than she had been. She could, of course, be right, and I'd have it all to do again in less than three weeks' time.

I felt very vulnerable standing in the hall, watching the well-upholstered rear of the sour one disappear on the corner of the stairs. From the geography of the house I guessed that the first door on the right opened into the surgery, and I found my eyes riveted on it, like the eyes of a rabbit hypnotised by a snake. It seemed like hours, although it could only have been a few minutes, before I heard a brisk tread on the stairs and a familiar voice call out to me.

'How nice to see you again, Miss Corbally.'

How relieved and glad I was to hear the voice and see the dumpy white-overalled figure of Sister Stevens, with her round glasses on her round face framing the kindest eyes, and her round arms, designed by Nature as a comforting refuge for tiny babies. Like all good monthly nurses, Sister Stevens worked in family groups and local communities, being passed, like the maternity smocks, from sister to sister, cousin to cousin, and neighbour to neighbour, and we had met at fairly frequent intervals in the nurseries of the big houses of the surrounding villages. She took my hand, leading me towards the stairs.

'Come along up. Mrs John is expecting you.' The round eyes beamed at me. 'Such a sweet girl, and she's so thrilled with her baby. It does you good to see her.'

'The baby's all right?'

'Fine little chap. Feeding well. No problems.' She opened a door at the top of the stairs.

'See for yourself.'

Mrs John had finished feeding and was sitting on the nursing chair, the baby in her arms, freshly bathed and fed, smelling sweetly of milk and talcum powder, unseeing blue eyes fixed on the lovely face, radiant with tenderness, that was bending over him.

'So you've come . . .' she said, holding out her little son with a gesture of such fond pride that it brought a lump to my throat. It was the 'look what I've done' gesture of a child thrusting its first crude painting into its mother's hands. She had every reason to be proud. All new babies are beautiful in their own way, but some are more beautiful than others, and little Christopher John was rather special. All babies have enchanting button noses, rosebud mouths, shell-like ears and big trusting eyes, yet all are different. Some are bald, some have hair. Christopher had hair, the silky down of the newborn, his perfect ears lay flat against his head, his skin was flawless.

There was as yet no sign of the unsightly rash caused by the richness of his mother's milk, which was to cause a difference of opinion, to put it mildly, between his father and Sister Stevens. Forewarned by me, and with my guarantee that the spots would disappear by the sixth week, when the baby would be able to tolerate the creamy milk she was providing, Mrs John stood her ground. It was only thanks to the mother's natural imperturbability to her indestructible happiness in her baby and to the firm support of Sister Stevens that Dr John did not achieve his aim. The controversy was fierce enough not only to undermine the resistance of a weaker woman, but to engender a degree of distress and tension which could well have caused the milk supply to fail. But that was in the future, and had resolved itself before I returned, by mutual agreement, the day before Sister Stevens was due to leave, to receive a progress report from her, and be appraised of any problems that might require my attention.

Christopher had no problems, but, at his mother's insistence, I continued to visit him at regular intervals. It was at my third visit that I met Dr John. His wife and I and Christopher were discussing the gradual introduction of solid food into his diet when I heard the stairs being noisily negotiated, two at a time, and a harassed-looking young man in a white coat burst into the nursery. Black unruly hair denied all his obvious efforts to smarm it down, the greyness of the prominent chin denoted a hasty shave (perhaps he had slept late after a disturbed night), the deep-set brown eyes were slightly veiled as they met mine, anxious and unsure. In that instant I understood the lack of self-confidence underlying his veneer of omniscient arrogance. Under the white coat I saw an uncertain boy, striving to prove himself a man, a boy whom I need not fear, whom I could not resent, whom I was henceforth committed to help in any way I could. He nodded briefly in acknowledgement of his wife's introduction.

'I saw you pass the surgery window. Lucky you're still here.' He perched on the low table, throwing a brief, paternal smile towards his small son. 'There's a baby downstairs with a bottom like a piece of raw steak. I've tried everything – boracic powder, various creams and ointments. It just seems to get worse.'

He paused, waiting, watching me.

'Are you asking for my opinion?'

'Of course I am. Why do you think I'm here?'

'I wouldn't have suggested powder, for a start. It gets lumpy when it's wet, and rubs the skin. Which baby is it?'

'The young Jones baby, from Frasset.'

193

I tried not to look smug. A bottom as sore as that would be a poor reflection on any health visitor.

'Frasset isn't one of my villages.'

'It wouldn't be!'

His voice was sharp, but he raised a conciliatory hand as my eyebrows went up.

'No, I mean that. I really wouldn't expect one of your babies to get into this state. Can you help me? What should I advise? I don't want to call in a specialist.'

No, you wouldn't, I thought. You wouldn't want to admit there was a problem you couldn't handle. You're not mature enough to understand how very much you don't know. Mrs John, on her way to put Christopher in his cot, lightly caressed her husband's cheek.

'You and your specialists! Miss Corbally is a specialist, darling. Health visitors are all specialists in their own field.'

The doctor looked rather startled, then gave me a small, ironic bow.

'So? What does the specialist suggest?'

'I'd ask what she's washing the nappies in. She's probably using Persil, or even Tide. No matter what treatment you prescribe, it will break down again unless she sticks to soap for the washing. If detergents are the cause of the trouble, and it's my guess they are, the nappies will be impregnated by now and she'll need to line them with clean pieces of rag.'

'What about treatment? Fullers Earth?'

I gave a slight shrug.

'If you like. Treatment's your department, prevention's mine. Personally I prefer the ordinary baby cream

194

with a little Friar's Balsam mixed in with it. It's wonder-fully healing stuff.'

He was already at the door.

'Thanks. I must get back to the woman, I told her I wanted a new prescription pad.'

'Just a minute,' I called, 'the Friar's Balsam. Be sure to warn her that it's a dye and lethal to anything she spills it on.'

He nodded, and, with a quick smile, was through the door and halfway down the stairs, as his wife shouted after him.

'Don't forget the prescription pad . . .'

So began a close and warm professional relationship. Dr John would often join us for coffee after his surgery, and we would discuss our mutual patients and their problems, correlating our theories, and adopting a unified approach with the practice.

When I visited Mrs Good a few months after her third baby's birth I saw a prescription on the table for Milpar.

'Same trouble again?' I asked.

'Yes. Doctor's been. Gave me a long talk about feeding. Baby needs more sugar.' Her eyes twinkled 'It could have been you talking, Miss Corbally!'

16

Little Drudges

I should have stopped to talk to her, a strange woman with a pram in one of my villages. I had driven past her with no more than a smile. The smile was instinctive, she looked so young and happy, and walked so lightly and proudly. It was already late in the morning and I had two visits to fit in before driving home for an early lunch before the afternoon clinic, including a first visit to a house at the end of the road in which I had passed the stranger with the pram. It was a new baby, but not a new mum; she already had seven children, five of which I had seen in the village school the previous week, and fine, healthy, well-turned-out children they were, ranging from five to fifteen years. The family had moved into the Chesford village a few months before the baby's birth, and, by the time I had caught up with the news of their arrival, Mrs Keith was already in hospital, and I learnt from the elder children that the two younger ones were in Margate with their grandmother. I was so impressed by those children that I looked forward to meeting their mother, and was disappointed when there was no answer to my knock. The house felt empty. Over the years of knocking on doors I had developed an instinct about empty houses. An unanswered knock could mean that no one had heard, or that the owner didn't wish to be disturbed, or that no one was in, and I somehow could sense the response and knew when to persevere and when to abandon hope. As I left a card through the letterbox I was comforted by the knowledge that Mrs Keith was in no urgent need of my advice or help.

I was knocking on the same door the following morning about half past ten. It was opened by the young pram-pusher of the day before.

'Is Mrs Keith at home?'

The pram pusher smiled, opening the door wide and welcoming.

'I am Mrs Keith, I'm sorry I missed you yesterday. You passed me in the road.'

'But you can't be Mrs Keith. You can't have eight children and a fifteen-year-old daughter and look like that.'

She laughed.

'I am, you know. I've got my marriage lines to prove it. Coffee's just ready, then I'll introduce you to Mark 8.'

She took me through to the sitting room. Everywhere was newly decorated. The furniture glowed with polish, and a freshly arranged vase of flowers stood on a small table. In the dining end of the L-shaped room I noticed four tapestry-covered chairs, and a sewing machine by the window had obviously been in use when I had knocked. The coffee was excellent, freshly ground. 'No instant brew in this house,' I was told as I commended the flavour.

'Everything is freshly cooked. I don't feed my family from tins or packages.'

'Lucky family!'

I was admiring the gay print in the sewing machine.

'Were you sewing when I interrupted you?'

'Yes. I make all the girls' dresses, and knit for them all.'

'How do you do it?'

'I suppose it's because we are so many. We're a family, and we all pull together. Each one, from four years upwards, has their own little job to do, including my husband. We're all up in time for about fifteen minutes' work before leaving the house, and, when they come home, another half hour all round, less for the young ones of course, in the house or the garden, before settling to homework or playing or going out with their friends.'

'What sort of jobs do they do?'

'Depends on their age. There's the breakfast to be got and washed up, beds to make, shoes to clean, dusting, vegetables to prepare, odd jobs in the garden, a bit of mending or ironing; well, you know what jobs crop up in a home. With myself and five full-time workers and two part-timers, that's nearly five hours' work accounted for, and quite painlessly, and I'm free to do extra things, like making their clothes, and we can all have fun together at weekends.'

'Do they rebel sometimes?'

'Of course. They're only children, but I'm not a slave driver. They all have their turn of a lie-in in the morning or a free evening, and they see the point of it. The home belongs to all of us, so we all help to look after it.'

We were walking down the garden to the pram under an old apple tree, which formed a canopy of green and white chintz above the head of Mark 8, a sturdy little eight-pounder. I gently touched the plump cheek, flushed with sleep.

'Rest while you can,' I admonished him. 'It won't be long before you're shinning up this tree on a half-hour stint of apple picking.'

Mrs Keith laughed.

'That will be the day!' she said. 'The trouble is that by the time this fellow joins the workforce it will be depleted at the other end. He'll probably be on over-time before he's twelve, poor little drudge.'

Her eyes were laughing, such gentle, kind eyes. I smiled at her.

'Somehow I don't feel I need waste much sympathy on him, nor on any of your little drudges. I think it's a splendid idea of yours.'

'I'm glad you approve. Some of our neighbours used to criticise me for "putting on" the children, as they described it, but I think my lot were as healthy and happy as any in the street.'

The baby still slept. Mrs Keith adjusted a blanket before turning back to the house, still talking.

'I heard a slogan recently. I rather liked it. "The family that prays together stays together." Actually we do pray together sometimes, and we work together and play together, and it works.'

When the Keiths had settled down, they became a great asset to the village, where they were much liked. It was Mrs Keith who ran to the assistance of her neighbour when she fell on the icy road the following winter. The grocery van had skidded to a halt and the housewives were emerging cautiously to make their purchases. Mrs Hackett, whose second baby was imminent, lost her balance stepping off the pavement and fell heavily on the hard road. Fortunately, I was on my way to visit Mrs Keith, and I found Mrs Hackett very shaken, being revived with a cup of tea by the fire. After making sure there were no broken bones, and no evidence of the onset of labour, I escorted the pregnant woman back to her own house. It was fortunate that she had not been badly injured, nor knocked unconscious, for, to my horror, on opening the sitting room door I saw her two-year-old girl stretched out on the hearth rug, fast asleep, in front of an unguarded fire.

'I only slipped out for a second, just to buy some sausages for tea.'

'You fell, Mrs Hackett. You might have been taken to hospital, and no one would have known about Peggy. Suppose a log had fallen out, or she'd flung out an arm while dreaming? Never, never leave a fire unguarded with a small child in the room.'

I had the pleasure of seeing Mark 9's arrival in the Keith family before I left the district, and she was welcomed with as much joy and love as if she had been Mark 1. By that time Mark 6 and 7 had joined the work-force, and one needed to look twice to distinguish between Mrs Keith, mother of nine, and her eighteen-year-old daughter.

Her ladyship at the Hall took a dim view of the Keith family.

'Disgusting!' she snorted down her aristocratic nose. 'Breeding like rabbits. No self-control.'

She had asked me to call and see her about the Conservative fete that was held each year in her garden.

'We're planning a baby show this year and I have told the committee that you will be judging it.'

I shook my head. 'Sorry, but no.'

'But you must. I mean, who else is there? Nurse Smart isn't dependable. She might get called away for a delivery or something inconvenient.'

'No, Lady Merlin. It's kind of you to think of me, and I appreciate being asked, but I can't possibly.'

'But it's a Saturday. You won't be working.'

'I do have a life apart from my work, and weekends are the only time I can live it. But apart from that, I can't judge a baby show in my own district.'

'Why ever not?'

'They are my babies, that's why not. I know them all. I know their mothers. How could I possibly say any one of them was better than all the others?'

She looked peeved, but had the grace to acknowledge that my argument was a reasonable one. The coffee was brought in. As I moved a book off a low table to make room for the tray, I noticed it was a history of my brother's regiment, written by him.

'I see you've got Pat's book.'

The remark was spontaneous.

'That, yes, I am interested in regimental histories, and that is a particularly good one.'

She picked it up, glanced at the title page.

'Colonel Corbally. Is he a relation of yours?'

'My brother.'

She was alert, interested.

'Your brother? Are you an army family?'

'Service. My other brother is an Air Vice-Marshal.'

'Really? And your father?'

'He was killed in 1915 at Ypres.'

She beamed at me

'So you're a war orphan.'

The way she said it made it sound like a peerage.

She stood up, refilling my cup on the way to the door.

'Just wait here a minute. I won't be long.'

She wasn't long. She came back carrying two dowdy navy-blue dresses over her arm.

'These nurse's dresses came in the last consignment of clothing. I think they're about your size.'

She was so pleased with herself it was difficult to disillusion her.

'You're very kind, but we have to wear the uniform provided by the county council. It's like being in the army, we must all be dressed alike.'

That made sense to her. She saw me to the door, taking my hand in both of hers.

'I hope you'll come to the fete anyhow. I'm inviting a few friends to stay on for a drink afterwards. I'd be glad if you could join us.'

The fete was most enjoyable and everyone was so pleased to see me there. All the village turned up, regardless of their political views. I kept well away from the baby show, which was judged by a chemist's wife from Warwick. Whatever qualifications, if any, she had to judge babies, she had the good sense to award the first prize to Mrs John's beautiful baby, rather to the embarrassment of the proud father. He was running the coconut shies, where Father Abbot and the Reverend Hughes were running an inter-church war, and from the roars of laughter between contests, I gathered their conversation was not entirely theological. Mrs Roche-Anderson had come over to help her friends, and the twins were enjoying themselves and raking in money giving donkey rides. The bottle stall was run by the schoolchildren, supervised by Miss Hodgkin, resplendent in a grey silk frock and a large white hat with grey roses falling over the brim. I won the prize for guessing the weight of an outsize marrow; it was fun watching how the competitors assessed the weight. To the village grocer it was a sack of potatoes, to the farmer, a sack of corn, to the nurseryman, a load of fertiliser. To me it was a two-month-old baby, and I got it right. I missed Helen Smart. She rarely failed to turn up at any village function, but I presumed, like her other friends, that she was held up 'with a delivery or something inconvenient.'

17

The Bravest Couple

I think the bravest couple I ever met were the Craigs. Michael was still working when I first visited Maureen with her first baby. She told me how desperately they had wanted this child, as she knew, and her husband knew, that he had only a few years to live. He was in the early stages of Hodgkins Disease, a progressive and incurable form of cancer affecting the glands.

The little girl was walking and a second baby well on the way, to Maureen's delight, before I met Michael. The door was opened before I reached it and he came out to welcome me, a tall man with dark curly hair and gentian blue eyes. There was such warmth in those eyes, such honesty – and how they could sparkle with fun! As always, at my approach, Maureen had put the kettle on, and, for the first time, the three of us sat together in the cosy sitting room. How often we were to sit together in that room during the coming months.

No longer able to sustain full-time work, Michael had taken a part-time job which Lady Merlin had arranged for him, helping with the estate accounts. When he was working, he was given lunch at the Hall, and never came home without some fresh vegetables or eggs, a home-made cake or freshly baked pie. He was not one of the Hall's tenants, as he owned the L-shaped house by the presbytery, which Mrs Nathan had once shared with her sister. Father Abbot still lived the other side of the hedge, white-haired now, no longer able to climb the steep hill to visit his flock at the top, but still totally involved in village life, which he continued to supervise from the presbytery gate. He was neighbour, father, comforter and pastor to the Craigs in their time of trial. The job at the Hall only lasted a few months. Michael found even that short walk up the drive was getting beyond his strength. Already the handsome mobile face was developing a hollow look, and his clothes looked as if they had been borrowed from a bigger man. In spite of Maureen's excellent cooking and the good fresh food which Lady Merlin still supplied, he was rapidly losing weight and strength.

Six weeks after the birth of their second girl, Maureen, a trained nurse, started a full-time job at Warwick hospital, commuting by train from the nearby station. For a short while Michael managed the house and the children, then his parents moved in with them to take most of the burden off his skeletal shoulders. I visited frequently, fitting in my timetable, when possible, to be available with the car when Michael was due at the hospital for treatment or a check-up. Generally, I would make them the last visit of the day, and stay on, regardless of time.

Sometimes Maureen would be at home when I called, depending on her shift. Often Michael would be alone,

or playing with his little girls, who, after a short interval, would be retrieved by their grandmother, as the
chatter of the elder girl and the crying of the baby could
soon become unbearable to the sick man.

After the Keith family arrived in the village there was
always help available. The babies would often be
collected in the afternoon by Mrs Keith, while Michael
rested, to be returned, if Maureen was on a late shift, by
one of the older Keith children, fed and washed and
ready to pop into bed. Other children from the school,
encouraged by Miss Hodgkin, took in a rota of pram-
pushing at weekends for the girls, gardening for the
boys.

Dr John visited constantly and became, like myself,
an honorary member of the household, spending far
more time with the sick man than his professional
duties warranted, ensuring that every possible comfort
and support was channelled into the house. Dr John
would never take 'no' for an answer. If Michael needed
a check-up at the hospital, a hospital car, a home help,
an airbed, a free supply of coal or extra milk, the doctor
would override all objection, cut all red tape, disregard
rationing shortages, waiting lists and such tiresome
obstacles, and everything that Michael needed, Michael
got.

No doubt people sometimes ask themselves what
they would do if they were told that they had a short
time to live. Many would not want to be told, but those
of us who prefer the truth to deception, how would we
react? How many would give up their jobs while they
still had the strength to enjoy life, to do the things they

had always dreamt of doing, to travel, to spend the money they could not take with them on the luxuries and pleasures which had always eluded them? There would be reunions with friends and loved ones, nostalgic visits to places one had loved.

For Michael it was too late for travel, for visits, for having fun. Knowing he was leaving a wife and two small children behind, he had been concerned with earning while he had the strength, not in spending. No one, least of all Maureen, would have blamed him if he had sought to enjoy, or ease in some way, what little life was left to him. The decision to have the children was a courageous one. She would be left alone to rear them. He would have to share her with them at a time when a lesser man would, understandably, have demanded his wife's undivided attention. To support them she had to work when he needed the comfort of her presence, but, as he pointed out, in the years ahead, when she would miss the comfort of his presence, his children would be there to help fill the gap and counteract the loneliness of widowhood. His parents were there, with their loving solicitude, and he had his books.

He showed me his books. The thrillers and whodunits of earlier years had been put away, while he delved into history and biographies, books about people long since dead, the 'greats' of the past, saints and explorers, poets and kings, statesmen and generals, pioneers and churchmen. 'After all,' he explained, 'these people will be my companions in the very near future. It seems a good idea to start getting to know them.'

We would discuss the characters that particularly appealed to him.

'What fun it will be to meet him!' And his face would light up, the sunken eyes would sparkle, or a dreamy look would come into them.

'I wonder if it really happened like that . . . or why he behaved in that way. It will be interesting to find out.'

There is so much in the past and the present that one doesn't know, that one can only speculate about, and our discussions would sometimes draw a frustrated sigh from me.

'I wish I knew!'

Michael would smile sympathetically, a little smugly, 'Poor you. You'll probably have to go on wishing for a long time. I'll soon know all the answers – lucky me!'

And his heroic wife and I would laugh with the dying man at the original and unusual brand of one-upmanship in which he indulged.

Towards the end, our conversations would be interspersed with:

'I can't wait to meet him.'

'I can't wait to find out.'

He hadn't long to wait. When he was too weak to get up, and I sat by his bedside, we would talk together of the joys of Heaven and the heart-warming promise. 'Eye hath not seen nor ear heard, neither hath it entered into the heart of man, what things God has prepared for those that love him.' And the sunken blue eyes would look past me, through the window, fixed on the far horizons to which he was travelling so inexorably.

Death held no terrors for Michael. It was a boring interlude to be coped with, like a journey that precedes a holiday. It was what came afterwards that mattered, that filled his thoughts and dreams.

'If it wasn't for leaving Maureen and the children,' he told me, 'I'd be so excited that I couldn't contain myself.'

Maureen often joined me in his bedroom, sometimes with one of the little girls in her arms, and together we'd discuss their future. Both parents were determined that the mother should know what the father wished and hoped for his children at every stage of their development. Details were discussed, like birthday presents, First Communion dresses, the keeping of pets, hairstyles. Every thought and suggestion was treasured by Maureen, as she said to me when we were on our own.

'I won't really feel that I'm bringing them up on my own. So many decisions have already been made together.'

It was very near the end when I sat with Michael one evening, waiting for Maureen to come home. Talking was an effort, so I had been reading to him, and we had lapsed into silence. His eyes were closed, and I thought he had dozed off, when a soft voice asked me.

'Tell me your idea of an ideal house.'

Thoughtfully I described my dream house. He wanted to know every detail, colour schemes, furniture, everything.

'What about the garden?'

That had to be described, plants, shrubs, flowers, all filled in.

'What's all this in aid of?' I asked.

The eyes snapped open, twinkling with laughter, the grey lips parting.

'Just thought I'd like to know, so I can keep an eye when they start building your mansion up there.'

I was with him at the end. The journey was quiet and easy, the passage calm towards the new world to which he had reached out so eagerly, with such faith and courage and intelligence.

Both little girls were at school before I left the Midlands. When Maureen spoke of future plans, she always spoke for Michael and herself. 'We would like . . .'

Sadly, the dreaded cancer claimed another victim that year.

When Helen Smart had talked about her funeral she had spoken with the certain knowledge of its nearness. She knew then that she had abdominal cancer, too far gone for an operation. How could it have happened? Helen was not one to be afraid to face the truth. Too many people are afraid to see a doctor, afraid to be told what's wrong with them, as if giving it a name could make it worse. But Helen wasn't one of those.

'Why on earth didn't you see Dr John?'

We were sitting together in her cottage. I'd made the tea and a cauliflower cheese was prepared to be popped into the oven for her supper.

'I had no idea. I thought it was just indigestion, so took an odd Rennie, or a dose of Andrews, and got on with the job.'

'Didn't you notice your tummy was swollen?'

She gave a little shrug.

'Middle-age spread. I wasn't worried.' She chuckled. 'My patients might have had other ideas. I was desperately tired, of course, but weren't we all, after that polio business.'

I put a log on the fire. The room was warm, but she had so little flesh on her, except for that enormous stomach. She was due at the hospital the next day to have some of the fluid removed.

'When did you really suspect?'

She laughed.

'You won't believe this, Molly, but I didn't, not until Dr John came to examine me. I'd had to call him to a delivery the day before, and he was a bit cheeky, asked which of us was having the baby! He suggested I should go on a diet, but I told him I couldn't eat much less, I had no appetite, so he looked more closely at my face and arms, and arranged to call. He's marvellous, comes every day.' She looked at the clock. 'I'm expecting him about now.'

As we heard the car draw up I fetched another cup and went to the door to let him in.

'Glad to see you here, Miss Corbally. How's my favourite patient today?'

Helen smiled, patting the chair beside her.

'A bit uncomfortable. It feels like triplets.'

'You'll be a lot better after the treatment tomorrow. No pain?'

She shook her head.

'I've arranged for you to stay in for forty-eight hours. It left you a bit shaky last time, didn't it?'

'Thanks,' she smiled her gratitude. 'That would be nice.'

'You know, anytime you say, I can get you a bed in the private wing. It's all laid on, just whenever you like.'

She shook her head, now nearly white.

'Not yet. I'm happy here among my own people. They couldn't do more.'

The flower-filled room, the get-well cards on every table, the new-laid eggs in the larder, the home-made cakes and pastries in the store cupboard, the fruit piled high on the dining room table, were all evidence of the caring love poured out on the sick woman by those she had succoured and nursed and comforted for nearly thirty years. So many of them had been brought into the world by those now weak emaciated hands.

'Which of your chauffeurs is driving you tomorrow?' asked the doctor.

'Mrs Roche-Anderson,' she fingered the shawl round her shoulders. 'She knitted this for me. Isn't it beautiful? And you should see Mrs Keith's bed jacket. How she finds the time, I don't know.'

I grinned. 'I do. I'll tell you her strategy. It's fascinating, but first, where's that bed jacket, Helen?'

'Top right-hand drawer. Thanks, Molly.'

It was duly admired, new cards were noticed and commented on, including rather basic but touching drawings by two small children. I saw Dr John to his car.

'How long?' I asked.

He shook his head. There was deep sorrow in his eyes.

'A few weeks, no more. I doubt if they'll send her home again.'

'Oh please. She'd rather it happened here. I've only got to let the village know and she'll get all the help she needs. People will sleep in. Mrs Roche-Anderson already has a list of volunteers and Dr Brand will lay on as much nursing care as she requires.'

He looked uncertain.

'You think that's the way she really wants it?'

'I'm sure it is. It's what the village wants too. She's given them so much for so long, now they want to do the giving.'

On Dr John's insistence the hospital sent her home, and he was at her bedside when she died, peacefully and without pain, surrounded by tributes of love from the village which she had served so long and so thoughtfully.

18

Sweet and Sour

The Reverend Roger Hughes was an all-round sports-man, and I wasn't surprised to run into him at the Warwick races one Saturday afternoon. Justin was with him, a handsome thirteen year old in the green blazer of Leamington College. How I wished they had sent him away to a good boarding school where he would have been toughened up and cut down to size. Although he was still an utterly charming and delightful boy, he was basically the same Justin, the 'boy who stayed in bed', and was shamelessly indulged by his doting parents. He still expected all his wishes to be gratified, provided they did not clash with anyone else's, and they usually were. His need to be successful in all he did was almost a phobia. He hated losing at games, and had the brains and application to be unusually good for his age as a bridge and chess player.

Justin recognised me first and called me over to join them at the paddock. Eileen was introduced, and we all compared notes as the horses paraded past us, while Justin was instructed on form and breeding. I decided to back a hunch. I often did. No form, I just thought the horse looked good. Justin backed Lester Piggott, and we made our way towards the course.

'Racing's good for the lad,' said his grandfather, as we looked for a good place on the rails. 'It's one thing that doesn't always go his way. He's got to learn to lose, and this seems as good a way as any, and more enjoyable than most.'

I watched Justin as Lester came up from the back, moved into third place, then second. The boy was shouting, willing him to win.

'Come on, Lester! Come on! WIN! You must win!'

But Lester stayed second. My hunch was the winner at 33–1. There was a brief struggle while Justin mastered his disappointment, then his fist unclenched, his hand seized mine, and his face lit up with a smile of genuine pleasure.

'Congrats, Miss Corbally. I'm so glad you won.'

As we watched the parade before the next race, the vicar turned to me with a chuckle.

'Did you hear about the Englishman who went to the Curragh?'

'No,' I said. 'Tell us.'

'The course was solid with priests,' he told us. 'One of them was blessing a horse in the paddock, a nice-looking animal which won easily. Next race, another blessing. Didn't look such a good bet, but it made it by a short head. The Englishman decided he was on to something good, and would back the next 'holy' animal. Surprisingly the priest chose an outsider. Didn't look as if it had much of a chance, but it got an extra-long blessing, so he backed it anyway, put his shirt on it and waited for the very large sum of money which was coming to him. It didn't come. The horse collapsed and died halfway round. Furious, he sought out the priest and asked what had happened, why the others had won and this one had died. The priest looked surprised. "Sure, man, don't you know the difference between a blessing and the last rites?"'

We laughed. It was a good story, in the right setting.

'You've got a great fund of stories,' I told him.

He nodded.

'I try and remember them when I go and see some of the poor lonely old people in the village. I like to make them laugh. Does them good.'

I agreed.

'Talking of old people,' he said. 'Have you seen Mrs Beck recently? She seems to be failing. Might be an idea if you could look in next time you're in the village . . .'

'How nice to see you dear.'

Mrs Beck was always glad to see anyone. She lived alone in a small cottage in Hornsborough Green and was imprisoned in her little home by crippling arthritis and a tired heart. She could potter around in the garden with the aid of a stick, was able to do little jobs around the cottage and cook simple meals for herself on the days when 'meals-on-wheels' didn't call. A home help came over from Dodsworth twice a week to clean, and neighbours called in occasionally, when they remembered. Her married daughter came down from Yorkshire twice a year, bringing the grandchildren for her to see, and there were letters and postcards from various nephews and nieces whose photographs filled every corner of the sitting room. Pride of place in the portrait gallery was given to her husband, in the uniform of a serving soldier in the First World War, and her son, who was shot down in a Spitfire in the Second.

'How are you today, Mrs Beck?'

'Not so good, dear. A bit puffy.'

She looked a bit blue round the lips and her breathing was laboured.

'Have you taken your heart pill this morning?' I asked.

'Oh yes, dear. I take them twice a day, regularly, like the doctor said.'

She inclined her head, with the neat little grey bun, towards a small table in the corner.

'There they are. I always keep them there, so I won't forget.'

I unscrewed the bottle to confirm with my nose that the flat, brownish tablets were in fact Senokot, a mild laxative prescribed for elderly people.

'Are these the only tablets you have?'

'There are some little white ones the doctor gave me, for my bowels, but I don't need them, I'm very regular.'

I bet you are, I thought, as I opened the cupboard. There, sure enough, was a little bottle of Digoxin. I brought it over to her, taking out one of the tiny pills and handing it to her.

'There's been a bit of a mix-up, Mrs Beck. These are your heart tablets, which you should be taking twice a day.'

217

She swallowed it, reaching for a glass of water.

'Then what are those others?'

I smiled. 'Those, my dear Mrs Beck, are for your bowels, to be taken only when you need them.'

She chuckled.

'I suppose they wouldn't have helped the old heart much, would they?'

'Not much, but they've kept your insides healthy. I'm putting them away in the cupboard, and I'll leave these on the table.'

I always checked the drugs when I visited elderly people, and made sure they knew what they were taking, and why. It could be very confusing when some pills were to be taken once a day, others twice, some three or even four times a day. We would devise a plan of coloured labels, arranging them in separate groups. My nightmare would be the duplication of drugs, when a new prescription would be made up before the current supply was exhausted, and the new bottle would be carefully labelled and ranged behind its mate, and a pill from each religiously taken at the appointed time.

I once discovered an old lady in such a state of depression and lethargy that she was unable to move from her chair, and her poor, semi-blind husband was trying to cope with the housework and the cooking and the shopping. A quick look at the array of bottles on the bedside table revealed a double supply of tranquillisers, not only those her doctor prescribed regularly, but also a different variety a locum had put her on. In view of the seriousness of her condition, I rang the doctor and asked permission to remove all the tranquillisers. He demurred, but eventually agreed. To relieve the husband I arranged for the services of a home help and meals-on-wheels. Within a fortnight she had cancelled both, and I found her in the kitchen doing the week's ironing, while an appetising meal was simmering on the stove.

Mrs Beck's drug situation was certainly simpler, just Digoxin, Senokot and painkillers for when the arthritis was unusually bad. She rarely took them and wouldn't have a sleeping pill in the house, let alone tranquillisers.

'The old brain's dull enough without making it duller,' she said. Her prescription for a good night's sleep was a mug of hot milk and honey and 'a little quiet read of a good book to switch your mind off things.' Certainly, her mental alertness and surprisingly good memory did bear out my theory that tranquillisers and sleeping pills can fuddle the brain and lead to early senility.

Another one who wouldn't have a drug in the house, apart from aspirin, was eighty-two-year-old Mrs Fenton. Mrs Fenton was everyone's pet. Before the stroke which had left her semi-paralysed she had busied herself with everyone's problems, and was always the first on the doorstep if a neighbour was ill or in any trouble. The local children adored her. While she was still driving, her car, filled with youngsters, was a familiar sight on its way to Stratford for a quick bathe in the river, or up to the Cotswolds for a picnic.

For the last six years she had been in a wheelchair, more able than most people thought to look after herself, but accepting graciously and gratefully the avalanche of help and kindness and goodwill that came her way. It hadn't been easy, at first, for such a compulsive giver to become a receiver, for such an active person to accept a passive role, but she learnt to curb her impatience, hide her frustration, and to genuinely enjoy the loving care of her many friends.

'Who am I to complain?' she would say, when I commiserated with her at the loss of her independence. 'Didn't Christ himself have to accept another man's help to carry his cross?'

She was one of the happiest people I knew.

'Aren't I lucky!' she would exclaim, showing me the flowers from a neighbour's garden, a dish of freshly picked raspberries from another, a newly published book, a home-made pie, a child's drawing. 'Everyone is so kind.'

Her day would start with a cup of tea and toast made for her by the newsagent across the road, who called every morning before he opened his shop. The nurse would help her to get up and dressed and settled in her chair before the home help, or a neighbour, came in to clean through, and make the bed, and cook her lunch if it was not a meals-on-wheels day. The afternoons were never lonely, there was always someone calling in for a chat, or a game of cards. The children who had filled her car when they were small took it in turns to stop at her house on their way home from school and get her tea. She was able to get herself into bed, and one of her closest friends would drop by in the late evening to make her a hot drink and tuck her down for the night.

Every little service, every gift, every visit was appreciated. Her warm smile, her repeated thanks would have been reward enough, but she kept a drawer full of little gifts close at hand – sweets for the children, pretty hankies or lavender bags for the grown-ups.

Love breeds love, gratitude inspires further giving . . . but there were those with no love and no gratitude, who had the same statutory right to the care and the visits of their health visitor. Such a one was Mrs Foot.

Poor Mrs Foot, she must have had much sadness in her life to make her so bitter. Even when her husband was alive they 'kept themselves to themselves', never mixed with their neighbours, nor joined any local organisations, nor supported any social or fundraising activities in the area. After his death she firmly, even rudely, rebuffed every friendly approach, every attempt to offer companionship, to draw the lonely woman into the community life. Now, housebound by arthritis, she complained bitterly that no one came near her. I knew her immediate neighbours, kind, helpful people who, in spite of earlier snubs, had offered to help with shopping, but nothing had ever been quite right. Their purchases on her behalf would be the wrong size, the wrong brand, the wrong price, until each in turn had been told, 'If you can't do things right, better not do it at all. I'll manage.'

Meals-on-wheels lasted a few months. The food was, according to her, uneatable, dull, badly cooked, only fit to give a dog. Having no dog, she threw it in the dustbin, and the hard-pressed driver heaved a sigh of relief when another awkward customer was taken off her list.

Home helps came and went. None of them lasted longer than six weeks. They couldn't stand her nagging, her criticism, her perpetual grumbling, and deeply resented her nasty little habit of leaving pound notes or bits of jewellery around the house 'to test their honesty'. Before long she had exhausted the patience of even the most long-suffering of those wonderful women and there was no one left to send.

She now had something else to grumble about when I called. She kept the place reasonably clean, and the butcher and baker and grocer delivered to the house, so her situation was not desperate, but how much more comfortable, how much happier it could have been. I suggested a Red Cross visitor, knowing they could have rung the changes so that all the burden didn't fall on the same visitor.

'I want no do-gooders coming here. I've always minded my own business, and I'll thank other people to mind theirs,' was her reply, which I interpreted as: 'I've never raised a finger to help anyone else.'

When the flu epidemic hit Dodsworth, Dr Mary Gibson rang the office to ask if I would look in on Mrs Foot, who was pretty ill. She had been put on antibiotics, but the doctors were all too busy for follow-up visits. Unfortunately, the message was put through late on a Friday afternoon and didn't reach me until the following Monday, by which time the treatment was having its effect and the old lady's temperature was down. I found her sitting up by the fire, in her dressing gown. She was, understandably, aggrieved that no one had been to see her since Friday, and continued to grumble while I made up her bed with fresh sheets, and checked the larder to ensure she was well stocked with soups and eggs and the light, nourishing, easily prepared food she would be needing for the next few days. At her request, or, more exactly, on her orders, I made a small pot of tea and brought the tray through to her. It was, of course, the wrong tray. I should have used the round one with the flower pattern on it. However, she conceded that the tea was drinkable.

'At least you make a better cup of tea than that stupid doctor. All those letters after her name and the woman can't even make a decent cup of tea.'

'How do you know that?' I asked from the kitchen, where I was washing up the breakfast things.

'How do you think I know? I had to drink the muck on Friday, when she was here.'

I came through the door, tea towel in hand.

'You mean, Dr Gibson made you a pot of tea?'

'Yes. Weak, horrible stuff. Silly woman.'

'Mrs Foot. Have you any idea how busy the doctors are just now? Dr Gibson is working all out from early in the morning until late at night, and is probably being called out of bed during the night. She's exhausted. I doubt if she's taking time to get proper meals, yet she found time to make tea for you, and you can't even appreciate her kindness.'

I could have said more, a great deal more. I was angry, indignant and resentful at this mean little woman's attitude to everyone who tried to help and befriend her. I had to call on my professional training to restrain myself, remembering that she was a sick woman, protected by her age and infirmity against my anger.

I had to call again, but kept my visits to a minimum, since there was nothing I, nor anyone else, could do to help her. I shed no tears when, frightened by her recent illness, Mrs Foot agreed to Dr Gibson's suggestion that she should move into one of the warden-supervised flats that had recently been built the other side of Kenilworth, outside my district, and, I noticed with glee, outside the boundary of Dr Gibson's own practice.

Inevitably, I too succumbed to the germ. Eileen avoided it, having been given anti-flu vaccine by the works doctor. I could have had it – it was on offer to all the district nurses and health visitors – but somehow I never got round to calling in at the clinic in Warwick. There always seemed something better to do, somewhere more important to be. Dr Brand was not pleased, and I was severely reprimanded when I next called at the office.

'Preventing illness is your responsibility, and that includes yourself.'

My excuse – that as I didn't happen to live in my own district I was exonerated from professional responsibility for my own health – was received with a grunt.

Mrs Wilson was noble, and came in every day while I was ill to get me 'a bit of lunch' and make up the fire in my room. I had once told Eileen that my dream of happiness was lying in bed with an open fire crackling in the grate, and she had remembered. Every morning, while I was bed-bound, she would be up at

6 a.m. to light the fire, carry up the coal, get my break-fast, and take Solow across the road to the dog minder who fed and exercised and cared for our little dachs-hund until Eileen collected her on the way home. Vainly, I protested to Eileen about the fire, to Mrs Wilson about her daily visits. I'd be all right with a thermos and some sandwiches. She might catch the infection, and my job was to prevent illness, not be the cause of it. She was imperturbable, shovelling coal onto the fire.

'And how did you pick up this lot but through look-ing after other people?'

'That's different. I was only doing my job.'

'And that's what I'm doing. You're my job, you and Miss Newton. Always looking out for other people, the two of you. Someone's got to look out for you.'

Sadly the flu had hit me just before the coming-of-age party of Eileen's nephew, in Kenilworth. It was a big occasion and a cousin of hers with his wife had come down from the North and were staying with us. As Eileen, in evening dress, brought up my hot water bottle and a mug of hot milk, our guests put their heads round the door to say goodnight, and I felt very sorry for myself as I heard the car drive away.

I was woken by the ringing of the doorbell and pebbles rattling on my window. Eileen must have forgotten to take her key. Bleary-eyed, I switched on the light. Grabbing my dressing gown I padded drunk-enly down the stairs, unlatched the door, and hurried back to my warm bed before coming face to face with the revellers. I had turned out the light and settled back under the blankets when I heard them creeping up the stairs. There was a loud whispering.

'Take your shoes off.'

'Shh . . . mustn't make a noise'

'Shh . . . we mustn't wake Molly!'

The utter absurdity of the situation was some compensation for being roused from a deep sleep at 2 a.m.

19

Individuals

As I walked up the rose-lined garden path to meet Mrs Warman and her first baby I paused to admire the superb blooms and disease-free foliage. It was twelve years since I had prescribed Epsom Salts for Mrs Roche-Anderson's roses, and I had long ago outlived the amused question with which the Lapfold mothers greeted me. 'Have you come to see the roses, or the dog, or perhaps the baby?' My mothers knew that I came to see everything, baby, toddler, school child, dog, garden, altered décor, a new washing machine, holiday snaps, a letter from the eldest son in the Merchant Navy, the lot.

The twins – now referred to as 'the girls' or 'Phillida and Patricia' – had gone away to boarding school. In their smart grey uniform, white blouses and red ties, for the first time they were dressed alike, but it no longer mattered. Their differences had developed over the years, and their individual characters were already stamping themselves on their faces, so there was no difficulty in distinguishing one from the other. The playgroup experiment had worked when they were very little. While the twin-bond held them firmly together, each had imperceptibly grown closer to her mother during those precious few hours of one-to-one companionship. Patricia's undivided attention had been a source of great joy, and Phillida, no longer overshadowed by the favourite, revealed a gentle affectionate side to her character, and, showing herself to be utterly lovable, had become exceedingly beloved.

I was rather surprised, on reading Mrs Warman's record card, to see that she had been discharged from a nursing home. The pleasant modern bungalow on top of Chesford Hill didn't look as if it belonged to the nursing-home income bracket. Most nursing-home babies were in the category of big houses, two cars, servants and nannies, or at least a monthly nurse. No servant opened the door, not even a daily, but Mrs Warman herself in a bright blue overall which matched her eyes. She explained that her husband had been left a small legacy by his godmother, and had decided that their first baby should be born in style. Having paid the nursing-home fees, there was still enough money left for a champagne christening. 'The rest of our children will arrive in a more plebeian manner,' she assured me.

As nursing homes are apt to assume that a nanny or monthly nurse will take over from them, they do not give the mothers the sort of instruction in feeding and bathing their babies that they receive in the hospitals, but Mrs Warman had got the idea from watching the nurses at work. Unfortunately, she had not attended the antenatal classes, as she had been working until the last two months, but she seemed quite confident and declined my offer to come over at bath time the following morning. The baby was sleeping, so Mrs Warman filled me in on all I wanted to know regarding weight, and feeding, and general condition.

'No nappy rash, I hope?'

'No, my husband's getting me a jar of St Martin's Chunky Marmalade this morning.'

I blinked. However, it was her home, and if she wished to discuss marmalades and preserves, I'd go along with it, for a short time.

'I find it rather bitter. I prefer Golden Shred myself, or better still, home-made marmalade. Do you ever make it yourself?'

We discussed recipes for a few minutes, then I returned to my subject.

'Have you a good baby cream?'

She looked surprised.

'But, I told you, my husband's bringing the marmalade home this evening, St Martin's Chunky. He couldn't get it yesterday.'

I stared at her.

'You don't mean? You can't mean? You're getting St Martin's Chunky Marmalade to use on the baby's bottom?'

'That's what they used in the nursing home. I saw the label.'

My lips were twitching. Laughter was oozing out of my eyes, my ears and the top of my head. It took all my professional training to restrain myself from exploding. I tried to talk.

'I think someone forgot to remove the label,' I croaked.

Mrs Warman's eyes widened, her mouth dropped open, then we were both laughing helplessly, tears pouring down our cheeks.

❧

I found Mrs Poynter's little girl waiting beside my car.

'Mummy says will you please come to our house. It's about Jimmy.'

The Poynters lived in the next street, but the four year old was delighted to be driven home in my car, with Solow on her knee. Her elder brothers were at school, but eight-year-old Jimmy had a problem that Mrs Poynter needed help with.

'He won't go in the mornings. I always like them to go before they leave home, then I know they're all right.'

'But it's easy enough when he gets there. They'd let him leave the class, wouldn't they?'

'He doesn't like to ask, and he gets himself all bunged up. I have to keep dosing him at weekends.'

'That's how lazy bowels start, with regular dosing. We must get him back into good habits again.'

'What do you suggest?'

'I'd try getting him up in time for an early breakfast of prunes or apple puree and All-Bran, then ten minutes running, or other exercise. It should do the trick.'

It didn't, and Jimmy went to see his doctor, who referred him to the paediatrician, who admitted him to the hospital for investigation. While in hospital he was as regular as clockwork, and he was sent home with the laconic diagnosis of 'laziness'. Within a few weeks the cycle had started again, and Mrs Poynter rang me up. I remembered, from my own childhood, the utterly revolting taste of liquorice powder with which I had been dosed at school. Even today I am allergic to that particular shade of greenish yellow. I collected a small bottle from the chemist on my way, and deposited it on the kitchen table.

'Send him upstairs, as usual, after breakfast, and, if nothing happens, give him a dose of this. There are three doses here, but I doubt if you'll need them.'

I called round the following week for a progress report. Mrs Poynter was beaming.

'It worked. The second time, when he didn't go, I picked up the bottle. He yelled: "No, Mummy" and fled upstairs again. He's regular now, goes every morning just like he used to.'

When I got home, a little later than usual, I found a note from Mrs Wilson. Mrs Dean had phoned to ask for a visit. I was puzzled. Christopher had seemed well enough when I saw him at the clinic two weeks previously, the feeding satisfactory in quantity and quality. What had gone wrong?

'He keeps crying. It's not like him.'

There was nothing obviously wrong with the baby, no distension, no local tenderness, no injury, no signs of early teething.

'Any particular time?'

'About an hour before his feed's due. I can't understand it. He used to sleep right through.'

'Does he take his feed all right? The full eight ounces?'

'He's not getting eight ounces now. I've cut it down since the last clinic.'

Since the clinic? I didn't remember suggesting any change in Christopher's feeding when I weighed him. Why should I? Could I possibly have muddled up the records? It had been a particularly busy afternoon.

'Did I suggest cutting him down?'

'No. Not to me, you didn't.' She sounded almost reproachful. 'But I heard you telling Mrs Hollis that eight ounces was too much fluid for her baby's tummy, and to give him less milk and some cereal, but I cut down the milk, like you said.'

She put the baby back in his cot.

'You never told me about the eight ounces being too much for his little tummy.'

Her voice was challenging and there was resentment in her eyes as she turned back to me.

'But it isn't, Mrs Dean, not for Christopher. He needs his eight ounces, and he's crying because he's hungry.'

'But you said . . .'

'Not to you. To Mrs Hollis.'

She looked puzzled.

'But surely, if eight ounces is too much, it's too much. If it's bad for her baby it must be bad for Christopher. I mean, babies are babies, aren't they?'

I shook my head.

'Not the way you mean, Mrs Dean, not to me they're not. I don't see "babies" at the clinic, nor visit them at home. I see Christopher Dean and Paul Hollis, and they're separate and individual people, and what suits one doesn't suit the other.'

Mrs Dean glanced towards the cot, and back at me.

'I never thought of it like that. I thought you sort of had certain rules and dished them out to us at different stages.'

I laughed.

'If it was that simple I could give you all printed instructions at my first visit and save myself a lot of time. Every baby is different from every other baby, so is every mother. Paul Hollis is a sick baby, I mean literally sick. His tummy can only hold a small amount of liquid, and he's a lot better since he's been having more solid food.'

Mrs Dean looked thoughtful.

'Christopher's hardly ever been sick.'

'I know, but he does tend to put on a little too much weight. If you start him on cereals too soon you'll have a fat baby, and nobody wants that.'

The sullenness had disappeared. A quiet happiness replaced it, irradiated by a sudden smile.

'What you said, about not visiting babies, I like it. It makes my Christopher seem sort of special.'

I returned her smile.

'He is special, Mrs Dean. Every one of my babies is very, very special.'

At the door I turned to remind her.

'Don't forget, if I have any advice to give you about Christopher, I'll give it to you, not to Mrs Hollis or anyone else.'

As I drove away, I was still wondering how much harm was done by people overhearing advice given to others and acting on it, and by patients recommending to fellow-sufferers treatment or drugs which they had found helpful. Advertisements have a lot to answer for, with their infallible remedies for back sufferers and headache sufferers. There are not such people. There's Mrs A with arthritis, and Mr B with sciatica, or Mr C with a hangover and Mrs D with migraine, each needing a totally different approach to their problem.

There were, however, occasions when I generalised. Some basic principles are applicable to all, and these were propounded and driven home at antenatal classes, in talks to Mothers' Clubs and Parent–Teacher Associations, and occasionally in not-too-busy village clinics, with a ten-minute chat backed up by an arresting poster or display. Apart from these rare talks, and the distribution of leaflets and booklets, I did not use my clinics as a platform for health education. That was best done in the homes, person to person, often over a cup of tea. The clinics, for me, were an occasion for seeing the babies and checking on their progress. They were so often asleep and tucked up in prams and cots when I called on their mothers. At my clinic they were not only untucked, but undressed, except for a vest. I liked to see every baby under a year old in his birthday suit. The weighing was a matter of form, and the mothers liked it. The weekly or monthly gain was a talking point with daddies and grannies and neighbours. I could tell by looking at a baby if his weight was correct, and, when he was placed on the scales, could, from long practice, guess the weight to within an ounce or two, particularly if I had held him, however briefly, before lying him on the tray. (I found this experience paid dividends at village fetes in guessing the weight of giant marrows!)

Some mothers, rushing in and out of the clinic between shopping and collecting the schoolchildren, wanted to dump their babies on the scales fully clothed. I always discouraged this, as no baby always wears the same clothes, so any variation in weight does not give a true picture. More important to me was seeing the baby undressed. A quick look at a naked infant as I juggled with the weights would reveal so much: the tone of the skin, the movements of uncluttered limbs, rashes, hernias, sore bottoms, and – not least important – from the corner of my eye I would be watching how new young mothers were handling their babies as they dressed and undressed them, how they related to them, how confident or insecure the babies appeared under their ministrations.

I always held out against any of my clinics becoming just a place to weigh babies – that can be done at any chemists – or to come for injections – those are available at a doctor's surgery. For me, the essential work of the clinic was to ensure the good health and progress of the babies. Of course vaccination and immunisation were encouraged, they were an essential part of preventive medicine, and were given as routine as they became due. Health visitors have a motto: 'It is better to build a fence at the top of the cliff than to maintain an ambulance at the bottom.' And the injections were an integral part of that protective fence. But Dr Lang was far more than just a pricker of small bottoms. She examined every baby thoroughly at the first visit, at six months and a year old, the toddlers at yearly intervals, and, of course, at any time on referral from me of any problem discovered at the scales or on a home visit. The knowledge, the expertise, the caring and concern of our clinic doctors are beyond praise, but, in addition to these qualities, they have the blessing of time, not always available to a GP in a busy surgery.

Two health visitors ran our busy bi-weekly clinic in the town, to which the mothers came from a wide area, and many were unknown to me. The country clinics held monthly in three of my villages were all my own, and everybody came: mothers from the big houses in expensive cars, prams wheeled from cottages, caravans, and canal barges, nannies and foster mothers with their charges. There was a wonderful, utterly dependable committee of local ladies who prepared the hall, sold the baby foods and vitamins, served the tea, and sat beside me to find record cards and fill in weights. They knew of my terrible secret – I was totally unable to remember names! Seeing a mother, I could visualise her home, know all about her baby, what breed of dog she had, and what brand of tea she used, but I could not remember her name.

All the mothers had small weight cards which they handed in at the scales, and I would call out the name to my helper who passed me the record card. No problem, until the card had been left at home, and Mum would wait expectantly, the baby already on the scales. I needed the record card, to check on the last weight and any comments made by me or the doctor, but I could not possibly ask her name. My loyal helper could, and did, and my mothers never guessed my dark secret. In most cases the committee members knew the mothers, had seen them grow up in the village, and called most of them by their Christian names, and the arrival of a new baby at the clinic was an occasion of great interest and excitement.

At Lapfold, where she lived, the local midwife was a frequent visitor, dropping in to see how 'her' babies were progressing, and to give me the rundown on the latest baby which she was about to hand over to my care. Nearing retirement, she had brought most of the children in the village into the world, and some of the younger mothers, and she was always a familiar figure at all village events, Christmas parties, sports days, school concerts etc., to all of which I was also invited.

In these days of hospital confinements, the passing of the district midwife is a sad loss to the community. Having a baby at home was a family event, and babies seemed to survive even the most unhygienic conditions. Childbirth in those days was such a joyous occasion, unhurried, not timed to suit the convenience of a doctor or midwife. Babies came when they were ready and were welcomed into their own homes, however simple. During her labour the mother was attended, comforted, encouraged and helped by a midwife with whom she had been in frequent contact all through her pregnancy, a midwife so caring that she would have nightmares lest one of her mothers should go into labour while she (the midwife) was on holiday. The mother–midwife relationship was one of absolute trust, and invariably of very real mutual affection, which helped to dispel the fears and tensions of labour, so, by a natural process, minimising its pains.

I remember helping a midwife at a home delivery. I knew the family well and spent most of the day with the mother, was having supper with Dad, when the midwife called to see how the labour was progressing. To our great amusement, the mother was so relaxed that she had fallen asleep, and had to be woken up as the baby was ready to be delivered. Later that evening, when it was all over, and the tiny new person lay snugly beside the radiant mother, flanked by two baby dolls, Dad carried in two sleepy elder sisters, woken by the noise, to see the baby and receive their dolls. I can still hear the three-year-old's exultant cry.

'Mummy's got a new baby, and I've got a new baby, and Kate's got a new baby, and we've all got new babies!'

That is what home confinements were all about.

And after the birth? Daily visits from the midwife, one's own midwife, only a little less thrilled and proud than the parents themselves. Then, after ten days, a visit from the health visitor, met and known through the antenatal classes, and the continuity of the baby's well-being safe in the hands of known people, of caring people, of friends, from the day the pregnancy was confirmed until the child reached school age. Nowadays how many people are involved in one pregnancy? How rarely is a mother delivered by the same midwife who supervised her in the early months, and how rarely does the midwife who delivered her see her or the baby after the event?

Health visitors being also school nurses, there used to be continuity even after school started, and a mother would find a friend at the school medical inspection, and, probably, the same doctor she had seen at the clinic, and her child continued under the care of people who knew about him, people who cared, because her child, her baby, had been their particular concern from the very beginning.

Knowing every baby in a clinic and every child in a classroom, I saw not a crowd of babies, nor a roomful of schoolchildren, but *individual* babies and *individual* children. The health and well-being of each individual was of supreme importance to me. A village, a town, a nation, the world, is made up, not of babies and children, men and women, teenagers and pensioners, not of ethnic groups, political parties or religious denominations, but of individual people, each one separate; each one, from the first moment of conception, special and unique, the like of which has never existed before and never will again.

20

School Nurse

At a school medical inspection just before my retirement, I experienced a phenomenon which would not have been possible in my early days as a school nurse. A school leaver was late for her appointment with the doctor, and I wandered out into the corridor to look for her. Seeing a long-haired, mini-skirted youngster hurrying towards me, I hailed her.

'It's Margaret, isn't it? Come on, the doctor's waiting for you.'

The young woman stopped in her tracks, drawing herself up to her full height of five foot nothing.

'He's not waiting for me . . . I am one of the teachers!'

I returned to the medical room, where the doctor was amused at my discomfiture, but, pressed for time, he sent me out again on another foray. Waiting on a chair outside the door was another long-haired, jeans-clad customer. I smiled a welcome.

'Come on in, Margaret. The doctor's waiting.'

The figure remained seated. From under the wavy locks emanated a gruff voice, full of indignation.

'I'm not Margaret . . . I'm a boy!'

When I started my career in health visiting, teachers looked like teachers, boys looked like boys and children looked like children. It was not uncommon for eleven-year-old girls to strip down to their pants for weighing in the corridor – in front of waiting parents and their male classmates. Now the scales have to be screened off, because today's little girls seem to be developing into big girls much earlier and, rightly, like to be private about their budding womanhood.

In my opinion it was the long-haired boys who were responsible for an outbreak of head lice in our schools in the early 1970s – a scourge which years of routine head inspections had practically eliminated. I used to enjoy those visits, every term to every school, and more often if summoned by an anxious headmaster. It was the sort of job one could keep up one's sleeve for a rainy day, or to break up a week when no clinic work interrupted the monotony of home visiting. Not that visiting was really monotonous. It was as varied as people are varied, as houses are varied, and each visit was a separate adventure, with its own individual approach, its own particular need to be met, its own message to be conveyed in a suitable manner. The variations of the health-visiting theme were summed up by one of the student health visitors who occasionally accompanied us on our rounds. Asked for her impression of the day's work, she replied, 'What struck me most was to see how many different people you become. You're a completely different person in every house.'

I suppose work that elicits such a comment can't really be described as monotonous.

Head inspections were not the sole object of the term-by-term visits to the schools. I welcomed them as an opportunity to see each child. As each child approached, I could rapidly assess their general appearance, colour, stance, cleanliness, the state of the clothing. On one such occasion I spotted an early case of muscular dystrophy as a plump little boy waddled towards me with the distinctive gait. I enjoyed the brief conversations as I combed through each head of hair, hearing news of success in school, of holidays, of parents and younger brothers and sisters, all of whom were known to me. After my first five years in the district, every head I inspected in school had once been cradled in my arms in the downy softness or baldness of early infancy.

Any infected child was given a note to take home. The only way to prevent a rapid spread of the problem was the immediate exclusion from school of the infected children. Whenever possible I tried to visit the parents before the children returned home, bringing the special shampoo and lotion to treat the infection, and arrange for a return visit forty-eight hours later. There would sometimes be a crisis situation, such as an imminent exam, or a leading part in a school play, which did not allow for forty-eight hours absence from school, and on such occasions I would deal with the situation personally, washing, disinfecting, fine combing through the hair, strand by strand, until every nit had been removed. During my training as a health visitor I had worked my stint in the cleansing stations in north-east London. Unlike some of my colleagues I had not found the work unduly repellent. I have always found pleasure in handling the silken texture of a child's newly washed hair.

The council school I visited in Kenilworth served not only the council estate but an adjoining estate of private houses, and the intake of children from the better-class homes slowly but surely raised the standard of cleanliness, dress and behaviour. When I was in the school, I would wander round the classrooms, talking to the teachers, noticing and observing. The time soon came when a shabby, dirty child would catch my eye, and later I'd be knocking on the mother's door . . .

'I've just come from the school . . . I noticed your Johnny had holes in his shoes . . .'

If financial help was needed I would contact the school welfare officer for a grant for new shoes, or give the mother a note to take to the WVS for pullovers, dresses or shorts. It was very rarely that I 'noticed' the same child a second time.

One of the most valuable moments of the school visit would be the tea break, when I joined the headmaster or mistress to discuss any health, social or behaviour problems that had come to his notice. In those days of smaller schools, every child was known by name to the head, who was conversant with his family background and any particular circumstances that might affect his progress or behaviour in school. I was the link between the school and the home, and sometimes even my close relationship with my mums would be strained at the seams when such problems as stealing or bullying were dumped on my lap, or, worse still, such problems as our best friends refrain from mentioning. Of course the children's friends *did* tell them, in no uncertain terms; classmates refused to sit by them, and even the teachers instinctively withdrew at their approach. I could cope with head lice – they were often not the parents' fault and could be caught by the cleanest children – but smelly children with soiled and badly washed pants were quite another matter, and the child's humiliation and embarrassment had to be brought home to the mother to induce her to improve her washing techniques.

A recurrent problem was the child who fell asleep in class, due, usually, to late nights, or sleep disturbed by a crying baby, or a restless young brother or sister sharing the room or the bed. There were the no-breakfast children who began to 'droop' by the middle of the morning. There were two droopers, in particular, who puzzled me – a brother and sister of seven and nine. They lived on a private estate and I knew there was no shortage of money in their house. The mother was an intelligent woman who, before her marriage, had a responsible job in an office in Coventry. The children's clothes were of good quality, and clean, although the buttons were all awry and half undone. Their trailing shoelaces were attached to expensive shoes, their hair was unbrushed and faces often dirty, and their mid-morning droops indicated an inadequate breakfast, if any.

I wondered, was their mother ill? Had she left her husband? I was sure that, in either case, their father would have engaged a housekeeper, or sent them to a relative to be cared for. I felt this was a case when both parents needed to be seen, so I called one evening about seven o'clock. The children were in bed and the parents seemed surprised to see me. The father was even more surprised when he learnt the reason for my visit. It transpired that his wife had recently gone back to her very interesting job. What he had somehow not understood was that her early start in the morning left the children to get themselves dressed, breakfasted, and into school with no help or supervision.

Being a liaison between the school and the home could work both ways. Sometimes it was the parents' complaints that had to be investigated. Occasionally there were complaints about the school dinners, which surprised me, as I enjoyed many a school dinner when engaged for a whole day on a medical inspection, and had always found them excellent. I was investigating such a complaint in one of my junior schools, where the relevant child was tucking in with relish to a delicious stew, when I noticed how dirty the children's hands were. I checked with the headmistress on the washing facilities, which appeared adequate, and was assured that they would all be having a good wash after their dinner so that the schoolbooks didn't get dirty or sticky. She accepted, in good part, my suggestion that, in the interest of hygiene and good social training, they should wash their hands *before* their dinner. Damaged books were more easily replaced than damaged stomachs.

I had the privilege to work with a generation of teachers who brought a sense of vocation to their work.

There were no crises of discipline in those schools. It was taken for granted by the teachers and by the children that orders were obeyed and rules kept. In the days when country children completed their education at the village school, I remember seeing big boys in the top class ruled, with great affection and inflexible discipline, by the immovable Miss Hodgkin. The relationship between the little woman and the hulking country lads who towered above her was a joy to witness. In those days, before village children were bussed into town at the age of eleven, they were none the worse for being versed in country lore, for learning about soil and crops and stars and local wildlife.

Lapfold was the official weather station for the district, and knowing how to read the weather portents was to be of practical use to tomorrow's farmers. For those who wanted a more academic career there were always scholarships available to the excellent grammar schools in Leamington, Warwick or Coventry, and any promising pupil would be assured of the concentrated tuition required to ensure that scholarship. I was always struck by the courtesy of the children, in and out of school. Good manners were not only taught, they were learnt from the staff. The children were never shouted at; 'please' and 'thank you' were part of the teachers' vocabulary, from the head downwards. Receiving courtesy, the children learnt to give it in return. I well remember my distress after the retirement of the beloved headmaster from Lapfold, when I overheard, from the medical room, a child being sworn at by a new teacher. Predictably, within a few months, the children were swearing at one another, at the teachers, even at their parents. I remain convinced that most children will respond to love and trust and respect. If they received a little more of these in our modern schools, the classrooms of today could be as calm and as happy and as productive as they were in the 1950s.

In those pre-ecumenical days, one of the problems for mothers of daughters was that by far the best girls' school in the area was the convent school at Kenilworth. That was, of course, just splendid for Catholic parents, but it was a difficult decision for some of the others. Like all other family problems, I would often be consulted on this one.

'As I see it,' I would advise, 'if you decide to send her to the convent you must be prepared to have an open mind, and accept the fact that she might become attracted to the Catholic Church and want to change her religion.'

I assured the parents that there would be no coercion, the non-Catholics were under no compulsion to attend services or religious instruction, but 'religion is caught, not taught', and if they did not wish to expose their child to the risk of 'catching' Catholicism, it would not be fair to send her to a convent school.

'It would be wrong to put her in a Catholic atmosphere and then oppose her wish, if she expressed it, to become a Catholic.'

Many Protestant girls passed out of the convent school without changing their religion. A few did, and their parents respected their choice.

I was glad when Crackley Convent invited us to carry out routine medical inspections on their children. This service, compulsory in state schools, was not normally extended to private schools, although we were only too delighted to include them. The first medical inspection Dr Lang and I carried out in a private school was at a very good-class and expensive prep school in Warwick – not my district, but I happened to be available that day. It was patronised by many professional families, including the local doctors, and one medical father had been watching the children in the playground from the headmistress's study, when he was suddenly aware that the physical condition of the little rich children in the playground compared unfavourably with the average state school pupils. At his suggestion we were invited to do a full medical inspection, and the toll of minor defects we unearthed was rather disconcerting. The word got around, and twice-yearly visits to every private school in the area became an accepted routine, and our doctors, solicitors, stockbrokers, works managers and all could watch their children in the school playground confident that they would be going up to their expensive public schools with a clean bill of health.

21

Mixed Relations

When a child is first examined medically in school, at the age of five, the statisticians in some county or government office require a great deal of information about his (or her) background, living conditions, financial situation, personal and family history of illness. An extensive questionnaire on each medical form has to be filled in before the child appears before the doctor. When I had been on my district for five years, the school entrants had been my babies, and there was no longer any need for questions. I knew all the answers, and the medical inspections were occasions of joyful reunion with my little friends and their mothers and the current toddlers or babies in each family. With both Dr Lang and I being in attendance at the schools and the local clinic, the line of demarcation between the Infant Welfare and the School Medical Service was very vague and frequently breached. Schoolchildren with problems would be brought to the clinic, while advice would be asked about the babies and toddlers who, of necessity, accompanied their mothers to the school where an older brother or sister was being examined.

It wasn't always like that. There was once a time when I knew very little about the school entrants, and had to elicit the necessary information from the mother while the doctor's stethoscope moved over the child's chest. It wasn't Dr Lang in those days, but a kind, fatherly Scot near to retirement. How gently he handled one very scared, undernourished and not over clean little boy while I questioned his mother, pen in hand. All went well until I came to 'Father's occupation?'

She hesitated, looking puzzled. I put it another way.

'What work does your husband do?'

She looked even more puzzled.

'That's it,' she said. 'That's the problem.'

'The problem? Is he, perhaps, out of work at present?'

I was getting a bit worried. Was he, perhaps, in prison? I was about to pass on to the next question when she answered slowly.

'That depends, Miss . . . on who you'd be wanting to know about. Would it be my husband? Or Jimmy's dad? Or the man I lives with?'

Nonplussed, I looked across at the doctor. His wise grey eyes twinkled at me under the shaggy eyebrows.

'The wage-earner,' he mumbled.

It was, of course, the financial aspect of the situation that concerned the statisticians, so the job of the man she lived with was duly inscribed on the form.

That was my first introduction to the complexities of family relationships on the council estate in Kenilworth. Married couples had children and were divorced, both subsequently remarrying and setting up establishments of 'his' children, 'her' children and 'their' children. In the next street, or further down the same road, the other partner of the original marriage might have one or two of her own children with her, to which would be added his and theirs. A child would be living in one house with stepbrothers and sisters, while his full brother or sister could be in another house, with Mum or Dad, with another set of steps and mutual halves. People talk today about having 'a crisis of identity'. If such a thing had been known in those days, such children could certainly have laid claim to it. A child's name was no clue as to whose house he lived in or even who his parents were, as they would often take the surname of their stepfathers, 'to save confusion'. It certainly never saved me from confusion, nor the unfortunate headmaster, struggling in a maze where even full brothers and sisters in his school had different surnames.

A further complication of relationship was added in one family in which the child's mother was his grandmother and his sister was his mother. It was, in fact, the only complication in an otherwise straightforward family, and one which I had been instrumental in bringing about.

I was on holiday when Mrs Barry came to the clinic to look for me, in obvious distress. The kind colleague standing in for me suggested calling round for a talk, but her offer was politely but firmly refused.

'It can wait another week till Miss Corbally's back. It's a family matter, you see.'

Oh, the inestimable privilege of a job through which one is accepted as an honorary member of one's families, and a recipient of confidences that even parents are not told! Mrs Barry's youngest child was not yet three, so I had been in close touch with her over the last few years, and had seen her at the school when we examined the elder ones, including her eldest, fifteen-year-old Margaret. It was Margaret who was the trouble. She was pregnant. It was before the days of easily accessible abortion, and I doubt, anyhow, if such a solution would have occurred to the Barrys. The question was not whether there'd be a baby or not – the baby was already there – but what to do with it when it came. They thought Margaret was far too young to accept the responsibility of motherhood. Adoption? The child had broken her heart when her mother suggested it. Then there were the neighbours. These were still the days when it was considered shameful for a girl to have a baby outside marriage. The Barrys were a decent, self-respecting family who felt themselves disgraced by their daughter's condition. I had a suggestion to offer which could solve both the questions: 'What shall we do with the baby?' and 'What will the neighbours think?'

As the time drew near when careful dressing could no longer conceal the fact that Margaret was pregnant, and her mother was not, Mrs Barry took the girl and her own little son for a prolonged visit to her sister in Kent. When they came home the Barrys had another little girl, and Margaret returned to school, thrilled and excited about her 'new baby sister'.

There were, of course, other families where unmarried mothers lived with their parents, leaving their babies with Mum while they went to work. It was often not a happy situation. Mum, having brought up a family of her own, was resentful at starting all over again with nappies and bottles and all the paraphernalia and upset of a small baby in the house. In my experience it sometimes resulted in the toddler being dumped in a day nursery, and the child growing up belonging to everyone and no one, often resented by the mother for spoiling her chances of marriage. In these cases, I do not go along with the modern assumption that the natural mother is automatically the best person to look after a child. An illegitimate baby is not always wanted by its mother. An adopted baby is always desperately wanted, otherwise why bother to adopt?

One of the exceptions was Rita, from the camp. One day, Lady Merlin's 'most reliable evidence' was discovered by her employer vomiting in the pantry. She admitted that she was pregnant. I suspected the father was married, because she absolutely refused to give his name. Whoever he was, she loved him and wanted to keep his child. Lady Merlin was indignant and very displeased about the whole thing.

'The stupid little creature! If I only knew who it was I'd see to it that he paid up.'

I bet you would, I thought. What a fighter she was in any cause that remotely concerned her.

'If, as I suspect, he is a married man, her silence is to her credit,' she sniffed, 'but that's no reason why he should get away scot-free. It takes two to make a baby.'

'But what about his wife, if he has one? It could break up a marriage. There might be children.'

The gold pen tapped imperiously on her desk. 'Whatever the circumstances, he should be made to pay.'

'Oh, Lady Merlin, have you less compassion than Rita? How would you have felt if it had been your husband?'

She bridled. 'How dare you! Fancy even suggesting such a thing, but . . .' the pen was still. 'Well, I suppose you've got a point. If there's a wife, it's not her fault, poor woman.'

'If she won't tell,' said Lady Merlin, 'we can't get a maintenance order, so she'll have to get the baby adopted.'

I shook my head. 'No way. She wants that baby more than she's wanted anything in her life. I have the impression that this really is a love child.'

She snorted. 'Nonsense! This sort of thing has nothing whatsoever to do with love, just animal lust. Disgusting!'

'Whatever you call it, Rita's keeping the baby.'

'Little idiot! How does she think she'll manage for money?'

'She can work.'

'She's not working here anymore, that's for certain. I've already given her notice.'

Lady Merlin didn't tell me, but I heard later from Rita of the very generous 'golden handshake' that accompanied the little maid's dismissal.

It was about that time that I met Mrs Adams at the antenatal clinic in Kenilworth. Her fourth child was well on the way and she felt the time had come when she needed help in the big farmhouse a few miles outside the town. Did I know of anyone? It was not unusual for me to be used as an unofficial employment agency. People were always looking for 'comers-in' to clean and cook, and would ring me up or write during the summer, hoping to catch one of the mothers whose youngest child would be starting school in September.

Mrs Adams wanted a girl to live in as one of the family, a girl willing to help with the housework, the children, if necessary on the farm. She had no objection to an unmarried mother; on the contrary she liked the idea, as the babies could grow up together. Rita and her parents were delighted. Her condition was not yet obvious, and, although the camp dwellers were perhaps more broad-minded than the average village community, they were quite glad for the neighbours not to know. Rita and her baby integrated into the Adams family so happily that I was sometimes left wondering which baby belonged to which mother.

Before the establishment of the Children's Department and the eruption of the welfare and social services, adoptions were our responsibility, and we worked closely with the adoption societies who placed the babies. We always knew in plenty of time when an adoption was pending, so were able to prepare the mother with basic instruction in baby care. We were informed of the date, even the time, when a baby was due to arrive in its new home, and would be there the next morning to help with the first bath, to encourage and reassure the mother who had missed out on the ten days in hospital or with the midwife during which natural mothers learn to feed and bath their babies. Today a health visitor can learn of an adoption quite by chance. It may be weeks before the official notification arrives on her desk, and by that time inexperience and total lack of preparation could have made havoc of an occasion which should be, and always used to be, one of great happiness and fulfilment. Adopting mothers deserve better than this hit-or-miss approach. People who take into their homes, and into their hearts, babies which are not their own, give proof of a rare and special kind of generosity and caring. In all the adoptions I have supervised I have never known one to fail, not even, as happens not infrequently, when a fulfilled and satisfied woman conceives and gives birth to her own child after all hope of doing so has been abandoned. I have always advocated being honest with children about their adoption, and the knowledge that they have been chosen by their parents can be a source of great happiness and pride to them. I was delighted to overhear the following conversation during a childish quarrel.

'I belong to Mummy and Daddy. You're only adopted.'

'Of course I'm adopted. They *chose* me. They *had* to have you!'

The worst part of the adoptive process was the last month of the probation period. By that time the baby was a deeply loved and integral part of the family, yet it was still possible that the natural mother might change her mind at the eleventh hour and refuse to sign away the child to which she had given birth. Each time I would wait anxiously for the telephone to ring and the jubilant voice at the other end of the line to announce: 'He's ours!'

22

Other People's Children

Mrs Silkins was never happy unless she had a baby in her arms. It had always been so, ever since the day when she had been seated safely in a low chair and allowed to hold her baby brother 'just for a few minutes'. Those few minutes had become a lifetime. As soon as she left school she had taken a job as nursery maid, and within a few years, was a nanny with her own nursery.

Now there are some nannies who become deeply attached to their nurslings and dread the day when they outgrow the nursery and go off to boarding school. Of such are the devoted family friends who sometimes remain in the household, in another capacity, until their babies marry, have babies in their turn and open a new nursery in which to install the nanny who had watched over their childhood. On the other hand, there are other nannies who only love small babies, and become frustrated and unsettled when the last baby of the family has outgrown the cradle. These move around, from family to family, and soon lose touch with the children who they cherished in infancy. Mrs Silkins was such a one. Married, with a pleasant, roomy house, she was God's gift to the county council. It is not every woman who wants to take charge of a baby for a few months, while an adoption is pending, or during the prolonged illness of the mother. The inevitable heartbreak of continual partings is an obstacle difficult to overcome. It is more rewarding to foster children on a long-term basis, when they grow up as your own.

Before Mrs Silkins's own children were even born, she was taking in babies. There were never less than three in the house, ranging in age from two weeks to two years, at which age, if there was no likelihood of returning to their mothers, they would be removed to a more permanent foster home before they became too attached to Mrs Silkins, who really no longer wanted them.

When I first met Mrs Silkins, her own son and daughter were already at school. We soon became close friends, as the constant turnover of babies necessitated frequent visits on my part, and she attended the clinic with successive babies for the regular check-up demanded by the law. I was with her one afternoon when her children came home from school. The current baby, a little 'prem' on three-hourly feeds, had just finished its bottle and was being winded when the eight-year-old boy burst into the room, his eyes shining, waving a large sheet of paper in the air.

'Mummy,' he shouted breathlessly, 'I've won first prize for my drawing.'

She nodded absently, her eyes on the fluffy golden head against her shoulder.

'Well done, darling. Take it to your room, and I'll come and look at it later, when Baby's settled.'

'All right,' he said, and turned to leave the room, but the light had gone out of his eyes, and the spring from his step, and I was worried at the malevolence of the look he gave the baby. I was not unduly surprised. The headmaster had reported to me instances of naughtiness in school, and continual showing off by both children, obviously seeking elsewhere the attention their mother failed to give them. I had been concerned about the situation and had been waiting for an opportunity to discuss it with Mrs Silkins. As she laid the baby back in the cot, I asked conversationally, 'Do your children resent having these babies in their home?'

'No. Why should they?'

'Because you're their mother, and you give so much time and so much love to the babies which they might feel should be given to them.'

She looked surprised.

'But the babies need my time. They're helpless and dependent, the darlings. As to love, the children know I love them.'

'Do they?'

The question hung in the air. She looked at me, a thoughtful anxious frown between her eyes. 'You mean . . . that drawing just now?'

I nodded. 'Brian was so philosophical. That resigned little sigh he gave. I got the impression that it was a fairly normal pattern.'

She was quiet, still thinking.

'If that's so, Mrs Silkins, do you think it's quite fair? They're your very own, and surely should have first and undisputed claim to your love and attention at all times?'

'Yes,' she said thoughtfully. 'Yes, I suppose you're right, but the babies . . .'

Her voice trailed off.

'The babies' needs are physical; they can be fitted in. This little fellow's feeds, for instance, couldn't they be adjusted so that he's back in his cot before the children come home and you can be all theirs just for a short time? Of course I know you love them, but what's important is that they should know it.'

She listened carefully as I told her of the trouble at school.

'I never thought . . .' she murmured. 'I never realised. Do you think, all these years, they've been jealous of my babies?'

'I wouldn't blame them, Mrs Silkins. Couldn't you have a break some time, during the school holidays, and just be together, the four of you as a family?'

She smiled.

'You may not believe it, but I have tried. Then they ring up from the Shire Hall. There's a baby needing a home.' She shrugged her shoulders. 'What can I do?'

'You can say no. We're nearly into June now. A month should see this baby strong enough for adoption, and the West Indian parents are collecting their little son in July, aren't they, when the university closes? That leaves you with one.'

'Her mother should be out of hospital in two or three weeks.'

'There you are then. Be firm, and if they try to bully you, put them on to me.'

She laughed.

'It does seem a good idea. I'm glad we've had this talk, Miss Corbally. I just hadn't thought about my children minding. You're quite right, they must come first – even if it means no more babies.'

She looked lovingly at the three tiny people asleep in their cots, and then straightened her back resolutely.

'I must go and admire that drawing of Brian's. Like to come?'

We went together to her son's room. It was empty. His sister called through her open door.

'He's out. He's taken his drawing round to show Mrs Evans.'

It is not unusual for children to turn to kind neighbours, or loving aunts, when their mothers aren't around, and it does not take long for these substitute mothers to supplant their own in the children's affections. It can happen so easily, even when the children are dearly loved. A mother who is too busy catching up with domestic chores to have time to listen to them, to discuss their problems, to show interest in their achievements. Again, there are women who are genuinely afraid of the sight of blood, who can't even bear to watch their children's injections. I have always tried to coax such mothers into the doctor's room, to persuade them to hold their babies instead of handing them to me.

'If your child is hurt, frightened or in pain, it's your arms that should comfort him, not a stranger's, not a neighbour's. That's what being a mother is all about.'

I had a special affection and regard for all my foster-mothers. I was fortunate never to meet a bad one. I realise there are such people, but I've always found it hard to understand. It's not a financially rewarding job, and, if a woman doesn't genuinely love children, why fill her house with them? Sometimes there'd be one child or two, brought up in the foster mother's own family. Then there was the Universal Mother, with a house always full of children; her children, foster children, neighbour's children, a visiting nephew or niece, filling every room and every corner of the garden with their games, their models, their jigsaws, and their exuberant presence, the bigger ones helping the little ones, hindering in the kitchen where Mrs Powell baked cakes and home-made bread, and prepared nourishing, appetising meals for as many children as happened to be there. No child would be sent home at dinnertime, all were welcome in this children's paradise of fun and gaiety and warmth.

The arrival of immigrants created a great need for foster mothers. It was customary, in their family orientated societies, for all young people to work, leaving the children in the care of the grandmother or other senior member of the family group, and the parents sought other substitute mothers in this country. They needed to work, they had homes to buy, businesses to set up, a new life to build. There was also a rise in the number of overseas students getting married at the universities and needing to have their babies fostered until their studies were completed and they could return, with the children, to their own country. They were, on the whole, devoted parents, regular in their visits, generous in their supply of clothing and toys.

Today, foster children are under the care of the social workers. It all started with one tragic case when a foster child died in a remote farmhouse, one tragedy so rare that it made headline news. A year later I found a small child placed for fostering with a mother so unsuitable that her own children had had to be removed from her care for a time. My protest was ignored. I was firmly told, by the Children's Officer, that fostering was no longer the concern of health visitors. She was wrong, of course. Children will always be the concern of health visitors, children of all ages, in their own homes or in foster homes; because the health and welfare of children is what health visiting is all about.

Perhaps my very favourite foster parents were Mr and Mrs Biggs, who were on their second generation of foster children. Unlike Mrs Silkins, Mrs Biggs preferred her charges to be mobile and reasonably independent when they came to her, which usually obviated the risk of adoption, or of reclamation by their mothers. She aimed to offer her children a stable and secure home, and a family to which they would truly belong. None of her children ever lost touch after they left her, and the grown-up members of the large family were immensely kind and helpful with the younger ones, whom they regarded as real brothers and sisters and treated accordingly. Birthdays and Christmases would bring cards and presents from all over the world, and, like many other parents, Mr and Mrs Biggs loved to gather as many of their children as possible round their

An Armful of Babies and a Cup of Tea

fireside on Christmas Day. The feeding of their large family was made easier, during the post-war rationing, by parcels of goodies from a 'daughter' in America, with ham and butter brought over from Ireland. The first year I knew them I was shown, with pride, an enormous turkey, ready stuffed, sent by a married 'son' in Ireland. Unfortunately the donor's Christmas letter was delayed in the post, and the splendid bird was put into the oven in the early morning, with no one aware of the bottle of whiskey concealed by the sausage meat stuffing. Tragedy! The bottle shattered in the hot oven and splinters of glass rendered the succulent flesh unsafe to eat. I hope, if any customs officer should read this, he will not be so hard-hearted as to say 'Serves them right!'

I'd had my own trouble with a turkey that Christmas, a gift from one of my farms. It had not been 'dressed'. (Personally I think a bird looks far more naked after being dressed than in its natural state, clothed in its feathers.) It was our first year in our kitchen, and such rituals were new to us.

When we had collected up the feathers from all corners of the house, Eileen installed herself with our big new cookery book and slowly read out the instructions, while I delved and probed and removed that which had to be removed. 'Drawing' a bird is not the pleasantest of occupations, and my own innards were doing a bit of a dance by the time the nauseating job was finished. Eileen smiled encouragement.

'Nearly done. Only the claws to remove. Take a sharp knife . . .'

I should have known better. All those anatomy lectures! As I struck the tendon the claw contracted, grabbing my hand in a cold vice-like grip. With a yell that must have been heard four doors away I dropped everything and shot through the door and halfway down the garden.

That was our first Christmas in our own home. For years Eileen and I had spent Christmas in hospital, making it a happy occasion for our patients. We had fun too, of course. There were parties on the wards and a belated Christmas dinner, but Christmas Day itself was the patients' day. Our first very own Christmas was sheer magic, and it contained everything that makes Christmas in any home in England; the crib and the tree, the cards and the holly, the crackers and the turkey and the lighted pudding, the mysterious parcels hidden away until Christmas morning, even stockings, just for that first year. My sister was with us, on holiday from the prep school in Sussex where she was a house-matron. It was her first visit to 149, the very first time ever that one of us had been hostess to the other in our own home. She arrived at Leamington station clutching a large shopping bag full of gaily wrapped parcels. She thought that was Christmassy, until she got into the car. I think she laughed all the way to Kenilworth, an exuberant puppy on her lap, a Christmas tree leaning on her shoulder, holly pricking her in the back, and a large turkey falling off her suitcase every time I braked.

Of course there was the midnight service. Eileen went, with her family, to Stoneleigh parish church, while Biddy and I walked through the crisp star-studded night to St Austin's. Later, while we warmed ourselves with mugs of hot cocoa before going to bed, chairs were being piled high with gaily wrapped parcels, and stockings, bulging excitedly, were tied to the foot of the beds.

Solow enjoyed the parcel opening as much as any of us, playing ecstatically with the wrappings as they were torn off. In her excitement she even forgot her manners, but quickly concealed her lapse under a large sheet of festive paper. She had her presents too, of course: a new collar, a rubber bone, and, joy of joys, a roll of loo paper which, chased round the house, and twisted round table and chair legs, added quite considerably to the general confusion. In time all the presents were unwrapped, admired, tried on (if wearable), tried out (if practical), the paper was collected up, Solow's lapse discovered and repaired, and a festive table was prepared for the traditional feast which already permeated the house with delicious aromas.

Then there was the hamper. Eileen had given up her job with the Ministry for Labour and was working as sister in charge of the surgery of a Coventry factory. It was a good liaison, as some of my fathers worked there. Just before Christmas, Mr Hazel, from the council estate in Kenilworth, had come to see her almost in tears. His wife had been taken to hospital with a perforated ulcer. There were three children from five to ten years old, and nothing had been prepared for the holiday. Mrs

Hazel had been feeling too ill to cope. No cooking had been done, no dinner laid in, no presents bought or wrapped, no stockings filled. All they had was a tree from previous Christmases. Eileen thought quickly.

'Don't worry,' she told him. 'Get the children to help you decorate the tree, and have a word with the fairy on top of it. Fairies are clever people. You'd be surprised what they can do.'

When Eileen told me the situation I drove into Warwick to collect toys and books from the Red Cross while Eileen rang up the Smalleys. Leonard received so many gifts of birds at Christmas from grateful patients and was only too glad to supply a nice fat capon. Our pudding recipe made three good-sized puddings, so there was one to spare. Eileen was home early on Christmas Eve, and we spent a happy hour collecting stocking fillers from Woolworth's, nuts and fruit and sweets, orange squash and crackers, and sprouts from our own garden. It didn't take long for the three of us to pack the complete Christmas dinner in a large box, wrap the presents (including cigarettes for Dad and a bed jacket for Mum) and deliver them to the Hazels' home with love from the Christmas fairy. Thus started a custom which was repeated in succeeding years, as there were few Christmases when some family I know wasn't in need of help, and our third pudding hardly ever graced the table of 149 on Easter Sunday.

The shining excitement and laughter of children adds its special magic to the Christmas feast, but, where there are children, it is their day, and the grown-ups plan and work for their happiness. That is an important part of Christmas, but not the whole of it. One day, when the children have grown up and are themselves decorating trees and filling stockings for their own children, the parents who thought that Christmas without children could not be Christmas will sit happily by their own fireside among the holly and the greeting cards, on a Christmas Day which is their very own, and remember past Christmases, and understand that the feast is not only about the happiness of children, but about love and peace and togetherness. Their own laughter will bubble up, as ours did, and they will discover, as we did, that they have never really stopped being children.

People who say that Christmas without a child in the house is no Christmas are talking nonsense. Firstly, Christmas celebrates the birth of the Eternal Child, reborn in the hearts of everyone who loves him. So, basically, there can be no Christmas without a child. Secondly, Christmas is a family festival, and families come in all ages. I'm certain that the birthday of the Christmas Baby was still celebrated at Nazareth when Jesus had grown to manhood, and there had long ceased to be a child in the house.

23

Dogs and Me

I would rate a love of dogs very high among the quali-fications needed for successful and happy health visiting, or at least the absence of fear of dogs. Dogs are an intrinsic part of the work of visiting babies, because babies live in homes, and about seventy-five per cent of English homes contain a dog. The dog is usually there before the baby, and has already dug itself into the affections of the mother while the baby is still 'a twin-kle in its father's eye'. To resent the dog, to repulse its rather wet and not over-clean advances, or to show fear of it, does nothing towards winning the respect and confidence and friendship of its owner.

In many houses the first response to one's knock would be an excited barking on the other side of the door, then the sound of a scuffle while the dog was removed and shut away before the door was opened. From behind the kitchen door, barking and scratching and whining would interrupt the conversation, and my request to release the prisoner would be received with pleasure by the owner and with wild enthusiasm by the dog. Getting to know each other could be a hilarious and totally enjoyable process, which had a disastrous effect on my navy-blue suit or overcoat, not to mention my stockings. On the occasions when I called in at the office at Leamington on my way home, the Senior Nursing Officer would shake her head in despair.

'Just look at your uniform!' And out would come the clothes brush she kept in a drawer of her desk for the dog-lovers on her staff.

'We shouldn't wear navy-blue, not in the country,' I grumbled as she brushed my coat. 'People don't have navy-blue dogs and babies don't wear navy-blue shawls. Besides, it feels silly, walking across fields. Why can't we wear grey or brown in the country?'

Some of my colleagues would have preferred not to wear uniform at all. I never advocated that policy. I felt it was important that we should be recognised by the people on whom we called, and known to be nurses, and the uniform somehow inspired confidence and lent an air of authority when dealing with awkward customers. It was also an invaluable asset if the car broke down. A nurse in uniform, stranded by the roadside, would stop any passing car or van or lorry, and I must confess that I was never honest enough to disillusion the helpful mechanics who were obviously convinced that I was on my way to an urgent confinement. I had only to look worried and murmur: 'Oh dear, I'm going to be late . . .' and feverish efforts would be made by every man within call to repair the fault. Nobody ever thought to ask me what I was going to be late for!

I had many four-legged friends on my district, and their names were all inscribed on their babies' record cards. I was only bitten once in all my years of health visiting, and that was a mistake. Flossie and I were the best of friends. She always met me at the gate of the farm and, after an exuberant greeting, escorted me across the yard to the farmhouse. She was a well-bred and highly trained collie, who had distinguished herself at local sheep trials. I felt slightly deprived one afternoon when, on opening the gate, I did not have to brace myself against her violent greeting, and, walking unescorted across the yard, I was wondering at her absence, until I saw a sudden flash of black and white project itself from the door of the shed, and I felt her teeth sink into my thigh. Fortunately I was wearing an overcoat and she didn't break the skin, but it was still painful, and I yelled as much from surprise as from pain. The instant she had attacked, Flossie recognised me, and slumped at my feet, grovelling and whining, pleading abjectly for my forgiveness. I had great difficulty walking the short distance to the house as my contrite friend crawled along at my feet, rolling over in front of me in an anguish of self-reproach. Her owner was most concerned and apologetic, explaining that Flossie had three newborn puppies in the shed I had passed, and her protective instinct was such that she would attack on sight anything or anyone that could be a threat to her precious babies.

That protective instinct of dogs and their fierce possessiveness is so often underrated by their owners. Mothers who would take every precaution to prevent an elder child from being jealous of a new baby would fail to foresee the effect a first baby could have on a cherished pet. A resentful and jealous dog could be a real danger to the baby who had supplanted him in the affections of his adored master and mistress. I have seen lack of thought and imagination result in a poor animal being given away, or even put down, a poor repayment for its faithful and devoted love. On the other hand, I have known dogs that so adored their babies that they spent all day beside the cot or pram defying anyone to approach it. I knew one family where even the father was not allowed to go near his own baby, so fiercely protective was the dog, which had belonged to the mother before their marriage. Sadly, the loyal guard had to go, to be replaced by a spaniel puppy whose loyalties and affections were equally shared, and who became the devoted friend and play-mate of their little boy.

Although I loved dogs I respected their right to refuse entry to a stranger. The only creatures that really terrified me were geese, although I approached a house with great caution if I knew it contained an Alsatian, and I have never tried to argue a point with a dachs-hund, although I had a particular love for these game little dogs. There were no dogs on my rounds with whom I did not, in time, make friends. Most animals know when they are loved, and respond accordingly. My most remarkable conquest was made as a result of my ignorance and complete lack of fear. As I opened the gate of a large house one afternoon two brindled boxers came galloping towards me down the drive. My first reaction was to shut the gate quickly before they reached it and got through it onto the busy road. It never occurred to me not to stay on the same side of the gate as the beautiful animals. As they leapt up at me I talked to them, patted them, caressed them, laughing as they impeded my progress up the drive. As I waited for the door to be opened they slobbered over me, their great paws on my shoulders, trying to lick my face. When their owner opened the door she gave a cry of horror and turned quite pale.

'I didn't know the dogs were out,' she squealed, grabbing at their collars.

'Why shouldn't they be?'

She dragged my new friends, protesting, across the hall, and shut them behind a door, explaining breathlessly, 'They have already attacked two people and are under a police order to be kept shut up.' She looked at me anxiously. 'Are you sure you're all right?'

'Perfectly all right. They couldn't have been friendlier.'

'You're lucky, so am I, and so are they. If you'd been afraid, and they'd sensed it, it could have been awful.'

I had always heard that animals could smell fear and reacted to it by attacking, especially if two or more could gang up on a victim. I was indeed fortunate that I had never had any cause to mistrust a boxer.

Perhaps my worst experience was being shown into the living room on a first visit while the mother went upstairs to fetch her baby. Crossing to the window to look at the small garden, I heard a low growl behind me, and turning, saw a basket in the corner of the room containing a large, nondescript bitch, with her heckles up, and, horror of horrors, two very small puppies. I froze, not daring to move, scarcely to breathe until her mistress rejoined me, completely unaware of the danger inherent in such a situation.

On another occasion, taken short in an Alsatian's house and escorted to the downstairs cloakroom, I heard the front door bell ring while I was occupied. Nelson was barking furiously, and there was a scuffle in the hall. I emerged from the loo as the dog was being shoved through the cloakroom door.

'The electrician,' gasped his mistress. 'Nelson hates him, he'd tear him to pieces.'

She banged the door and disappeared, and I was shut in with the enormous dog, bristling with rage, barking, growling, snarling, hurling its huge weight at the door that separated it from its enemy. Now Nelson and I had enjoyed many a friendly chat in the company of his mistress, but this enraged beast was not the Nelson I knew. I retreated rapidly into the loo and shut the door, and there I stayed until the electrician had finished his business and Nelson and I were released!

My dachshund, Solow, was as well-known as I was on the district, and, when her puppies arrived, everyone wanted to see them. As soon as they were old enough to leave their mum, I used to take one or other of the small sausage puppies in the car on my rounds, to the delight of all the children. Our little hand-reared runt and his beautiful, naturally-fed brothers were used at my clinics to demonstrate the advantages of breast-feeding. I used up outdated packets of Ostermilk to wean the puppies, and was delighted when one of them was being admired by the mother of an overweight baby fed, against my advice, on National Dried Milk. I had failed to persuade her to change to the less fattening Ostermilk, and it was with great pleasure that I informed her that the healthy, firm little puppy she was raving about was being fed on Ostermilk.

'But he's perfect!' she exclaimed. 'Look at that coat, at that lovely firm little body.'

She handed him back to me, and gave a sudden wide grin.

'You've convinced me, Miss Corbally. If Ostermilk's good enough for this puppy of yours, it must be good enough for my baby.'

And Ostermilk her baby had, from that day onwards.

Solow, like all dachshunds, was fiercely protective. She always mistrusted men, and our builder friend Jim Aitken was nearly bitten when, discussing a new house, he leant over Eileen's shoulder to point out something on the plan.

❧

The garden at 149 had become too large to fit into our increasingly busy lives, and the field across the road had been sold for building. There was also talk of the Birmingham Road, on which we lived, being widened, so a move seemed advisable. The Aitken brothers had a plot of land available on a secluded site just off the next street. The plan for what they considered the 'perfect small house' only allowed for a small garden, backing onto the grounds of a big house with a magnificent copper beech and a huge silver birch whose naked branches, lit up by moonlight, were to enchant us on winter nights.

The grief of losing our first-ever home was balanced by the excitement of planning the new one, discussing minor adjustments with Jim and the architect, choosing carpets and curtains and bathroom fittings. Coming in halfway through a discussion between Eileen and Jim, I heard he had opted for a white bath, washbasin and loo. Now, nice bathrooms are things I get quite excited about, and I liked the shiny black fitments at 149. Noticing my despondency, Eileen questioned me as to its cause. 'It isn't important. I just don't like the idea of sitting on a white lavatory seat forever.'

How she laughed, as she reassured me that I should spend my future sitting on a shiny black lavatory seat, soaking in a bath with a shiny black surround, but the insides would be white, which was much, much cheaper than coloured baths and loos.

Selling a beloved home is always sad, but it can be fun. One learns to shrug off the snide remarks from would-be purchasers; it's all part of the business of trying to get the price reduced. It was interesting assessing the callers, sorting out those who meant business from the casuals who had seen our board while driving past, or to whom looking at houses was just a hobby, one with which we had a certain sympathy. We both knew what the wives were looking for, and what advantages to point out to them, and, having handled every aspect of the property, we also knew how to interest the husbands. We thus discovered that selling a house is another sphere in which two women can have the edge over a married couple, as each of us could operate on our own. We played a guessing game as to which couple we would hear from again, or which man would return with his wife, or vice versa. We were seldom wrong. Our profession had taught us to judge people fairly accurately, and to read their real thoughts behind whatever veneer they adopted. We knew it was the most critical who were the most serious, so did not resent them. Why bother to be nasty about a house in which you had no financial interest? Praise is easier, and we received plenty of that and lapped it up, because the house was very dear to us.

The new house was at the end of a cul-de-sac and, as Eileen and I passed up and down the short road to watch the building, we talked to our future neighbours as they worked in their front gardens, promising that they should see the completed house in which they showed such interest. We had hoped to be in by Christmas, but at the last minute the plasterer fell ill, leaving the hall and kitchen unfinished. What house-wife could face Christmas without a kitchen? Jim had promised and Jim would not let us down. The trade union leaders would have been horrified to see, as we did, a builder plastering, and a carpenter painting, but the house was finished on time.

Soon after Christmas we gave a small party for our immediate neighbours. Ours was the last plot on the estate, and those people had been living in close prox-imity for at least a year. To our horror, and their shame, we found ourselves introducing them to each other. That evening, in that new house of the newest residents, the road became a neighbourhood, and a seed was sown that developed within weeks into shared hospitality, mutual help, and the forging of deep and lasting friendships.

About this time I acquired a new baby of my own. When the first Mini was on view in the Austin show-rooms in Leamington I went to see it. It was love at first sight. While I yearned over the enchanting little car, I heard Dr Brand's voice behind me.

'Playing truant this morning, Miss Corbally?'

I turned to meet the twinkling eyes of the MOH.

'Not really, it is a baby, after all. May I chalk it up as an official visit?'

'You may not, this isn't your district,' he grinned. 'What do you think of her?'

'Heaven.'

Man-like, he was examining the engine.

'Why not have one?' He emerged from under the bonnet. 'Have you paid off the loan on your present car?'

'Two years ago.'

'Good. Then you can trade it in, in part exchange, and get a loan for the balance. I'll fix it with the treasurer if you like.'

Did I like? He fixed it, and in due course I took delivery of my blue Mini, and drove it proudly from village to village, the envy and admiration of all. Filling her up at a garage in Lapfold, I received a delightful tribute.

'If she goes as pretty as she looks, she must be a good goer.'

24

Sons and Mothers

Letters were easier to deal with than telephone calls, provided they explained all the problems clearly and were explicit about the needs to be met. They allowed time to think them over and form some sort of plan before visiting. A telephone conversation could trap one into unwise decisions or promises.

Mrs Pitman's letter was perfectly clear. Her mother-in-law had just come down from Manchester to be near her son and his family, and had bought a flat in Dodsworth. She was nearly eighty and not very strong, so would I please arrange for the services of a home help, and meals-on-wheels, and anything that might contribute to her comfort and well-being.

It was a charming flat on the first floor of an attractive block, surrounding a peaceful secluded garden. The flats consisted of a good-sized bedroom, sitting room, a small kitchen and bathroom. Mrs Pitman senior admitted to having been 'a bit tired and rundown' after the effort of packing up the Manchester house, and her daughter-in-law was inclined to fuss a bit anyhow. She agreed that she was well able to keep her little flat clean and would enjoy doing a bit of cooking in her tiny kitchen. She didn't eat big meals, and would be having her Sunday dinner with her family, and there was a little café round the corner if she was feeling lazy. She smiled self-consciously.

'I am a bit of an old lazybones, you know, but I mustn't pander to "No, Mrs Pitman, you mustn't or you'll become really old." There's nothing more ageing than having nothing to do all day.'

I rang her daughter-in-law to tell her I'd been to the flat.

'Oh good. So you have everything laid on for Mother?'

'Actually, no. I've laid nothing on. Your mother-in-law seems perfectly able to do her own bit of cleaning and cooking, and is quite happy to do so.'

'But she's nearly eighty. She's entitled to have help.'

'It isn't a case of what she's entitled to, but what is the best thing for her. If she has to shop she'll go out and meet people and get exercise and fresh air. Besides, she admits to being lazy, and if she has nothing to get up for she probably wouldn't bother, and nothing could be worse, at her age, than staying in bed all day.'

I promised to look in every few months, and if the old lady deteriorated any help would, of course, be provided as it became necessary. But I felt, and was proved right, that old Mrs Pitman had many years ahead of active and fully independent living.

I always found it heart-warming when sons and daughters showed concern for their elderly parents, but it wasn't always easy for them to see that their careful plans, with so much caring love behind them, were not only resented by the old folk but were often not, in fact, conducive to their well-being or happiness.

'I can't put my mother in a home,' said some, when the alternative was loneliness or the torment of knowing herself to be a burden on her family. There was also the chorus, 'She can't live by herself.'

It was late in the afternoon when I called on Mrs Owen, at her son's request. Would I try and persuade her to move, he had asked, she wasn't fit to be alone and they knew of a nice home where she'd be well cared for. I was warmly welcomed and led into the sitting room – an old lady's sitting room – full of bits of furniture collected over the years, of treasures and souvenirs from long-past holidays, of useless little gifts made or given, with love, by children and grandchildren, of photos, photos everywhere, of her dead husband, of her children's weddings, of her grandchildren, of a succession of beloved dogs. I admired the treasures, enquired about the children and listened to the histories of some cherished knick-knacks.

'You'll stay and have lunch with me, my dear?'

The invitation surprised me, and I glanced at the old carriage clock on the mantelpiece; it said 12.15.

'Haven't you had lunch, Mrs Owen? It's nearly three o'clock.'

She walked over to look closer at the clock, picked it up and held it to her ear.

'Dear me, it must have stopped.' She gave a little chuckle. 'Nearly three o'clock, you say? I wondered why I was feeling so hungry. I thought the morning had seemed unusually long.'

I would have left her to get her long overdue meal, but she insisted that I should accompany her to the kitchen, where I sat at the table and watched her make some toast and scrambled egg.

'You can't run away yet, you've only just come.'

The dust lying thickly in the sitting room, the unswept carpet, the dingy curtains hanging crookedly, framing grimy windows, had not prepared me for the filth of that kitchen. Grease lay thick over the cooker, it was splashed over the walls, mouldy sandwiches lay beside an open bottle of sour milk on the stained table-cloth, bundles of old newspapers covered every available chair and spilled onto the dirty floor, and, in a corner, the decaying body of a mouse was squashed in a trap. Although the window was open, the smell was indescribable. Mrs Owen seemed quite unaware of the squalor as she put a second cup and saucer on the tray and carried it through to the sitting room.

'I never eat in the kitchen,' she explained. 'One must keep up one's standards.'

Standards! I observed her closely as she poured out the tea. Tall and gaunt, thick glasses indicating bad eyesight, long fingers knotted with arthritis, a once-good tweed skirt, soiled faded jumper and matching cardigan from which two buttons were missing. The thinning grey hair was well brushed, her skin clean, and a faint scent of lavender emanated from her. There was a gentle happiness in her smile, and utter serenity in her manner.

'Did Elsa ask you to call?' she asked.

'Your daughter-in-law? Yes. I think they're a bit worried about you.'

'I know. They keep on at me to move. I'm not moving anywhere.'

For a moment her hand tightened on the ivory-handled knife.

'This is my home. My children were born here. My husband died here. All my life is contained in these walls.'

As I put down my cup, she reached out and caught my hand.

'You look a kind person. You won't let them put me out, will you?'

I laid my free hand on hers and pressed it.

'No one can put you out, but as to them worrying, that's as it should be. Your son ought to be concerned about you.'

She nodded slowly, helping herself to an overripe banana.

'Yes. Victor's a good son, but that wife of his . . . I'm sure she means well, poor girl, but I dread her visits. She does go on so, says the place is dirty. What business is it of hers?'

'None, really. It's certainly none of mine, but I could get someone to come in twice a week and clean through for you. Would you like that?'

The eyes behind the thick lenses roved round the room, perhaps seeing it as I saw it, and not over proud of what they saw.

'That would be nice. It's not easy to get anyone to help these days. I can afford to pay.'

I knew the type, proud, independent. She'd pay her way if she had to starve to do it.

'Would she cook?' she asked.

'I doubt if she could give you that much time. It's quite a big house to keep clean. But I could arrange for meals-on-wheels to be brought to you, that would be three good dinners a week.'

She smiled a gentle, happy smile.

'That would be a treat. I've never liked cooking.'

She took my hand in both of hers.

'I'm glad you called. I had no idea such nice things could happen to me.'

I returned her smile.

'I'm glad too. What about your shopping? Does your daughter-in-law do it for you?'

'Sometimes, but she doesn't always get what I want, but what she thinks I ought to have.' She laughed, a delightful, naughty little laugh. 'It's like being a little girl again. "Eat up your vegetables, they're good for you", remember? And we had to eat our crusts, to make our hair curl. Mine never did. I used to think how lovely it would be to be grown-up and eat what one wanted.'

'What sort of food do you like?'

'Cakes and biscuits. They're easy, don't need cooking. But Elsa will buy me meat and vegetables and fish. Luckily I have a kind neighbour who always looks in before she goes to the shops.'

A kind neighbour, a home help, meals-on-wheels and a caring son in the vicinity. We seemed to have all the ingredients needed to keep Mrs Owen in her own home for as long as she chose to stay.

I went straight round to the daughter-in-law to tell her I had called on the old lady. She was most grateful.

'And has she agreed to go into the home?'

'I didn't suggest it, Mrs Owen. She made it quite clear that she wants to stay in her own house.'

'But she can't. The place is a pigsty. You've seen it.'

'I agree it's not very savoury at the moment, but I'll arrange for a home help to go in – she'll soon get it cleaned up.'

'She's not getting enough to eat. She's like a scarecrow.'

'The meals-on-wheels service will provide her with three good meals a week, and the home help will keep an eye on the larder. If she has plenty of eggs and cheese and milk and a few tins of soup she'll not do so badly.'

Young Mrs Owen looked disappointed.

'Oh well, if you think she'll be all right, I suppose we can let her stay there a bit longer. [As if they had a choice!] But I'm telling you I'm not happy about it. I've enough to do looking after my own home without running over to Mother every day.'

And much good your rushing to Mother has done her, I thought.

'That really won't be necessary. If I may give your telephone number to the home help she would let you know if your mother-in-law needed anything.'

She had kept me standing in the hall, and now moved to open the door.

'I'll visit her from time to time and keep in touch with you,' I promised.

Next time I called, the home help, Mrs Power, was just leaving. She had done wonders with the house, washed the curtains, cleaned the windows, and tidied up the kitchen, from which drifted the savoury smell of fish pie cooking in the oven for Mrs Owen's lunch. Mrs Power came on the days when the WVS didn't call, and usually found time to prepare a little dish. On Sundays the neighbours would often ask Mrs Owen to share their lunch with them, or would bring a ready-cooked meal across the garden, and occasionally her son would fetch her in his car to spend the day with them. Already the frail body was beginning to fill out, although her clothes still hung loosely, often torn and buttonless, held together with large safety pins. Although she wouldn't admit it, I guessed her sight was so poor that she was unable to thread a needle. Mrs Power was very concerned.

'When I come early and she's still in bed, I see her underclothes on the chair, so neat she puts them, but they're all torn and raggedy, not fit for a lady like her to be wearing.'

I called at Jermyn Street in the evening when Mr Owen was at home. He asked me in, calling to his wife, who was putting the children to bed, to come and join us. While we waited for her, he expressed his gratitude for the help I had organised for his mother.

'I still think she'd be better in a home,' said Mrs Owen as she came into the room. 'I grant you the house is cleaner, but she looks such a mess, so uncared for.'

'That's what I've come about, Mrs Owen. Perhaps you don't realise how bad her sight is. She can't manage things like sewing on buttons and mending torn hems, just little jobs that would make all the difference to her appearance. I thought, if you understood, you could do those little things for her next time you're over there.'

She sniffed, but said nothing. I hoped she felt ashamed. I turned to her husband.

'I was wondering about your mother's financial situation, Mr Owen. Mrs Power tells me her underclothing is in a shocking state. I'd gladly buy her the things she needs if she can afford them, but don't like to ask for the money in case it embarrasses her. Or perhaps your wife would prefer to see to it herself?'

I turned enquiringly to Mrs Owen. She looked at her husband, who appeared rather shocked.

'I had no idea. Did you know about this, Elsa?'

Another sniff. 'How could I know? You don't think I undress your mother when I go there, do you? Or go through her drawers?'

I didn't like the implication.

'Mrs Power often arrives before your mother is up. She brings a cup of tea to her room, and she noticed the clothes by the bed. Our home helps are encouraged to be observant.'

'Of course. Excellent woman.'

I could see Mr Owen was embarrassed by his wife's attitude.

'Mother's not rich, but she has enough to pay for what she needs. I've never interfered, although sometimes I wonder what she does with her money.'

'I was going to ask about that. I've explained to her about having the lunch money ready when the WVS call, but they tell me she is one of their worst defaulters.

Sometimes she seems to have no money in the house, and another day she'll be offering them wads of notes "for the poor old ladies who can't pay".'

'Oh dear. That sounds serious.'

'It's not an unusual picture. Old people do get careless about money, and your mother is, I imagine, a very generous person. She'd be an easy victim for any unscrupulous hoaxer who happened to call.'

'There you are!' Mrs Owen thumped the arm of her chair. 'I told you she was getting senile. That's it. She goes into the home.'

Mr Owen raised an admonitory hand. 'Quiet, Elsa dear. There's no need to get excited. Let's hear what Miss Corbally has to suggest.'

'The usual solution, in these circumstances, is for a member of the family or a solicitor to assume power of attorney. I was wondering if your mother would agree to such an arrangement.'

He nodded slowly. 'I don't see why not. It certainly seems the sensible thing to do. I'll look over on Saturday and have a talk, and go through her papers, and cheque book, make sure everything's in order, rates and taxes and all that, and no bills outstanding.'

'You were taking us shopping in Leamington on Saturday.' Mrs Owen's voice was shrill.

'I'm sorry, my dear, but this is important. You can go with the children, on the bus, and, while you're there, you can buy the new vests and other things for Mother. I'll give you the money.'

Mrs Owen was nearly in tears. 'I'll have my hands full with the children's shopping. Oh why can't she go?

It's one thing after another, nothing but worry. I can't stand any more of it.'

Mr Owen leant over and patted her hand. 'My wife's not very strong,' he said apologetically. 'I'm afraid, with me being at work, most of the burden of looking after Mother has fallen on her.'

Mrs Owen was crying now. 'All this worry, it's making me ill,' she sobbed.

Her husband withdrew his hand, his shoulders slumped. 'It is a worry,' he said to me. 'I know she's being properly cared for now, thanks to you, but at the back of our minds there's always the fear that something might happen. She could have a stroke, or fall down the stairs. One hears of old people being found dead. The thought of Mother being there alone, perhaps hurt and helpless . . . We'd never forgive ourselves.'

I shook my head.

'You wouldn't have anything to forgive, nothing to blame yourselves for. Such things can happen to anyone, of any age. If your mother was living here with you she could die of a heart attack while you were at work, and your wife out shopping. Of course you worry about it, but it's a risk she has chosen to take. She knows as well as you do what could happen, but whatever happens she wants it to be in her own home.'

'Does she really appreciate the risk she's taking?'

'She does. We've talked about it. Death, for the elderly, is often swift and merciful. Even if it is not to be, your mother is willing to take her chances. She considers a short spell of pain and fear preferable to months of homesick misery pining for her house and all her treasures. I say months, because I think the move would kill her.'

Mrs Owen remained in her home, and there was no more talk of moving her. Mrs Power found her one morning. She had died quietly in her sleep, happy and at peace, surrounded by all her beloved possessions, her cherished memories, in the room she had shared with her husband, where her children had been conceived and born.

It was to Mr Owen's credit that he was genuinely concerned to do what he thought was the best thing for his mother. He gave no thought to his own interest, and was happy that the money from the sale of his mother's house should keep her in comfort in the home he had chosen for her.

Mr Pugh's ideas were quite different. His mother lived in a modern three-bedroomed house in what the agents describe as 'a desirable residential area', and he was determined that there she should stay, lonely and unhappy though she was, struggling to exist on a breadline income, her pension drained away by exorbitant rates. Mr Pugh knew the value of that little property, and, as the only child, he knew it would be his when his mother died.

The old lady had come to hate the house. Most of the neighbours were out at work, and too busy with their own lives to bother with the lonely old lady in their midst. There was no money to spare for entertaining, for outings or holidays, barely enough for food, and heat was rationed, however cold the weather. Money wouldn't stretch to the twenty-four-hour all-round warmth needed by a rheumatic old body. I had told her about Mrs Gould, and taken her to see the house. She was just the sort of gentle frail little person that Mrs Gould loved to care for, and she was given the option of the next vacancy. The sale of her house would provide an annuity more than adequate for Mrs Gould's fees. Mrs Pugh was charmed with the set-up, and, on her return home, hobbled round the house selecting the furniture she would take with her.

'I can sell the rest, the money will come in handy when I move. My son has all he needs.'

It was good to see her pleasure at the prospect of a new life, a life of comfort and warmth and companionship.

'I've never minded waiting if there's been something good to wait for, to look forward to.'

Alas, her joy was short-lived. Her son would not hear of the move. She was too old and too tired to assert herself. He was all she had in the world, and she dared not risk a quarrel with him and his family. For her, his rare visits with her adored grandchildren were worth any sacrifice.

A long hard winter took its toll. The old lady was barely able to drag herself out of bed and crawl from room to room. How I wished Father Pat was still with us to support her with his practical kindness, his invigorating humour, and, literally, his strong arms, but, sadly for Kenilworth, the Irish curate had left us many years ago and was now in charge of his own parish in Ireland. The kindly bishop had left him with Canon Swift until his death, because 'the old man loved the boy', and the happy partnership had been replaced by one priest from a busy Birmingham parish which he no longer had the health to administer.

When Mrs Pugh was found on the floor, nearly dead from hypothermia, Leonard decided that she was really unfit to live alone. Loneliness, continual pain, and the heavy sedation necessitated by it, had begun to affect her mind, and she lived more and more in the past, unaware of where she was. Leonard asked Mr Pugh to call and see him. He told me later of the interview. He had recommended a nursing home, but Mr Pugh had appeared shocked.

'My mother hasn't got that sort of money,' he said.

Leonard suggested that if the house were sold, the money would be available. It wouldn't be for long. Mr Pugh wouldn't hear of it.

'What have I been paying National Health contributions for all these years? What are hospitals for?'

'Have you ever seen a geriatric ward?' Leonard asked.

'They're for old people, aren't they? My mother's old. You say she needs care, so it is up to you to find her a bed.'

It appeared his wife had the grace to look ashamed. She pleaded for some compassion.

'We can find the money. Doctor says it won't be for long. There is a tidy bit in the school fund, and we can put it back when you sell the house.'

It was to no avail. He chided her for her soft heart.

'It's a good thing our children have a father to look after their interests.'

How we wished that Mrs Pugh's solicitor, and not her son, had taken over the power of attorney when her mind began to fail. A humane man, he would have seen to it that his client's last months were spend in comfort and dignity. Leonard had no choice but to arrange her admission to a geriatric ward, where she died. Her son never visited her there. Perhaps, after all, he may have been just a little bit ashamed.

25

No Possible Answer

$$\approx\!\!\text{❦}\!\!\approx$$

I first met Phyllis Watts when I was visiting the rehabilitation huts at Hatton Mental Hospital, where one
of my mothers was readjusting to caring for her six-
month-old baby after a severe attack of post-natal
depression.

I had found Mrs Wills in tears when her third baby
was nearly four months old. With an extra child to
support, her conscientious husband was working over-
time, leaving her on her own evening after evening,
and the children virtually fatherless. It was patently
obvious that his family needed his presence in the
home far more than the extra income he was bringing
in, but no one, least of all his grateful wife, had thought
to tell him so.

Apart from the tears (to which I was accustomed, as
extra-busy days and disturbed nights succeeding the
euphoria of childbirth often causes a period of mild
depression which is relieved by a good weep on a
sympathetic shoulder) there was a trapped, hunted
look in Mrs Wills's eyes which worried me. I well knew
of this form of puerperal mania with its terrible risk to

both mother and baby, and, indeed, to other children in the family. One had read horrifying stories of mass murder of helpless children and of the mother's suicide in an attack of this nature, and I was always on guard for early symptoms. I would be alerted by more-than-normal depression, by too-frequent attacks of weeping, loss of appetite, agoraphobia with its complications of unreplenished larders, children missing school, and all the other non-happenings resultant on a mother being unable to set foot outside her own door. There was naked fear in Mrs Wills's tear-filled eyes as she pushed the trembling baby into my arms.

'Take him,' she whispered. 'Please take him. Don't let me hurt him. I'm so afraid.'

Dr John was out, and there seemed little hope of a visit before the evening, but a telephone call to her mother in the next village brought her hurrying over, and I knew the threatened family could be safely left in her care. I made her promise never to leave her daughter on her own with the baby, as the risk of her harming him was terrifyingly real. On the doctor's advice Mr Wills gave up overtime working, so that he could spend as much time as possible with his wife and share the burden of the children and the home under which she was breaking. Alas, it was too late. Sedation at home was inadequate, and, after an attempt to slash her wrists, Mrs Wills was admitted to Hatton Hospital.

As we walked together through the extensive and colourful grounds of the hospital on that sunny afternoon, wheeling the baby in his pram, I noticed a young couple sitting on one of the benches, deep in conversation, and was struck by the sweetness of the girl's smile as her eyes met mine. They both stood up as we approached, and came over to see and admire the baby, and the girl's lovely eyes were soft and moist with longing. I noticed, and was touched by the sensitivity of the young man's awareness of her emotion, and the gentleness with which he drew her away as Mrs Wills tucked up her little son again, and prepared to move on. Her cure was almost complete, and she told me of the happy afternoon she had spent the previous day with all her family round her.

Later that morning I was in the office of my friend and colleague, Miss Waldron, the hospital almoner. We were trying to arrange a date, mutually convenient, for her to visit Mrs Wills's home with me before the mother was discharged.

'I'm rather tied up at present, with the wedding on the twenty-fourth. Shall we say the twenty-sixth, in the afternoon?'

I marked it in my diary.

'A family wedding? What fun.'

'Oh no,' she smiled. 'Nothing so simple. It's young Phyllis Watts, one of our patients. She's marrying Paul Wenlock, also a patient.'

'Great Scott!'

No doubt I sounded and looked as shocked as I felt. She shrugged her shoulders.

'I know. We've tried to discourage it, but we can't refuse. Even mental patients have rights, and they're very much in love, always around together. You may have seen them? A pretty, fair girl with lovely eyes and the sweetest smile, probably wearing a pink blouse and linen skirt. Paul's a stolid young man, dark, with a small moustache.'

I nodded. I recognised the couple on the bench.

'They looked pretty normal to me. In fact, they struck me as rather delightful people.'

'They are. When they're normal they're particularly nice, but ... you know the old song "when she was good, she was very, very good, but when she was bad she was horrid". They're both depressives. Phyllis gets miserable and weepy, and suicidal, but Paul can be violent. We let him out from time to time, and he gets a job. We have contacts with employers, and he's a very likeable person. All goes swimmingly for a few weeks, then someone upsets him, and wham! He's back in again, via the police station on an assault charge.'

'What about Phyllis? Does she ever get home?'

'Rarely. Hopeless parents. There's a younger son, whom they adore. They never had much use for their girl, except as a nursemaid to her little brother, but they pressurised her at school. She's not stupid, but she's not all that brilliant, and couldn't take it. She was sixteen when she was first brought to us, after an overdose. Every time she goes home the tensions build up again. They do their best, so does the brother; he's grown-up now, but somehow it doesn't work out.'

I understood. I'd watched the beginnings of just such situations in other families, and tried to prevent a similar build-up.

'Where will they live after the marriage? Here?'

'Phyllis's parents have a small furnished cottage which they're going to rent to them. The wedding will be here. That's what's keeping me so busy.'

She smiled warmly.

'I'm rather enjoying it really. Not many spinsters get the fun of planning a full-scale wedding, and I'm really very fond of them both.' She sighed. 'I hope it works. I hope it will be the right thing for them. It just could be, but . . . one can't help wondering.'

My mind had leapt forward, remembering the pink-bloused figure yearning over the pram.

'Suppose there's a baby?'

My friend chuckled as the striking clock brought her to her feet, grabbing case notes from the desk for the meeting in a neighbouring office.

'If there's a baby, Miss Corbally, that will be your headache. The cottage is in Lapfold.'

Few villages look kindly on weekenders, but when Lapfold learnt that the cottage by the woods was to be occupied permanently by a couple straight out of Hatton, the village was less than pleased. How anyone found out about the Wenlocks I never knew, but a village grapevine is the most efficient finder-outer and distributor of news ever invented. There is a saying that if you want an item of news spread quickly you 'telegram, telephone, or tell-a-woman'. I would add 'tell-a-villager'.

The people of Lapfold were not unkind; it was, normally, a welcoming community into which newcomers were accepted and absorbed from the moment of arrival. But they were afraid of the Wenlocks. It was an unknown situation, which they treated warily. There had been stories of strange sights and happenings in the woods round Hatton Hospital and the children of Lapfold were forbidden to play in the little spinney behind the newcomers' cottage. In spite of the recent change of staff at the school, the village still observed the countryman's code of good manners. No bricks were thrown through the window, no slogans daubed on the cottage walls, but nobody called to see the newly married couple, and, when they appeared at the Post Office or the village stores, conversation would stop and other customers would drift away. The Wenlocks seemed quite impervious to their unpopularity. They were accustomed to far stranger behaviour in the community where they had been living, and they were happy to be left alone to enjoy the bliss of their own home, of their freedom, of the wide open countryside where they could wander at will, eating when they were hungry, going to bed when they were tired, emancipated from the regulations and routine of hospital life.

Three months after the marriage, Dr John sent for me.

'We've got a problem, Miss Corbally. Mrs Wenlock was in this morning. She's pregnant.'

He leant his elbows on the table, running his fingers through his hair. 'What are we going to do? She shouldn't have the baby, of course.'

I remembered the yearning eyes in the grounds of Hatton Hospital. 'Is she happy about it?'

'Ecstatic,' he moaned. 'She was so excited when I told her, I couldn't think of suggesting . . .' he paused. I knew how his mind was working.

'Termination? Oh no, you can't do that to her.'

'But it's an impossible situation, with that history. Both parents.'

'Is it? I mean, it just might be a good thing for her, the achievement of motherhood, and having someone dependent on her, needing her?' There was a question in my voice. He sighed deeply, reaching out a hand for the case notes.

'You could be right. A baby might help her, but . . . it takes nine months to make a baby.' He thumped the table as his voice rose. 'At least seven more blasted months to go, and she's a chronic depressive. What am I to do?'

'You mean the drugs?'

'Of course I mean the drugs, damn it! To withhold them could be disastrous, and yet I dare not keep her on them.'

The thalidomide tragedy was still fresh in all our minds, and all doctors were aware of the risk to the baby of prescribing any tranquillisers for an expectant mother. He jabbed a finger at the case notes.

'The mind boggles at what this lot could do to that baby. And then, what? Can you see that couple coping with a severely disabled child? That is, presuming there'd be a couple left to cope. The shock would probably drive her to suicide.'

Seven months. It seemed interminable. But . . .

'Have you stopped the drugs?'

'Yes. I've rung Hatton, and expect her psychiatrist to ring me this evening.'

'It's your decision though?'

300

He nodded. His eyes met mine.

'What do you think?'

'I think that you and I and Mrs Wenlock can see this through together. I think she's intelligent enough to understand the situation, and gutsy enough to co-operate as far as she can.'

'Agreed. But how far can she co-operate?'

'You say she's excited about her pregnancy, and I'm sure she is. Don't you think this euphoria could tide her over for a bit? One month anyhow? Perhaps two?'

He nodded slowly. 'Could do. She was certainly over the moon this morning.'

'I'll keep in close touch. There'll be the excitement of buying the baby clothes, and making them. There's not much money available, I can probably rustle up a second-hand pram, and a cot. We can take it slowly, spread it out over the weeks.'

He nodded thoughtfully. 'It could work, but not for ever. Two months at the outside. Then what? We've still have another five to go.' His shoulders slumped as his hand slapped down on the case notes. 'It's impossible. We'll never get her through.'

My mind had been working on all possibilities of excitement and distraction. 'I could probably arrange a holiday for them both. They never had a honeymoon. Couldn't afford it. I'll get in touch with the Rotary Club or the Round Table. A couple of weeks in the fifth or sixth month. If we can fix it. Looking forward to that should keep her head above water.'

He smiled suddenly. 'Marvellous idea! Could you really do that?'

'I'm sure I could. The only snag of this treatment would be the side effects, the post-holiday blues which are experienced by everyone.'

'I think it's worth it. By that time she should be well into the sixth or seventh month, and the risk posed by the drugs would be greatly reduced.'

Phyllis Wenlock was determined to have a perfect baby, and Paul supported her with his love, and his own bubbling excitement. Having been stripped of his self-confidence by so many failures in life, he regarded his paternity as his first real achievement, and for that reason alone it was vital that nothing should go wrong. With that in mind, coupled with her own longing for the baby and concern for its well-being, Phyllis fought against her illness. We fought together. When she felt threatened by a wave of depression she would ring me up and we would plan a visit to Mothercare in Leamington, or the WVS store in Warwick, to rummage among pram covers and tiny blankets, or I would just call round and let her talk to me. The holiday was a tremendous event and eagerly looked forward to by them both. Black moods were dispelled by looking at pictures of the guest house where they were to stay, and of the small seaside town. Phyllis had never had a seaside holiday and her excitement was a joy to see. How blessed are our charitable organisations that can provide such happiness, and how fortunate the health visitors and social workers who are privileged to confer it.

Naturally, Phyllis wanted to share her great news. She told the postmistress, who had always been kind to the shy, insecure young bride. The postmistress, need-less to say, told everyone, who told everyone else. New young life, lambs and calves, piglets, foals and chickens are of the very essence of country life, and a new baby is always an event in a rural community. Suddenly, the Wenlocks were acceptable. They had, after all, turned out to be perfectly harmless and inoffensive, and now the little wife was expecting a baby, and her husband wasn't working.

'Poor man, how could he, under the circumstances?' To my delight, Lapfold decided to 'adopt' the Wenlocks. The spinney echoed again to children's shouts and laughter. Neighbours dropped in for a cup of tea and a chat. Vegetables and fruit in season, eggs and bunches of wild flowers appeared on the doorstep, blackberries picked by the children in the hedges and kindling wood collected in the spinney. The village started knitting. The crafts class of the WI were making a basketwork cot, lining and decorating it. Mrs Russell, aware of the enormity of the problem, arranged to keep Phyllis occupied. She and Mrs Roche-Anderson planned little social afternoons in their houses, whist drives and beetle drives and housey-housey (which was to grow into bingo), while Paul was coaxed out by the boys onto the playing field, and Miss Waldron and I held our breath lest some cheeky youngster might inadvert-ently trigger off one of those dreaded rages.

The whole village might have been going on that holiday. It was the main topic of conversation, and little presents kept turning up at the cottage: cakes and biscuits and sweets 'for the journey', dark glasses, suntan lotion, toilet bags, books and magazines 'to read on the beach'.

At Hatton Hospital, a delighted Miss Waldron supplied a generous sum of holiday spending money for the couple, with whom she still kept in touch and in whose welfare she was deeply concerned. The sun shone for them, the landlady could not do enough for them, and they returned home relaxed and well, with pictures to show and stories to tell of their great adventure.

The baby, a girl, was club-footed, a minor deformity, easily corrected, but the effect on Paul of this small imperfection was catastrophic. He castigated himself. He couldn't do anything right, not even father a perfect child. He blamed his wife, who had been obliged to resume her treatment in the later months. He totally rejected the baby, and would not hold her, nor even touch her. Phyllis blamed nobody, and doted on her little girl, co-operating most efficiently with the hospital's instructions in gently massaging and manipulating the little feet. She breastfed successfully, and the baby was as healthy and contented as any on my district, and, fortunately, cried very rarely.

But if little Georgina did cry, Paul would walk out of the cottage, at any hour of the day or night. As far as possible, he ignored the fact of the baby's existence, and would not have her in the same room with him. His tenderness to his wife had in no way diminished, and he seemed unaware how deeply his attitude was hurting her. His antagonism to Georgina, who he saw as a blow to his self-esteem, was fed by his jealousy of

Phyllis's absorption in the baby. He resented any reminder of the child's existence, and even the sight of nappies drying on the line could send him into a paroxysm of rage. His illness showed itself in a ritualistic obsession. Everything had to be in exactly the right place, in exactly the same order, meticulously aligned, and Phyllis nearly broke down under the strain of caring for her baby and keeping her husband happy.

Miss Waldron rang me up to tell me that she had moved Phyllis and the baby to her mother's house as a temporary measure. It was not ideal. The grandparents were fond enough of Georgina, but not over-enthusiastic about having their comfortable lives disrupted for any length of time by a small baby and a temperamental daughter they had never really loved. Phyllis was intensely loyal to Paul and would go to the cottage every day to tidy it up and prepare a meal for him, leaving the baby with her parents. It was becoming painfully clear to us all that, the older the baby grew, the more important it was to keep her and her father apart. A small baby, immobile in a cot, was one thing. A toddler, interfering with his meticulous arrangements as she moved freely round the cottage, would be at risk of incurring his anger, that terrible sudden anger that could have tragic, even fatal results. It was a risk that could not be taken.

I attended a meeting at Hatton Hospital with Miss Waldron, the psychiatrist, and Dr John, and we all came away with aching hearts knowing that there was no solution to the problem of the Wenlock family. Phyllis herself had been with us for part of the meeting, to discuss frankly her own feelings and wishes. One thing was obvious. She would have to choose between Paul and Georgina. The three of them could not share a home. She was, understandably, unhappy staying with her parents, and that situation could not last much longer. She could not bring Georgina back to the cottage while Paul was there. She would not be parted from her baby, who was her whole world. She still loved her husband, and could not accept the only possible solution, a legal separation, which would enable her to bring her child up in peace in her own home.

I left the Midlands not long after that meeting, and so I never knew what happened to the Wenlocks. I have to confess, I could have found out, but I didn't really want to know. We always like there to be the perfect solution to these problems, but sometimes there is simply no answer.

26

Nannies and Grannies

The nannies of my acquaintance varied from the old-fashioned, grey-suited, white-aproned wise guardians who had watched over the childhood of my own contemporaries, to the young girl from the village, just out of school, who came in to help a young mother, not so long out of school herself. If I'd had my way, I would have teamed up the young and very new mother with the wise and experienced old nanny, and the mature mother of two or three children with the young girl from the village. Unfortunately such arrangements are not made on the ground of suitability, but, like many others, on the grounds of finance, and the income of a first-time father would rarely stretch to the wages of an experienced nanny.

The old-time nanny was hard to come by at the end of the Second World War, but I did have the good fortune to meet the odd one on my rounds. I never really got to know them, as follow-up visits in such establishments would have been an impertinence. While I was still in the cradle, these women knew more about babies than I would ever learn. They'd not learnt it from books or lectures, but from one another, and from the children themselves. I doubt if they could spell 'psychology', yet no professional could improve on the technique of one particular nanny who watched, in silence, a display of bad temper by a visiting cousin in her nursery. Stamping, banging doors and kicking at the furniture, the ten year old thought she had put up quite a show – but it didn't last. By the evening, having supper over the nursery fire, too old for early bed with her small cousin, too young for dining-room dinner, she remembered her naughtiness with a shamefaced little laugh.

'I was in a bad temper this morning, wasn't I, Nanny?'

'Eat up your soup dear, it will make you grow tall. Were you in a temper, dear? I hadn't noticed.'

No reprimand, no punishment could have supplied more salutary lesson, or more effectively cut a cross little girl down to size. I know. I was that visiting cousin.

When, as a health visitor, I was first confronted by this same, familiar white-aproned figure, I felt very humble. The mother was out, and Nanny listened courteously as I explained the reason for my visit, and brought me up to the nursery to see her charge. I thought, if I was very good, I might be allowed to hold the baby for a few minutes, if I sat in a chair and promised not to move. But the baby was asleep so we admired from the cotside.

'Just like her mother as a baby. She was the first baby I took from the mother.'

Lucky baby, I thought. Lucky mother. Tea was brought to us, strong nursery tea, and a slice of fruitcake, which I didn't want, but knew I had to eat.

Nannies like to see 'a clean plate'. I left a note on the hall table for the mother, enclosing my telephone number and the times of the local clinic, and the record card for vaccination and immunisation. Much that was new in baby care had developed since Nanny had taken her first baby from the mother and I hoped her one-time nursling would be allowed some say in the management of this new-generation baby.

Professional mothers who continued to work would be apt to confide their children to highly trained Norland Nannies, and I would enjoy meeting this new brand of nanny and hearing about their training and their theories. The children were safe with them if the mothers were out all day, but those in their first job always welcomed my visits and the knowledge that I was always available on the end of a telephone. I know how they felt. I remembered my first experience as a private nurse. You think you know it all. You probably *do* know it all. But it can be frightening to find yourself solely responsible for a patient, or baby, with no one to turn to for advice. It is important to appear confident and capable, to have an answer to all the questions, but it is comforting to be able to check with someone else that they are the *right* answers. Unfortunately, in our delightful but unexciting villages, Norland Nannies didn't stay long. The whole world was open to them, and, after a year or two gaining experience and self-confidence, they would turn their sights to London or the continent, or both.

More frequent were the mothers' helps – raw untrained girls whose only qualification was a love of children. Gay young mothers, busy with their social life or wrapped up in their charities and committees, were in blissful ignorance of just how little these girls knew. The mothers themselves were not all that knowledgeable, so I had a dual task in such establishments, making sure that I found the mother at home from time to time, and filling her in on the advice and guidance I felt she would do well to pass on to her nanny. These girls rarely lasted long. They would leave the village for a job with better prospects and more money, or get married, and the experience gained was invaluable when their own babies came along. Au pairs from France or Germany would fill in during the summer, and the 'poor little rich children' sorted themselves out as best they could with constant changes of guardians, of routine, of values and priorities.

It was a Norland Nanny who brought Lady Merlin's three-month-old grandson on a visit to the Hall while his mother accompanied her husband on a business trip to France. Granny rang me up.

'Could you possibly call and see me after the clinic tomorrow? I've got my grandson here, and I am a bit worried about him.'

My heart sank. I didn't know about the nurse.

'Why not bring him to the clinic? Dr Lang could give him a check-up if you like.'

'Oh no.'

Her voice was sharp. I smiled to myself. Clinics, to her, were for 'the cottagers', not for her grandchild. She had never seen Lapfold clinic.

'I would prefer it if you would call here. Come to tea.'

I went to tea . . . and what a tea! Scones, sandwiches, cakes. I was told about the nurse.

'The girl is taking a day off tomorrow.' She sounded aggrieved. 'How things have changed. My nanny never had a day off. She had her holiday, of course, by the sea, with the children, and spent a few days each year with her sister. The housemaid took over then, she was the eldest of a big family and experienced with children.'

So was Rita, I thought, but Rita had been dismissed.

'The trouble is, I don't know how I'll manage. I never looked after my own children. There will be napkins and bottles and things. What am I going to do?'

'Have you asked Nurse to show you?'

'Of course not. I would feel such a fool asking that chit of a girl to show me how to change a baby's napkin.' She paused, looking at me over the rim of her teacup. 'I thought perhaps you . . .'

I smiled, and put down my cup.

'Shall we go up to the nursery after tea? I would love to meet your grandson.'

The nurse was delighted to see us. It was nearly feeding time and the routine of changing and feeding was about to begin. A charming, intelligent young girl, she was obviously aware of the grandmother's inadequacy, but afraid of causing offence to the rather fierce old lady by offering to instruct her. Tactfully, slowly, she changed and cleaned the baby and made up the feed, explaining every detail of the process in response to my questions, while Granny watched and listened.

'I am so interested in your techniques,' I said, as we exchanged a wink behind her ladyship's back. 'Methods are changing all the time, and what I learn from you nurses I can pass onto my young mothers.'

The baby was ready, clean, sweet-smelling, yelling with hunger. The nurse held him out.

'Would you like to feed him, Lady Merlin?'

Before Granny could answer the baby was already in her arms, and, willy-nilly, she had the bottle in her hand. As the yells ceased and her grandson sucked happily, his blue eyes gazing up into her face, her tenseness eased, she smiled down at him, held him closer. The nurse was busy making up the cot. I tilted the bottle gently.

'Try and keep it at an angle, keep the base solid with milk so that he is not sucking in air.'

'Am I doing all right?' she whispered.

'You're doing splendidly.'

I was in the village next day and looked in to see how things were going. I found Lady Merlin kneeling on the floor where her grandchild sprawled, kicking and gurgling, reaching out to the multi-coloured knitted ball she was rolling towards him. She looked up at me, her face radiant.

'Grandmothering hour,' she said.

'No problems? He's been good?'

'He's been perfect.' She picked up the baby and cuddled him to her, her cheek resting on the downy head. 'Thank heaven for modern nannies and their ridiculous days off.'

Nannies I could get along with. I either left them alone or provided unobtrusive support as long as it was required. Grannies were something quite different.

Grannies had reared families, or a proportion of them. I never see why the claim to have 'had ten and reared six' qualified them to advise their daughters and daughters-in-law, who wanted to have three and rear them all. No doubt they thought, and sometimes said, that, having had none and reared none, I didn't qualify to give advice. At least I hadn't lost any, which perhaps balanced things up.

Granny Mills really terrified me. She always answered the door, and answered all my questions curtly, at times rudely, while her daughter-in-law sat silent and embarrassed. When, at last, I persuaded her to bring the baby to the clinic, it was Granny who undressed him. When I pointedly asked the mother to bring her baby to the scales, Granny marched up with him. She sensed my disapproval and was on the defensive.

'She's so ham-fisted. We'd be here all day if I didn't help her.'

Granny Mills didn't hold with clinics. She thought it unlucky for babies to be weighed, but I had been seriously concerned about the baby's feeding and had enlisted Leonard's help to overrule her superstition. But neither he nor I could get the baby to the clinic during the winter. When, worried by the infant's pallor and persistent cough, I had asked him to call in, he had found his patient sewn up for the winter in flannel, the removal of which was almost forcibly resisted by the grandmother.

He was almost knocked backwards by the reek of the stale goose grease, which was smeared over the tiny chest. The overheated skin was causing irritation and

313

was crisscrossed with scratches on the few areas where the baby could make contact. Granny Mills would not allow the baby's nails to be cut. To cut a baby's nails in the first year would 'turn it into a thief', she informed me, adding for good measure that her third child had grown up a stammerer because, while she was in hospital as a baby, some foolish nurse had cut her nails on a Sunday. I refrained from asking if she stole as well as stammered. The old lady had a poor opinion of nurses and midwives, particularly the one who had delivered her first grandchild.

'That child won't come to no good,' she predicted sourly. 'He'll come a cropper in life, never make anything of hisself, you mark my words. That stupid woman brought him straight downstairs to show his father. *He* should have gone *up*.'

I asked a silly question.

'But he was born on the first floor. How could he have gone up?'

She looked at me pityingly.

'On a chair, of course, same as all mine were carried. The first journey has to be up if they're to get on in the world, or rise to Heaven in the next,' she added darkly.

Granny Mills didn't hold with fresh air, or vitamins, or injections.

'None of mine ever had the needle, and look at that Perry child down the road, nothing but coughs and colds since her vaccination. Much good it's done *her*.'

'She wasn't vaccinated against colds, Mrs Mills, but against smallpox and she hasn't had smallpox.'

She snorted. Young Mrs Mills was hovering by the door. I moved to join her, and we walked to the car together. She was at the end of her patience. She was an intelligent girl and had read carefully the booklets I had left with her, and listened to the advice I had tried to get across, but she couldn't stand up to her forceful mother-in-law, in whose house they lived. Her husband was trying to be loyal to his wife and his mother, but he too was concerned about their baby's welfare, and the stress was beginning to show. The situation was becoming intolerable. If they didn't get a home of their own soon, where they could bring up their baby in their own way, the family would break up. She would have to take the baby away, but where could she go? They were a long way down on the housing list, as they had a reasonable home, structurally and statistically.

My friend, the housing manager, was understanding. Emotional stress was not an item that figured on his 'points' list, but he moved the Mills right up to the top, and they were given the very next vacancy, which, fortunately, was on an estate the other side of the town from Granny.

Grannies come in two packets. They are either mothers or mothers-in-law, and they all adore their grandchildren, spoil them outrageously, and many of them overwhelm the young mothers with their theories on how the grandchildren should be brought up, forgetting that their grandchildren are somebody else's children. Inevitably one granny's ideas would conflict with the other granny's ideas, with the doctor's, with mine, with anything the young mothers would have absorbed from reading and discussion, and conflicts would arise within the family, and a harassed young mother would pour out to me all the pent-up irritation.

'She forgets I'm grown-up now, and this is my baby.'

'I don't want to upset Richard, but I'm sick to death of hearing about his early years, how he was fed, and dressed, etc. This isn't her Richard, it's our Philip, Richard's and mine . . . not hers.'

My advice was always, 'The grannies only want to be helpful because they love you and the baby, so listen politely, make them happy by saying "yes" in the right places and appearing interested. There may be real wisdom in what they say. Accept what seems good to you, ignore the rest, and, when they've gone, continue to bring up your baby in your own way.'

I had no doubt that was precisely what was happening to my own advice in many of the homes I visited, and it was right that it should be so.

Perfect grannies lived too far away for dropping in, but near enough to be reached by an insecure and anxious young mother, to babysit in the evenings, or take over the children for a day. Perfect grannies were not too free with their advice, aware that ideas had changed since their own children were babies. Some would even ring me up.

'I wonder if you could drop a hint next time you call on my daughter. I don't like to interfere, but . . .'

Resident grannies would be out of their depth in a changing world of disposable nappies, unboiled feeding bottles, Babygros instead of flannel petticoats, open windows and daily baths. I remember one mother, a not particularly bright girl who lived with her parents, who was deeply resentful when a monthly clinic had to be cancelled.

'All that trouble bathing him and putting on clean clothes, all for nothing,' she grumbled, when I called at the house the following week.

I remember one highly intelligent young woman who had unwisely loved a married man and borne his child, and was living with her parents. She was a private secretary and continued her very interesting job after the baby's birth, while Granny coped with the help of her excellent 'daily'. Granny was a writer, and it had not been easy for her to surrender the peace and solitude she required for her work. Her little grandson was nearly two when I first met her. I called in the morning, a sunny June morning. The daily was busy in the bedrooms, and young Timothy was in the garden, outside the window of Granny's study and within sight of her desk. There were two large trees on the lawn, to one of which the small boy was attached by a long rope fixed to his harness. Bouncing about on another rope attached to the second tree was an enchanting Labrador puppy.

'They're company for each other,' explained the writer as we watched the two young things rolling over in a tangle of legs and arms and wagging tails, with a chorus of squeals and yaps and gurgling laughter.

'The ropes keep them both safely anchored, allow them to play together when they want to, and to escape at will to the refuge of their respective trees. Neither rope reaches to the other tree.'

Even as we watched, the puppy yelped as the play became too rough, and scurried away to lie panting just out of Timothy's reach. The child, who had obviously learnt that screaming would get him nowhere, settled philosophically to picking daisies on his own patch.

Timothy was four when his mother married and he moved, with his adored canine friend, to a new home with his stepfather, leaving Granny once more to pursue her literary career in peace and solitude.

In my early years as a health visitor I understood the reaction of grannies to my visits. Although well into my thirties, I looked younger, young enough to be their daughter, and what right had I to come into their homes and lay down the law to their daughters about their grandchildren? In those days there were quite a number of resident grannies. In the post-war housing crisis, young married couples were, only too often, forced to live in their parents' houses. Granny felt she had the right to make decisions in her own house, and 'what was good enough for my children is good enough for theirs'. 'Newfangled ideas' were resisted and it was almost impossible to speak to the mother without Granny's disapproving presence hovering in the background.

Over the years the picture changed. Young couples moved into their own homes. I became old enough to be a grandmother myself, while articles and broadcast talks on childcare began to infiltrate the public consciousness.

The time came when the dragon grannies of my early days became the frail old ladies on whose behalf my help and support was solicited. The clock had gone full circle. My babies had grown up and were having babies of their own, and my own mums were the new generation of grannies who welcomed me at the door of their daughter's houses, where they were helping out during those early weeks when I made my first visits to the babies of my babies.

27

Then and Now

In the 1970s the scene was changing rapidly. Cleansing stations for scabies and head lice had long been closed. Dirty heads were becoming a rare phenomenon, and young doctors would have been at a loss to recognise scabies. We had won the battle against smallpox, diphtheria and polio, and now measles too was being tackled in the same way. This new vaccine was untested, and viewed with some suspicion by parents and doctors, so, until it had stood the test of years, we refrained from pressing or even recommending it. Measles was not a killer in the same category as the other three scourges, and we didn't want to risk any distressing effects resulting from one vaccine putting our mothers off the well-proved and vital ones already in use.

By this time TB clinics and sanatoria were closed, and I no longer called on the Red Cross to send infected or threatened children for long stays in Switzerland. What a boon those Davos holidays had been, and how many tubercular children had come home cured, and other ailing and asthmatic children restored to health by the clear mountain air. The Red Cross were wonderful. No application for help was ever refused. The Swiss holidays, be they for a few months or up to two years, were mainly financed by the annual carnival in Dodsworth. Now other charities profit from this event.

The many voluntary organisations were unfailing in the help they could provide, each in their own field, assisting the elderly, the blind, disabled children, service personnel and their families. There were local charities, and the all-embracing BRCS and the WVS (now the WRVS). Fortunately, these so valuable organisations still flourish and continue their indispensable work, and until the end of my professional life I continued to rely on them and turn to them for help, which they never failed to give. By that time professional social workers had proliferated. Children's officers had taken from us the adoptions and fostering, and held a supervising brief for all 'problem' families. Relationships of trust and acceptance built up over the years with difficult parents could be shattered in one day by a keen, officious visitor from the Children's Department. If they had only contacted us in those early days, and profited from our knowledge of the families and our experience in the care of children. But they were new and enthusiastic; they thought they knew all the answers and needed nobody's help.

Now there is more co-operation, closer liaison, and less duplication of visits in the same household. In the early days of the mushrooming growth of the social services, it was possible for four or five different officials to be calling at the same house, if the occupants included the elderly, disabled, blind or children 'at risk' for whatever reason. Sadly, we health visitors were in danger of being regarded as just another of 'them visitors from the council'. When, in the course of time, things settled down and the new departments sorted themselves out, the specialised social workers, such as those who worked for the blind and the disabled, were to become extremely valuable to us with their special knowledge and expertise.

By 1970, the attachment of health visitors to doctors' practices was generally accepted, which left us with problems inherent from the serving of two masters – the MOH and the doctor in whose practice we worked. Local authority clinics had to be covered, school medical inspections attended and regular cancer-screening clinics for women were starting. All these commitments would sometimes clash with our surgery requirements, where well-baby clinics, immunising sessions and cancer-screening clinics were becoming increasingly popular. If a health visitor worked for more than one practice, as I did, less and less time was becoming available for the most important part of our work – visiting people at home. A health visitor is not primarily a clinic nurse. She should be, as the name implies, visiting – seeing people in their own background, finding and solving their problems at their source, offering help in a way that is impossible in the hurried, impersonal and public atmosphere of a clinic or a surgery.

Close liaison with GPs made for more varied and interesting work. As they gained confidence in us and realised how we could help, they used us in many follow-up visits to patients discharged from hospital, and we became involved in the diets of diabetics, the rehabilitation of stroke victims, the re-adjustment of colostomy patients and the supporting of cancer patients and their families. All of this was time-consuming but left the doctor free for more urgent work that only he or she could do. We became their 'ears' and might be sent to a garrulous patient with vague symptoms to let them talk things about with us. 'Go to Mrs X and assess . . .' I would be told, and I knew the best part of a morning would be spent assessing Mrs X.

In our new role as savers-of-doctor's-time we found our nursing skills, learnt long ago, and our basic, down-to-earth knowledge of the rules of positive health came in handy. A broken limb that took an unreasonably long time to knit suggested to me a lack of calcium. If sufficient calcium was being taken in the diet, why was it not being used? How did we ensure that babies' bones and teeth would grow strong and healthy by absorbing all the calcium in their milk? Vitamin D, of course, the essential sunshine vitamin. At my suggestion my doctors prescribed high concentrates of vitamin D for all their fractures, and recalcitrant bones began to knit together.

Elderly and handicapped people who needed help would contact their doctor, who would promise to send his health visitor 'to fix them up with a home help and meals-on-wheels'. In many cases such services were neither needed nor desirable, and I had to persuade him to promise only to send his health visitor 'to discuss the situation'. These discussions sometimes revealed problems of which he and his patients were totally unaware.

Mrs Pinkerton lived in a flat above her daughter, on whom she relied for her shopping, as she was trapped in her flat by painfully swollen legs. As the daughter was going on holiday, she rang the surgery about meals-on-wheels for her mother during her absence, and I was sent round to discuss the situation. I was shocked at what I found. Not only were Mrs Pinkerton's legs enormously distended, but her feet were nearly black and cold to the touch. Both enormous legs were encased in tight elastic stockings.

'I've worn these since my last baby was born,' she told me. 'I had phlebitis after the birth and the doctor prescribed them.'

'How long ago was that?' I asked.

'Fanny's twenty-four now. That's my daughter downstairs.'

Twenty-four years encased in elastic stockings! Those poor, poor legs. I explained the problem.

'The more your legs swell, the tighter the stockings get, causing further swelling from the restricted circulation. I strongly advise you to stop wearing them.'

I pointed to her blackened feet.

'Those feet are starved of blood. They're dying. You've heard of gangrene?'

She nodded.

'That's a terrible thing, isn't it? People lose their limbs from gangrene, don't they?'

'You're right, Mrs Pinkerton. You don't want to risk that happening. How would you feel if you woke up one morning and found your feet sitting on their own at the end of the bed?'

She laughed, but I could see she had got the message.

'You'll feel a bit lost without the elastic stockings for a while. I suggest you ask your daughter to buy you some good strong tights. They'll support the poor old legs better than ordinary stockings.'

She promised to do that, and I reported the outcome of my visit to her astonished doctor. Meals-on-wheels were arranged for the two weeks of her daughter's holiday, and I had no urgent reason to call again, although I intended to do so as soon as the pressure of work eased up.

It was about two months later, as I was having a quick lunch in a coffee house about half a mile from Mrs Pinkerton's flat, when I heard my name called, and, to my astonishment and delight, there she was lunching at the next table, her legs almost a normal size, and able to carry her down the stairs and into the town and a new, active way of life.

Practice attachment of health visitors had, like all changes, its good and bad points. In the villages, where nearly everybody belonged to the same practice, there was only gain in the closer liaison with the GPs, the free access to patients' medical records, the more varied and interesting work that came my way, and the added authority of my introduction to a difficult customer: 'Your doctor asked me to call.'

It was different in the town, where doctors' practices in no way corresponded to districts or streets, or even families. It was not unusual for husbands and wives to have different doctors, and it would be possible for me to be calling on a mother and baby while a colleague was making a hospital discharge visit to the father, and we frequently met one another in the same street, or block of flats. At the clinic, I was only able to advise the mothers of my own practice. There is more than one right way of feeding and rearing a baby, but they do not run concurrently, and conflicting advice can be confusing and harmful. Every school included children from all the practices, and I would attend medical inspections where less than half the entrants were known to me.

Seeing children in school, weighing them, testing their sight and hearing, filling in the record forms, the history of injections and illnesses and other problems, and preparing them for the doctor's examination: all this is a job. When every five-year-old entrant has been known to you since birth and you are greeted in the school by your one-time babies and their mothers as an honorary member of their families, it becomes something far, far more than just a job.

It would be sad if such days are gone forever; if today's health visitors, in their practice attachment, will not be able to experience the intense satisfaction I knew at one particular medical inspection at the primary school at Dodsworth.

As Dr Lang removed her white coat at the end of the day, she said to me:

'What a wonderfully healthy, clean and well turned out group of entrants. I haven't found one issue among them that could have been prevented.'

The headmaster, with whom she had been discussing her findings, turned towards me. He knew the answer before he asked the question.

'How long have you been working on this district, Miss Corbally?'

'Five years,' I replied.

That is what health visiting is all about.

About the Author

Molly Corbally served as a nurse in the Second World War, and on returning to England became one of the first District Health Visitors in the newly-formed NHS. She worked in the rural Midlands between the 1940s and the 1970s. She died in 2012, but her book was rediscovered and is being republished here by Two Roads.